The Chief Musician

Or, Studies in the Psalms, and Their Titles

E.W. BULLINGER

NEW YORK

The Chief Musician

For information, address:

Cosimo, P.O. Box 416
Old Chelsea Station
New York, NY 10113-0416

or visit our website at:
www.cosimobooks.com

The Chief Musician was originally published in 1908.

Library of Congress Cataloging-in-Publication Data
A catalog record for this book is available from the Library of Congress

Cover design by www.kerndesign.net

ISBN:1-60206-036-3

It is a great and acknowledged fact that the key to the Psalm-Titles has been lost for over twenty-two centuries.... Now, at length, we may say that the long-lost key has been found. And the explanation it gives is so simple that a child may understand it.

—from *The Chief Musician*

PREFACE.

THESE papers originated from reading the proof-sheets, and afterward, the remarkable book of Dr. James W. Thirtle, LL.D., *The Titles of the Psalms: Their Nature and Meaning Explained.**

Dr. Thirtle, in his great work, was bound, from the very nature of the case to be literary and scholastic: confining himself to interpretation, and leaving others to make the application.

Having a freer hand, I was able, in the pages of *Things to Come*, to treat the subject in a simpler manner; referring those who seek for further and deeper knowledge, and more exact evidence, to Dr. Thirtle's own work.

The importance of that work will best be shown in the words of a Review which appeared in *The Biblical World*, Chicago (Nov. 1904):—

> "He is a bold, brave man who will tackle a problem that has outwitted the sages of centuries. Translators, textual critics, and exegetes have always been more or less baffled whenever they have attempted a solution of this knotty problem of the Psalter.
>
> "From every evidence in the oldest of the versions, the Septuagint, the superscriptions of the Psalms were quite mysterious and unknown in the second and third centuries B.C. This shows itself by the fact that some of the terms are transliterated bodily without translation from the Hebrew into the Greek. The varied character and purpose of these titles would seem to furnish a clue to their complete explanation. But merely a glance at the latest and best commentaries on the Psalter shows that they still occupy quarters in the realm of the unknown. It is true that much in these titles, such as the names of authors of the particular kind of composition, and histor-

* London: Henry Frowde, Paternoster Row. Price 6/- net. Published in 1904, 2nd Ed. in 1905. Followed by *Old Testament Problems*: critical studies in the Psalms and Isaiah, 1907. 6/- net.

ical data have been measurably understood. But the so-called musical titles have been a sphinx to interpreters. The key to their real meaning must have been lost very early in the history of the Psalter. . .

"The main contention of the author is certainly true. He has found the key that has been lying within sight of scholars, but unseen, for long centuries. His discovery has opened up a series of questions that require re-investigation. Some of these are, (1) the age of the Psalter, (2) the compactness of the Psalter, (3) the character of the content of the individual psalms, in view of the meanings proposed for some of these new subscriptions."

This testimony is true, and it shows the great obligation under which Dr. Thirtle has placed, not only the whole Church of God, but the whole literary world.

I have been urged by several friends to republish these papers in a separate form; and, encouraged by Dr. Thirtle to do so, now present them, with some additional papers on the word "Selah" Dr. Thirtle's later work on *Old Testament Problems* (referred to in note on p. v.), has led to the addition and inclusion of Parts iii. and iv., on "the Songs of Degrees," for the further consideration of those who are interested in the study of Scripture, and who receive it, not as the word of men, but as it is in truth, the Word of God, which effectually worketh in them that believe (1 Thess. ii. 13).

I commend it to God, for without His blessing all the labours of His servants are in vain.

E. W. BULLINGER.

"BREMGARTEN,"
NORTH END ROAD,
LONDON, N.W.

November, 1907.

CONTENTS.

PART I.

SPECIAL WORDS IN THE TITLES OF THE PSALMS.

INTRODUCTORY.

"TO THE CHIEF MUSICIAN."

(1). WORDS RELATING TO SPECIAL OCCASIONS.

(2). WORDS RELATING TO SUBJECT-MATTER.

(3). WORDS RELATING TO SPECIAL CHOIRS.

(4). WORDS RELATING TO LITERARY FORM.

(5). WORDS RELATING TO PURPOSE AND OBJECT.

(6). THE ONE WORD CLAIMED FOR MUSIC.

(7). HISTORICAL TITLES.

(8). THE DOMINANT WORD.

The Psalm-Titles.

PART I.

SPECIAL WORDS IN THE TITLES OF THE PSALMS.

ILLUSTRATIONS.

PART I.

PART II.

PART III.

PART II.

SPECIAL WORDS IN THE TEXT.

PART III.

THE SONGS OF DEGREES.

PART IV.

THE SONGS OF THE DEGREES.

PART I.

INTRODUCTORY.

"TO THE CHIEF MUSICIAN."

It is a great and acknowledged fact that the key to the Psalm-Titles has been lost for over twenty-two centuries.

The value of our present work can be estimated, and its importance understood when we can start with the assertion that the long-lost key has at length been found by Dr. James W. Thirtle: whose name will be for ever bound up with this wonderful discovery; and handed down and remembered when the work of all those who have indulged in mere conjectural guess-work will have been forgotten.

No subject of Biblical study has appeared to be more incapable of solution.

This is the universal testimony of all who have ever written on the subject. No writer, ancient or modern, has ever professed to put forward a conclusive explanation, or one with which he was perfectly satisfied.

Bishop Jebb, who wrote a standard work on the Psalms (in 1846) confesses that "so great are the difficulties attending this enquiry, that, in many instances, little more than conjectures can be offered." (Vol. ii. p. 133).

Some give it up; or fall back on the assertion that these titles are not of any necessary authority, and are not all genuine, but often represent the caprice of editors, the fruits of conjecture, or of tradition.*

* Bishop Perowne, *Com.* Vol. i. p. cxi.

Dr. Thirtle quotes the late Franz Delitzsch, as saying* of these Titles, "The Septuagint found them already in existence, and did not understand them . . . The key to their comprehension must have been lost very early."

He also quotes Neubauer,† as saying :—" From all these different expositions of the titles of the Psalms, it is evident that the meaning of them was early lost."

Professor Kirkpatrick also says :‡—" Many of them are extremely obscure; and their meanings can only be conjectured."

With regard to two points, however, there is a consensus of belief:

(1) That these Titles form part of the primitive sacred Text: and,

(2) That they are connected, in some way, with the liturgical use of the Psalms in the Temple worship.

There have been three guiding principles underlying all the many interpretations arising from the loss of the key.

(1) The Septuagint, and other ancient versions, looked for a logical or mystical connection between the titles and their Psalms; and translated the words accordingly, though they could not see any such connection.

(2) Then came the School which looked upon the various words as denoting so many different musical instruments. And Commentaries, Dictionaries, and "Helps to the Bible," have called in the aid of modern musicians and ancient instruments to explain the terms used in the worship of the God of Israel. The translators of the Authorized Version partially adopted this view.

(3) The modern school sees in these titles only styles of singing; or, the catchwords of popular music. This view is reflected in the Revised Version.

---

* *Com. on Psalm.* † *Studia Biblica*, Vol. II. ‡ *Psalms, Introd.* xviii.

But all these interpretations are only mere guess-work; and, the key being lost, they have served only to extend this unprofitable field of conjecture; to divert Biblical studies into false channels, which could yield no satisfactory results; and to postpone any real enquiry as to what these Titles have to say for themselves, and what the Bible contains about them within its covers.

Now, at length, we may say that the long-lost key has been found. And the explanation it gives is so simple that a child may understand it. Indeed, with a Bible open before one, it could be pointed out with one's finger, without uttering a word with the lips.

We have often remarked that those who go back for their evidence seldom go back far enough. When we leave modern professors and interpreters, and go back to the oldest manuscripts and versions, and the earliest printed editions of the Hebrew Bible, we do not find many of the divisions which obtain in modern editions of the Bible.

To speak of the Psalms only: in modern Hebrew Bibles the Psalms are sometimes broken up; and a Latin word, with Roman numerals interpolated between them.

But no such division can be found in the manuscripts, or in the early printed editions of the Hebrew Bible, beyond the enumeration in the margin. In all these there is no break, or space, between the lines of the Psalms.

It is therefore, little less than impertinence to place them in any other order than that in which they have come down to us; or to make any other arrangement of them, based on their chronology, history, or subject-matter.

Not only is there no break between the Psalms, but there is not even a space between the lines. In its ancient form, the Psalter is written, and printed, in successive lines; without any space between those lines from the beginning to the end.

13 הָבָה־לָּנוּ עֶזְרָת מִצָּר
וְשָׁוְא תְּשׁוּעַת אָדָם׃
14 בֵּאלֹהִים נַעֲשֶׂה־חָיִל
וְהוּא יָבוּס צָרֵינוּ׃
סא לַמְנַצֵּחַ עַל־נְגִינַת לְדָוִד׃
2 שִׁמְעָה אֱלֹהִים רִנָּתִי
הַקְשִׁיבָה תְּפִלָּתִי׃
3 מִקְצֵה הָאָרֶץ ׀ אֵלֶיךָ אֶקְרָא בַּעֲטֹף לִבִּי
בְּצוּר־יָרוּם מִמֶּנִּי תַנְחֵנִי׃
4 כִּי־הָיִיתָ מַחְסֶה לִי
מִגְדַּל־עֹז מִפְּנֵי אוֹיֵב׃
5 אָגוּרָה בְאָהָלְךָ עוֹלָמִים
אֶחֱסֶה בְסֵתֶר כְּנָפֶיךָ סֶּלָה׃
6 כִּי־אַתָּה אֱלֹהִים שָׁמַעְתָּ לִנְדָרָי
נָתַתָּ יְרֻשַּׁת יִרְאֵי שְׁמֶךָ׃
7 יָמִים עַל־יְמֵי־מֶלֶךְ תּוֹסִיף
שְׁנוֹתָיו כְּמוֹ־דֹר וָדֹר׃
8 יֵשֵׁב עוֹלָם לִפְנֵי אֱלֹהִים
חֶסֶד וֶאֱמֶת מַן יִנְצְרֻהוּ׃
9 כֵּן ׀ אֲזַמְּרָה שִׁמְךָ לָעַד
לְשַׁלְּמִי נְדָרַי יוֹם ׀ יוֹם׃
סב לַמְנַצֵּחַ עַל־ידוּתוּן מִזְמוֹר לְדָוִד׃
2 אַךְ אֶל־אֱלֹהִים דּוּמִיָּה נַפְשִׁי
מִמֶּנּוּ יְשׁוּעָתִי׃
3 אַךְ־הוּא צוּרִי וִישׁוּעָתִי

משנבי

14 ° ס"א קְמֵינוּ או קָמֵינוּ וכן ר"ב ח"נ. סא. 1 ° ס"א למנצח וכן ד"ב, דיר ח"ש"ו. 1 ° ס"א נגינות או נגינת וכן תר, ח"ע וח"ר: 3 ° כן ברוב ספרים כ"י, ר"ב ר"ג, רו ח"נ. ס"א ימים וכן ר"י, ר"ב, ד"ד וד"ן. 9 ° כן בנע"א ברוב ספרים כ"י, רו, רי וד"ו. סב. 1 ° ס"א לידותון וכן ח"ס ות"ר. 2 ° ס"א מי־מטנו וכן ח"ע, ח"ס ות"ר: עיין לקמן פסוק ו'. 3 ° כן ברוב ספרים כ"י, ר"ב, ד"י, ד"ב, דייר וד"ו, ס"א אך ובלא מקף וכן ר"נ רו ח"ס.

Reduced *Fac-simile* of page 1208 of Dr. C. D. Ginsburg's Edition of the Hebrew Bible (Psalms lx. 13—lxii. 3).

To illustrate this we give a reduced fac-simile of a page of Dr. Ginsburg's *Massoretico-Critical Edition of the Hebrew Bible*, which is printed according to the manuscripts.

We have taken the page (1208) which contains the last two verses of Psalm lx., the whole of Psalm lxi., and the first three verses of Psalm lxii.

Psalm lxi. and lxii. both have titles: but it will be seen that there is no space between the lines; and that, what we call the title might just as well be (in whole or in part) the end of one Psalm as the beginning of the other.

The question arises:—Are we right in thus calling it a Title? Is it all *super*-scription? or is any portion of it *sub*-scription?

Can we find an answer to these questions? Is there a Psalm to be found apart from other Psalms, from which, standing alone, we can learn what was the principle adopted in the composition of a Psalm?

Yes, there is one. And to Dr. Thirtle belongs the credit of asking the question, and of finding, in the answer, the key to the whole matter, and the solution of the problem. The Psalm (or "A Prayer," as it is there called) is the third chapter of the prophet Habakkuk.

Here we have a typical Psalm, standing by itself, with no other Psalm going before or following it. Here, then, we can see for ourselves

(1) What part was the *super*-scription:

(2) What part was the *Psalm* itself: and

(3) What part was the *sub*-scription.

Thus, in Habakkuk iii., we have

v. 1. The *super*-scription, or Title proper. "A Prayer of Habakkuk the Prophet upon *Shigionoth*."*

vv. 2-19-. The Psalm proper.

---

* *i.e., consisting of loud cries* (see below, p. 86, under *Shiggaion*).

v. -19. The *sub*-scription. "To the Chief Musician* upon *Neginoth*."†

We see at once, from this, that the typical Psalm consisted of *three parts*, not two.

We have the same three divisions in "the writing of Hezekiah" (Isa. xxxviii. 9-20). It was his Psalm of Praise and Thanksgiving for recovery from his sickness.

In verse 9 we have the *super*-scription, or Title.

In verses 10-20-, The Psalm proper.

In verse -20, the *sub*-scription.

Hezekiah appears to have done what David did. Acting as his own "chief musician," he ordered the Psalm to be used in the Temple worship during the rest of his life.

During the seventy years of the Captivity in Babylon, the knowledge of the Temple worship must have become unknown to the bulk of the people; and by the time the Septuagint Translators came to their task, in 250-200 B.C., to turn the Hebrew into Greek, it must have been wholly lost. There was nothing to tell them of these three parts of a proper Psalm, unless they, like Dr. Thirtle, had thought of comparing Hab. iii.

The Massorites themselves, in editing the Hebrew text, were no better off; for they had no more personal experience or knowledge of the Temple usage than the Translators of the Septuagint had.

There was nothing between the lines to tell either of them where the break should be.

An illustration of this is seen in their treatment of the word "Hallelujah." The Septuagint Translators put all the twenty-four Hallelujahs at the beginning of the

* The same word as used throughout the Psalms.

† See below, under *Neginoth*, p. 90.

Psalms; whereas, in the English version (following the Hebrew text), they are put at the end of the Psalms in thirteen instances, and only ten times at the beginning. See, for example, Psalms cxv. and cxvi.; and Psalms civ. and cv.

In the case of the Psalm-titles, the Translators of the Septuagint took *all* that was written between the two Psalms as belonging to the Psalm that followed; and did not see that the first part of it was the *sub*-scription of the Psalm that preceded.

This mistake of the Septuagint has been perpetuated in every printed translation of the Psalms ever since; and is seen in our own Bibles to-day.

The consequence is that in the case of the fifty-five Psalms which have titles, many of these titles must be divided. We shall have to place the first part of the title at the end of the preceding Psalm: while the last part must be left as the title of the Psalm over which it already stands.

Psalm lxxxviii affords an example of the confusion which has ensued through not seeing this simple fact. As at present divided, two authors are named for that one Psalm, to the perplexity of all commentators; whereas, the difficulty is at once removed by noting that the first part of the title belongs to the preceding Psalm.

Many have observed that these Titles have little or nothing to do with the Psalm itself. And this is true: because they in whole or in part belong to the Psalm that precedes it. Several commentators actually notice that these titles seem more appropriate to the preceding Psalm, than to the one over which they are placed. And this is the case, because that is where they really do belong. Thus the commentators come right up to the point, and yet do not see it!

So far, the key to the solution is simple in the extreme; but there are far-reaching consequences to be noticed; and many precious expositions to be made.

Only one result must now be named, and that is, that *the "Higher Criticism" receives a death-blow.* For years past the Critics have been cutting the Psalms about, and telling us which were "exilic," and which were "post exilic": *i.e.*, which were written *during* the Exile in Babylon, and which were written *after* the Exile.

It is now obvious, that, had the authorship of these Psalms been "*post exilic*," and had that authorship been in any sense contemporary with the Septuagint Translators, these latter would have understood the titles, for the key would not have been lost. But it *was* lost, as the critics themselves confess, "very early."

Therefore, it follows, that the Psalms were, as we have them to-day, line for line, at least 2,500 years ago; long before the date of the Septuagint Translation (250-200 B.C.)

The typical Psalm in Habakkuk iii. shows that the expression "For the Chief Musician," etc., has its correct position at the *end* of the Psalm, and not at the beginning. This is clearly and easily seen in the case of isolated Psalms like Hab. iii. 19 or Isa. xxxviii. 20. But in the Psalter, where the Psalms follow each other so closely that no break occurs between them, it is as clearly seen how translators, from the earliest times, following the mistake made by the Septuagint Translators, have taken the concluding note of one Psalm and treated it as part of the title of the following Psalm.

This mistake is not without its great outstanding lesson; for, it establishes beyond a doubt, that the Psalms, as we have them to-day, are the same, line for line, as they must have been at least 250 years B.C. And, if there has been no change, even in the order of the lines, for more than 2,500 years, it is practically certain that no change took place in the comparatively much shorter time of about five or six hundred years, between the days of David and the days of Ezra, when the work of the Great Synagogue settled the canon of the Hebrew Scriptures.

The proper place of the expression "To the Chief Musician," is the key. As placed at the beginning of a Psalm, it does not fit the lock of that Psalm over which it stands. But it *does* fit the lock of the Psalm at the end of which it is placed, and with which it should therefore be connected.

The word itself is לַמְנַצֵּחַ (*lam'natzeach*) from נָצַח (*natzach*) *to lead* or *superintend*. Compare 1 Chron. xxiii. 4; 2 Chron. ii. 2, 18; xxxiv. 12. Ezra iii. 8-11.

When a Psalm, which may have been originally written in connection with other associations and had its origin in other circumstances, was formally handed over to the *leader* or *superintendent* of the Temple worship, it received a new status, and was thereafter associated with a new application for which it was peculiarly suited. That formal act was an epoch in its history which determined its future use. Not all the Psalms were adapted for such special use. That formal act shows therefore that we have no mere haphazard collection of poems, but that all is designed and ordered. That order was David's. Again and again, we have the record how all was arranged "according to the order of David": 2 Chron viii. 13, 14; xxiii. 18; xxix. 25-30; xxx. 21, 26. Ezra. iii. 10. Neh. xii. 24, 36, 45, 46.

(1) WORDS RELATING TO SPECIAL OCCASIONS.

"SHOSHANNIM." (LILIES).

Psalms xliv. and lxviii.*

THE SPRING FESTIVAL: PASSOVER.

AND

"GITTITH." (WINE-PRESSES).

Psalms vii., lxxx. and lxxxiii.†

THE AUTUMN FESTIVAL: TABERNACLES.

CERTAIN Psalms were specially adapted for special occasions, just as to-day there are some so designated as "Proper Psalms" for certain days.

The great Feasts of the Passover and Tabernacles would certainly have their own Proper Psalms; for they were the two great Feasts.

And what did they commemorate? As "feasts of the Jews" they are connected with the deliverance of the people from Egypt, and with the dwelling of the people in booths.

But as "Feasts of Jehovah" they are associated with Him, and were to commemorate His acts, and not merely the people and their benefits.

---

* Not Psalms xlv. and lxix. over which the title now stands, in the Versions.

† Not Psalms viii., lxxxi. and lxxxiv. over which this title now stands in the Versions.

Look at Lev. xxiii., where we have the declaration unto the children of Israel concerning these Feasts.

They are specially called "The feasts of Jehovah" (*v.* 2, 4, 37, 44); "My feasts" (*v.* 2).

The feast of Passover was "the LORD'S Passover" (*v.* 5). It commemorated His *Redemption* of Israel and the making of the nation (Ex. xv. 13. Deut. xxiv. 18).

The Feast of Tabernacles commemorated not merely the fact that they did dwell in booths, but that *the Lord kept them in safety*, even in the wilderness, though they did dwell only in booths. It commemorated not merely that they were exposed to privation, but that they enjoyed Jehovah's preservation; not merely that they were in the midst of danger, but that they were surrounded by Jehovah's protecting care.

The Feast was to be observed "that your generations may know that I MADE THE CHILDREN OF ISRAEL TO DWELL in booths" (Lev. xxiii. 43).

Yes, though they were in booths they dwelt in them for forty years, and the Lord was their defence. (See Deut. viii. 2-4, 15, 16; and compare Ps. xxvii. 5; xxxi. 21. Isa. iv. 6.

The word יָשַׁב (*yashav*) *to settle, sit down, abide*, is very strong. It is in the *Hiphil*, and means *to make to dwell* (safely and surely). It is used of the final settlement of Israel in their own land. See Jer. xxxii. 37, "*I will cause them to dwell* safely." Ezek. xxxvi. 11, "*I will settle you* after your old estates"; *v.* 33, "*I will also cause* (you) *to dwell* in the cities." Hos. xi. 11, "*I will place them* in their houses." Zech. x. 6, "*I will bring them again to place them.*" Thus is the sureness and safety of their dwelling in the wilderness in the past, to be the subject of Israel's observance of the Feast of Tabernacles, while it looks forward to the future Divine settlement of the People in their own land, in millennial days. It was to be observed "unto the Lord."

Now, these two Feasts divided the year into two equal parts. Passover was in the first month, and Tabernacles was in the seventh month.

Passover was the Spring Feast; Tabernacles was the Autumn Feast.

The universal symbol of Spring is *flowers*; and of the Autumn, *fruit*. In the Bible *Lilies* are the flowers of Spring; the *Vine* and *Pomegranates* are the fruits of Autumn.

Moreover, the nation of Israel is symbolized as a Vine again and again.* It was also spoken of as a Lily. Just as we have the Rose for England, the Thistle for Scotland, etc., so the Lily was the flower that represented Israel.

Dr. Thirtle finds a proof of this usage in the Apocrypha, where Esdras says in his prayer (2 Esd. v. 23-28, R.V.):†

Here the one subject is Israel, as God's "one People," under all these symbols; and among them we have the *Lily* and the *Vine*. This is in harmony with, and was probably

---

* Isa. v. 1-7; xxvii. 2-6. Jer. ii. 21; xii. 10, etc. Ps. lxxx. 8. Hos. x. 1.

† "O Lord that bearest rule, of all the woods of the earth, and of all the trees thereof thou hast chosen thee ONE VINE: and of all the lands of the world thou hast chosen thee ONE COUNTRY: and of all the flowers of the world ONE LILY: and of all the depths of the sea thou hast filled thee ONE RIVER: and of all builded cities thou hast hallowed ZION unto thyself: and of all the fowls that are created thou hast named thee ONE DOVE: and of all the cattle that are made thou hast provided thee ONE SHEEP: and among all the multitudes of peoples thou hast gotten thee ONE PEOPLE: and unto this people, whom thou lovedst, thou gavest a law that is approved of all. And now, O Lord, why hast thou given this ONE PEOPLE over unto many?" etc.

derived from, the Bible use of these symbols in the Tabernacle and Temple. Lilies and Pomegranates were everywhere seen (1 Kings vii. 20-22). The "knops and flowers" (Exod. xxv. 31-34) were doubtless the globe-like pomegranates and lilies. (The Septuagint says "globes and lilies.") The High-Priest's dress had "bells and pomegranates," the bells being the bell-like flower of the lily (Exod. xxviii. 33, 34; xxxix. 35, 36). Hosea xiv. 5-7 also uses the "lily" and the "vine" in connection with the nation of Israel.

In the Jewish Prayer-Book, to-day, at the Feast of Purim, Israel is called "the Lily of Jacob"; and at the Feast of Dedication (*Chanucha*) God is praised for delivering "the standard of the Lilies" (*i.e.*, of Israel).

The Hebrew Shekel had on one side, sometimes, a Lamb (Passover), and on the other a wine-bowl (Tabernacles). The Half-Shekel had a triple lily and a wine-bowl.

By the kindness of Messrs. Eyre and Spottiswoode we are able to give an illustration of the Shekel.

SILVER SHEKEL OF SIMON THE MACCABEE.

(Circ. B.C. 138.)

Obverse: A cup (perhaps the Pot of Manna). Above it, in old Hebrew characters: SHEQEL YISRA'EL. SH. G. *Shekel of Israel. Year 3. Reverse*: A flower (perhaps "Aaron's rod that budded"). YERUSHALAYIM HAQ-QEDOSHAH *Jerusalem the Holy.*

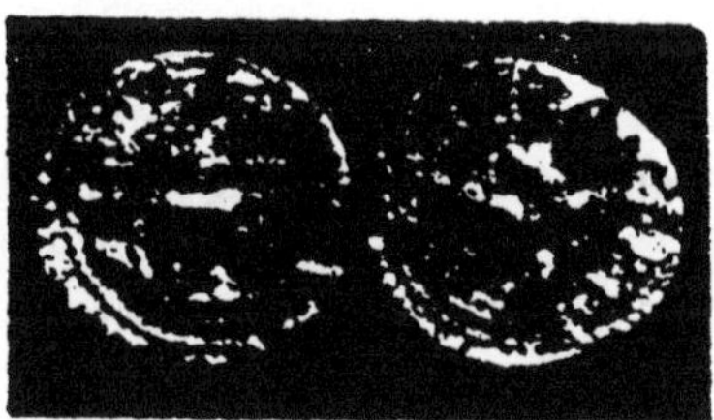

SILVER HALF-SHEKEL OF SIMON THE MACCABEE.

Obverse: HASI HASHSHEQEL *Half of the Shekel. Year 1. Reverse*: Same as the shekel.

(From the King's Printers' "Illustrated Aids.")

In Old Jewish cemeteries we constantly see on the tombs the seven-branched candlestick, with its "knops and flowers" (*i.e.*, its lilies and pomegranates), and sometimes we see a triple lily or a pomegranate.

Commentators (as will be seen above) suggest that the Bowl is "the Pot of Manna," and the Flower is "perhaps Aaron's Rod that budded."

Interpreters, who are guided chiefly by heathen traditions, see in the lilies only "*poppy heads*" that speak of eternal sleep! and in the pomegranates merely "*a round fruit*" or husk from which the kernel (the spirit) has fled. Thus, Egyptian and Babylonian heathenism is introduced in order to explain Divine Biblical symbols!

On the other hand, what *we* see in those simple figures engraved on the tomb is that which Scripture teaches: and for those who have ears to hear the *Lily* says, "*Here lies one of Jehovah's redeemed*"; and the *Pomegranate* says, "*Here lies one safe in Jehovah's keeping.*" The one symbolizes the Passover truth of Divine *redemption;* and the other the Tabernacle truth of Divine *preservation.*

Thus there is perfect harmony throughout.

And this is what we find in the two Passover Psalms, and in the three Tabernacle Psalms.

Shoshannim means *lilies*, and *Gittith* means *wine-presses.* These five titles, when they are taken from the Psalms over which they now stand, and are connected respectively with the preceding Psalms under which they should stand, will cease to perplex the reader by the irrelevancy which their present position gives them; and will shed wondrous light on the Psalm to which they properly belong as the *subscription.*

The two *Shoshannim* Psalms are xliv. and lxviii.*

* Not Psalms xlv. and lxix., over which they have hitherto stood.

The three *Gittith* Psalms are vii., lxxx., and lxxxiii.

All five Psalms are intensely national.

Psalm xliv. is appropriate to the oppression in Egypt, the Divine Deliverance, and Jehovah's redemption (*v.* 26).

In Psalm lxviii. we have the Passover story.† The "JAH" of Exodus xv. 13 reappears in Ps. lxviii. 4: while both these Psalms occur in the second, or Exodus book of the Psalter.

Gesenius fixes the meaning of *Shoshannim* as *lilies*. Other meanings are only guess-work. Fuerst thinks that it is the name of one of the twenty-four choirs, from a master named *Shushan*! Prof. Kirkpatrick thinks it is the tune of a well-known song beginning with this word! Wellhausen thinks it is the catchword of an older song (of course "older")! The Polychrome Bible thinks it means "with Susian instruments"! This is as likely (Dr. Thirtle truly observes) as that the French should set a patriotic song to a tune called "Waterloo," or "Fashoda," or that modern Jews should set it to a tune called "Kishineff."

Our readers must study for themselves the three *Gittith* Psalms (vii., lxxx., and lxxxiii.), in the light of the true significance of the Feast of Tabernacles, and they will see in them Jehovah's keeping, and the appeals to Jehovah the Divine Keeper; always remembering that the Heb. עַל (*'al*) rendered "to," has the much wider meaning of *relating to*. They will then see (and would smile were it not so serious and sad) that the guesses of human wisdom are as silly and childish as they are useless and meaningless.

---

* Not Psalms viii., lxxxi., and lxxxiv. over which they have hitherto stood.

† See this Psalm, under '*Alamoth* p. 67; and under "Selah," in Part II.

One thinks *Gittith* refers to a Gittite instrument; another, a Gittite melody; another a tune or march of the Gittite Guard; another to a body of Levites who lived in the Levitical city of Gath-Rimmon. But we, who recognise this as being "the Word of God," are prepared to receive and learn something more dignified and instructive; and something more worthy of the Divine authorship.

"SHUSHAN-EDUTH" AND "SHOSHANNIM-EDUTH."

(LILIES: A TESTIMONY).

Psalms lix.* and lxxix.†

A SPRING FESTIVAL: FEAST OF WEEKS.

BEFORE we pass to other Titles, there are two Psalms which are connected with *Shoshannim*, which we have seen means *Lilies*, and is used for the Spring Festival of the Passover.

These two differ from the other *Shoshannim* Psalms, in that the word is combined with another word, *'Eduth* or *Edoth*.

There is no question as to the meaning of this word. It is עֵדוּת (*'edûth*), and means *testimony*. It is from עוּד (*'eûd*) *to testify*; and is a common word for the Law, which is Jehovah's *testimony* to His people. It is also used in a more general sense of the whole of Divine Revelation. In Psalm cxix., it is one of *ten* synonymous words used of the Law or Word of God, and occurs in two forms twenty-three times.‡

The question here, however, is not so much what the word means, but what it denotes as used in connection with *Shushan* or *Shoshannim*.

To use the key again, which Dr. Thirtle has so wonderfully discovered, we shall have to disconnect these two

* Not Psalm lx. over which this title now stands in the Versions.

† Not Psalm lxxx. over which this title now stands in the Versions.

‡ Verses 2, 14, 22, 24, 31, 36, 46, 59, 79, 88, 95, 99, 111, 119, 125, 129, 138, 144, 146, 152, 157, 167, 168.

titles from the two Psalms over which they have been so long wrongly placed as the *super*-scription (*viz.*, Ps. lx. and lxxx.); and see in them the *sub*-scription to the preceding Psalms, *viz.*, lix. and lxxix.

The first words *Shushan* and *Shoshannim* refer to a *Spring* Festival, and the latter word *Eduth* refers to some special *testimony* in connection with it.

The A.V. has nothing to say on the matter. The R.V. says, in the margin, of the former, "That is, *The lily of testimony*": and of the latter, "That is, *Lilies, a testimony.*"

This "testimony" must be connected, however, with a Spring Festival. It can hardly be the Passover itself, of the title would be simply "*Shoshannim,*" like the other Passover Psalms.

It can be associated only with the Second great Feast, the "Feast of Weeks."

But there is a difficulty connected with this also: for, at first sight, neither of the two Psalms appears to be appropriate for the Feast of Weeks.

This difficulty, however, we submit, is only apparent, because, perhaps, the object of the Feast of Weeks is not fully apprehended by us. There is no difficulty as to the object of the Feast of the Passover, for this is plain and clear. But we have seen how the object of the Feast or Tabernacles became forgotten; and how that Feast developed into a commemoration of the bare *fact* that *their fathers dwelt* in Tabernacles, instead of the miracle that Jehovah "*made them to dwell*" safely in the wilderness. Was there a similar forgetfulness as to the design of the Feast of Weeks?

We can answer this question only from the Word of God. If we go to the Post-exilic observance of the Feast, or to its observance from that time to the present day, we see the usual accretions of Tradition, and a departure from the original institution. First, the Feast became practically meaningless, "a Feast of the Jews"; and then it became a commemoration of the giving of the Law of Sinai.

The Talmud declares that it was instituted with this object; and Jewish Tradition confirms it. Even Abravanel, who denies this as the *object* of the Feast, yet emphatically declares that the Law was given at Sinai at Pentecost. There can be no doubt as to the historical connection between the two; but it is quite another thing to say there was any such connection in the original design and object of the Feast. If we ask what Jehovah says about the object of this Feast, we note that its very name associates it with and links it on to the Passover in such a way that the one feast is the complement of the other. One is incomplete without the other.

Jehovah's redemption of Israel had two great objects. They are set forth in Jehovah's covenant at the Bush. "I am come down to deliver them out of the hand of the Egyptians, and to BRING THEM UP OUT of that land UNTO a good land" (Ex. iii. 8). In Ezek. xx. 6, Jehovah rehearses what he had done for them; and speaks of "the day that I lifted up mine hand unto them, TO BRING THEM FORTH of the land of Egypt INTO A LAND that I had espied for them."

In Deut. vi. 23, Moses testifies "He brought us OUT from thence, that he might bring us IN."

In Deut. xxvi., they are instructed to say, at the offering of the basket of first-fruits, "The LORD brought us FORTH OUT of Egypt, and He hath brought us INTO this place."

Now the Feast of Weeks was reckoned fifty days from the Passover; and thus became so closely bound up with it, that it was practically the real *conclusion* of the Passover.

So closely connected were they that, from the time of the Second Temple, Pentecost was called עֲצֶרֶת (*atzereth*) *closing*, *conclusion*, or *termination*, from עָצַר (*'atzar*) *to shut* or *close up* (Deut. xi. 17): and the feast is still so called.

In the Jewish literature of the present day, it is actually called "*the conclusion of the Passover.*"

The Feast of Weeks would be very inappropriately so called, if it did not stand in some fixed and essential relationship to the intervening weeks between it and the Passover; for the weeks themselves were not a feast, but the fiftieth day, on which they ended, was the culmination of the Passover.

The Feast of the Passover commemorated the goodness of Jehovah in bringing His people OUT of Egypt.

The Feast of Weeks celebrated the goodness of Jehovah in bringing them INTO the Land.

The Feast of Weeks was as peculiarly associated with the Land as the Passover was with Egypt. The counting of the fifty days was not to commence until they were come into the Land. This Feast could not be kept in the wilderness. The ordinance was: "*When ye be come into the land which I give unto you.*" The first of the fifty days was the morrow after the sabbath of the first-fruits. And, in Deut. xvi., we have the design of Jehovah, in instituting this Feast, and the special injunctions as to its observance. They were five (see verses 10-12):—

a | 10-. Thou shalt *keep*.
    b | -10. Thou shalt *give*.
        c | 11. Thou shalt *rejoice*.
    b | 12-. Thou shalt *remember*.
a | -12. Thou shalt *observe*.

It was specially a Feast when "thou shalt remember that thou wast a bondman in Egypt." That *remembrance* of whence they were *brought out* was to be the basis of their rejoicing at being *brought in*, and of the thank-offerings which they were to *give*.

Hence, two Psalms (lix. and lxxix.), written in connection with other events which called them forth, were handed to the Chief Musician for Liturgical use, because they laid firm and sure the basis of similar praise.

In both Psalms the People are *in the Land*: but enemies are there too, and those that rose up against them. These enemies are like "dogs" as to their *noise* and *greediness*. But Jehovah is the *defence* of His People; and they will praise Him for His deliverance which He will surely give.

The Structures of the two Psalms bring this out.

PSALM LIX.

A | 1-5. Prayer to the God of Israel. Enemies with them in the Land.

B | a | 6. Comparison to a dog. } Character
b | 7. Doggish character. Barking. } of enemies

C | c | 8, 9-. David's trust in Jehovah.
d | -9, 10. Reason. "God my defence."

A | 11-13. Prayer to the God of Jacob. Enemies with them in the Land.

B | *a* | 14. Comparison to a dog. } Character
b | 15. Doggish character. Greediness. } of enemies

C | *c* | 16-. David's trust in Jehovah.
d | -16, 17. Reason. "God my defence."

Hence, the Psalm concludes with the rejoicing required by, and suited for, the Feast of Weeks, in *v*. 16.

"I will sing of thy power;
Yea, I will sing aloud of thy mercy."

PSALM LXXIX.

A | 1-4. Complaint. Enemies with them in the Land.

B | 5. Expostulation.

A | 6-12. Prayer. Enemies with them in the Land.

B | 13. Praise.

Like Ps. lix., this Psalm also ends with the rejoicing required by, and suited for, the Feast of Weeks, in *v.* 13.

> "So we thy People and sheep of thy pasture,
> Will give thee thanks for ever;
> We will show forth thy praise to all generations."

Gesenius says, the title of these two Psalms denotes "a melody whose first line compared the Law, as the Testimony, to a choice flower."

Delitzsch thinks it denotes "a popular song which began 'A lily is the Testimony,' or 'Lilies are the Testimony.'"

Fuerst thinks it is perhaps the name of "a musical choir, whose president, Shushan, lived at Adithaim, in Judah (Jos. xv. 36)."

Wellhausen translates it "the tune of the Lily of the Law."

Perowne says, "In the great darkness which envelopes this and other inscriptions, it is impossible to explain the words satisfactorily; but they most probably denote the measure or melody to which the Psalm was to be set."

We may here pause, and reproduce some weighty words of Sir Robert Anderson, on the general subject. They appeared in *The Christian* of April 21st, 1904, and give the result of Mr. Thirtle's discovery as it affects the Higher Criticism. He says:—

"The crusade against the Bible which masquerades as 'Higher Criticism' claims to have established that the Pentateuch was compiled in the Exilic age, and Daniel and the Psalter in the Maccabean period.

In my 'Pseudo-Critcism'* I have shown that these questions are issues of *evidence*, which lie outside the province of the philologist; and, further, that no competent authority would accept the conclusions of the critics as regards Daniel and the Pentateuch. If Mr. Thirtle's book had reached me before mine went to press, it would have enabled me to formulate a still clearer case in regard to the Psalms. His discovery, of course, destroys the 'critical hypothesis.' As he has urged, the fact that the meaning of the 'Psalm-titles' had been forgotten when the Septuagint version was made clearly proves that the Psalter must have been much older. But how much older?

"There can be no doubt that the Psalter was framed at a time when Temple worship prevailed. Might it have been compiled for the post-captivity Temple? Such an hypothesis is improbable in the extreme. For the Sanhedrim of the Septuagint period was practically the same College as the great Synagogue which preceded it; and that such a College should have lost the meaning of the 'Psalm-titles,' if they dated from Nehemiah's age, is not credible. The student of evidence—the true 'Higher Critic'—who enters upon the inquiry without prejudice, will therefore come to the conclusion that the Psalter is pre-exilic. If proof were found that additions were made to it in the early days of the Second Temple, this would not affect the fact that the collection must have been already in existence. And the very latest date to which it can be assigned is the period of Josiah's revival; for it is certain that such a work could not have originated in the evil days of the last three kings of Judah.

"I do not mean to suggest that it was not much more ancient; but the argument based on post-exilic ignorance respecting the 'musical terms' will not carry us any further back. And this is enough to destroy the 'critical hypothesis.' Mr. Thirtle's discovery, therefore, has consequences which reach far beyond the Book of Psalms. It discredits the entire position of the Higher Critics."

We are thankful for this important pronouncement: for, as the "Higher" Critics are prudently treating this discovery with a conspiracy of silence, it is necessary for us to reiterate its value as bearing upon the question of the Psalm-Titles as a whole.

* *Pseudo-Criticism: or the Higher Criticism and its Counterfeits.* James Nisbet, London, 3/6.

THE PSALM-TITLES.

We have now to look at some special Psalms of a more private character and reference, but yet of national importance, as celebrating great events in connection with David's life.

(2) WORDS RELATING TO SUBJECT-MATTER

"MUTH-LABBEN."

(THE DEATH OF THE CHAMPION).

Psalm viii.*

DAVID AND GOLIATH.

IF we now turn to Psalm ix., in our Authorised and Revised Versions, we find as the *super*-scription.

"To the Chief Musician upon Muth-labben.
A Psalm of David."

Now, using Mr. Thirtle's key, we separate these two sentences; and read the first:

"To the Chief Musician: relating to Muth-labben,"

as the *sub*-scription of Psalm viii., and leave

"A Psalm of David,"

as the *super*-scription of Psalm ix.

In the same way we must deal with the title of Ps. viii., as it now stands in the A.V.; and, as we have already said (p. 5), the words "To the Chief Musican, upon Gittith," are the *sub*-scription to Ps. vii.

So that Psalm viii. in its three parts will properly stand thus:

(1) The *Super*-scription: "A Psalm of David."

(2) The *Psalm* proper: Verses 1-9.

(3) The *Sub*-scription: "To the Chief Musician, relating to Muth-labben."

---

* Not Psalm ix. over which this title now stands in the Versions.

But now comes the question, What does "Muthlabben" mean?

Here we are met by answers innumerable, and contradictory.

One thinks that it is the name of a tune. Another thinks it is the "catchword of a song." Another takes it as the name of a musical instrument. Another thinks it is the name of a man called "Ben" in 1 Chron. xv. 18, one of the Levitical singers. If so, then it must be about his death: for all are agreed that *muth* means *death*. Some suggest that the word *al*, which means *relating to*, should be compounded with the word *muth*, and treated as one word *alamoth*; which is a word found in another title. But all these, and many more, are only the merest guesses.

The natural meaning, as the words stand, is "*Death of the son*," or "*Death for the son*:" בֵּן (*ben*) being the Hebrew for *son*. But whose son we are not told. Some think it was Absalom, and others Nabal.

All this compels us to go to the Scripture instead of to the ingenuity of our own brains. But it is very curious that, in all such cases as this, Scripture is the last place that commentators think of going to.

It seems strange, on the face of matter, that, whether the words be taken in connection with Psalm ix. or Psalm viii., both Psalms are equally inappropriate to any celebration of a *son's* death. They consist of praise to Jehovah.

It is true that בֵּן (*ben*) means *a son*. But בֵּן may be the word בֵּין (*beyn*) written *defectively* (that is, transmitted without the expression of its vowel—which is often the case in Hebrew). In that case, it would mean *the separator*, and be related to בַּיִן (*bayin*)—*between*. The dual form of this word appears in the designation of Goliath, in

1 Sam. xvii. 4, 23, as אִישׁ־הַבֵּנַיִם (*'ish-habeynayim*) *the man between the two hosts; i.e.*, the man who came out *between* the hosts of Israel and the Philistines. Hence, לַבֵּן (*labben*) *for the son*, may be read לַבֵּין (*labbeyn*) *for the champion*, or *the one standing between*.

Indeed, this is how the title is read in the ancient Jewish commentary or paraphrase called the *Targum*: "To praise, relating to the death of the man who went out between the camps," *i.e.*, the champion, as he is called twice in 1 Sam. xvii., *viz.*: in *vv.* 4. 23.*

Read in this light, Psalm viii. stands out in a new light altogether; and we have to look at it as it relates to and celebrates "*the Death of the Champion*," Goliath of Gath. Indeed, "*Death to the Champion*" may have been the burden of the "shouting" of which 1 Sam. xvii. 52 speaks.

Goliath was a type of all the great defiers of God, and is stamped with and bears the "hall-mark" of *man*, as independent of God. Man was created on the *sixth* day; and *six* is the number which characterizes him.

Goliath had *six* pieces of armour mentioned: he was *six* cubits and a span in height; and "his spear's head weighed *six* hundred shekels of iron."

Nebuchadnezzar's defiance of God was marked by his image, "whose height was three-score cubits, and the breadth thereof six cubits": while six instruments of music summoned all to worship it.

The coming Man of Sin is stamped with the same number in the triple or concentrated form 666; while the numbers connected with him are all multiples of *six*: *viz.*, 42, 1260, 2520.

---

* The word "champion" in verse 51 is another word גִּבּוֹר (*gibbôr*) *a strong man*.

The death of Man's champion, the man who defied God and the hosts of His People Israel, was the turning-point of David's life. David was a "stripling," and but a babe compared with this Giant: and, in his song of praise, he is filled with thoughts of the excellency of Jehovah's Name, His greatness, and His condescension in noticing him and endowing him with strength.

From this point of view the Psalm is exquisite.

Look at its Structure.

PSALM VIII.

A | 1-. Jehovah our Adonim.

B | a | -1. His greatness in the heavens.

b | 2. His goodness and condescension to man on the earth.

B | *a* | 3. His greatness in the heavens.

b | 4-8. His goodness and condescension to man on the earth.

A | 9. Jehovah our Adonim.

Here we have *six* members; and, combined with the general structure, as thus exhibited, there is another, in which *Earth* and *Heaven* are alternate subjects.

The excellency of Jehovah Adonim, the Lord of all the earth, begins and ends the Psalm. Enclosed, between these declarations, there are four members, which contrast God and man alternately.

This is the form in which the praise of Jehovah is formulated.

In 1 Sam. xvii. this is the thought that breathes in every word that David uttered. He appealed to Jehovah who had delivered him from the lion and the bear (*v.* 37), and was assured that the same Jehovah would deliver him out of the hand of Goliath (*vv.* 37, 46, 47). His desire was "that all the EARTH may know that there is a God in Israel" (*v.* 46).

Is not this the one thought of this eighth Psalm, which celebrates this great victory, and embodies the same great thoughts of Jehovah?

It is remarkable that we have the same thought and the same words in Psalm cxliv. 3.

> "What is man, that thou art mindful of him?
> And the son of man, that thou visitest him?"

And this Psalm (cxliv.) is "A Psalm of David." It begins:

> "Blessed be Jehovah my strength,
> Who teacheth my hands to war, and my fingers to fight.
> My goodness, and my fortress;
> My high tower and my deliverer;
> My shield, and he in whom I trust;
> Who subdueth peoples* under Him†
> Lord, what is man, that thou takest knowledge of him?
> Or the son of man, that thou makest account of him?"

Is it not remarkable that in the Septuagint, this Psalm‡ bears the title "Τῷ Δαυὶδ πρὸς τὸν Γολιάδ." "*A Psalm* of David, concerning Goliath.

Whether there be authority or not for this Title, it is sufficient to show that there is something in the Psalm that makes it peculiarly appropriate to David's victory over

* An ancient reading (one of the *Severin*) reads *peoples*, instead of "my people." So, many MSS., the Targum and the Syriac.

† Some Codices read *him*, instead of "me." See Ginsburg's Heb. Text and note.

‡ There numbered cxliii.

Goliath, and that links it unmistakably with Psalm viii., *Muth-labben*, or *The Death of the Champion.*

There is also, in Ps. cxliv., a reference to the vain and false words of the strange children (Goliath and his Philistine "seconds"); and special reference to the event, in the praise of God, "who delivereth David his servant from the hurtful sword" (*v.* 10).

Thus we see how Ps. viii. belongs to David, and its *interpretation* to the circumstances which called it forth.

This will help us to understand any *applications* that it may have; and will, indeed, guide us to the right one.

The use of this Psalm in Heb. ii. 5-9 is one such application, which puts it beyond a doubt that the Psalm relates also to the true David; David's Son and David's Lord; and to the subjection to Him of the world to come. That world is not going to be put in subjection to angels, but to Him who is emphatically the "Son of Man." Both the Psalm and the Epistle tell us that all things are to be put as a footstool for His feet: "but now we see not yet all things put under Him. But we see Jesus, who was made a little lower than the angels (for the suffering of death crowned with glory and honour), that he, by the grace of God, should taste death for every* man."

It is in Psalm viii. that Christ is first called "the Son of Man." And this first occurrence of the title fixes for us its meaning. It refers to *dominion in the earth.* This is the one great subject of the Psalm. It is addressed to "*Jehovah our Adonim,*" and *Adonim* always expresses *lordship* in relation to the earth, while Jehovah is connected with Lordship in relation to Covenant.†

* *i.e.*, all, or every, *without distinction.*

† See *The Divine Names and Titles*, by the same author and publisher.

The Psalm opens and closes (as we have already seen) with a reference to the earth: "O Jehovah our Adonim, how excellent is thy name in all the EARTH."

Man was made "to have dominion" over the works of God in the Earth (*v.* 6 and Gen. i. 28). But man fell, and lost that dominion. This ruin is not to be repaired; but "the Son of Man," "the Second Man," "the Last Adam," is to have this dominion over a new Earth. As the Son of Man, He is heir to the whole Earth; as the Son of Abraham, He is heir to the Land; as the Son of David, He is heir to the Throne.

He who is David's Lord (Adonai) is also "David's son according to the flesh" (Rom. i. 3). He is "the root" from which David sprang, and He is "the offspring of David" (Rev. xxii. 16).

But there is another Goliath who has to be destroyed. There is another champion who is defying God, and keeping the People of God in terror, even as the People of Israel "were dismayed and greatly afraid" (1 Sam. xvii. 11, 24). "Give me a man, that we may fight together" was Goliath's cry. And God gave him a man—not a giant, but a "babe and a suckling," to whom He ordained strength, that He might "still the enemy and the avenger." Even so is it with that other champion. The Son and Lord of David took part of flesh and blood, and thus became "the Son of Man," "that through death he might destroy him that had the power of death, that is, the devil; and deliver them who through fear of death were all their lifetime subject to bondage" (Heb. ii. 14, 15).

But this we "see not yet." The work of Redemption has been accomplished. The *price* has been paid; but *power* has yet to be put forth to take possession. The sentence of judgment has been passed; a "judgment-summons" has been issued; but "execution" has yet to be "put in."

Another work has first to be done. He took part of flesh and blood. He came to this earth, over which He is to have dominion. He came "a little lower than the angels." He had to "taste death." And hence, "in the days of his flesh," He could say, with reference to this earth, over which He is to have dominion: "The foxes have holes, and the birds of the air have nests; but the Son of man hath not where to lay his head." This is the *first* occurence of the title (Son of Man) in the New Testament (Matt. viii. 20). The time for that dominion was "not yet." That time will come, and John sees a vision of it: he says (Rev. xiv. 14-16): "I looked, and behold a white cloud, and upon the cloud one sat like unto THE SON OF MAN, having on his head (that head which before had no place to lay on in the earth), a golden crown, and in his hand a sharp sickle. And another angel came out of the Temple, crying with a loud voice to him that sat on the cloud, "Thrust in thy sickle, and reap: for THE TIME IS COME for thee to reap; for the harvest of THE EARTH is ripe. And he that sat on the cloud thrust in his sickle on THE EARTH; and THE EARTH was reaped." This is the *last* occurrence of the title "Son of Man" in the New Testament.

All Psalms that bear the *super*-scription, "A Psalm of David," refer, in their fullest significance and highest application, to the true David.

Whatever may have been their primary interpretation; whatever may have been the circumstances with which they first stood in connection; the final reference is to David's Son and David's Lord.

The Holy Spirit, in Hebrews ii. 5-9, shows us the

application which exhausts the eighth Psalm, and in this we have a key to the application of other Old Testament prophecies.

In the original interpretation of Ps. viii., we see David, "the stripling," endued with Divine "strength." We hear his ascription of praise to the Great Giver of all dominion. We see him take his place of unworthiness: we listen to his prophetic words to Goliath; "This day will Jehovah deliver thee into mine hand; and I will smite thee, and take thine head from thee; and I will give the carcases of the host of the Philistines this day unto the fowls of the air, and to the wild beasts of THE EARTH; that ALL THE EARTH may know that there is a God in Israel. And all this assembly shall know that Jehovah saveth not with sword and spear: for the battle is Jehovah's, and he will give you into our hands" (1 Sam. xvii. 46, 47).

Even so will it be in the great closing scene of that coming day, when the great "Champion," who has so long defied God, shall have come down to this earth having great wrath, knowing that then he hath but a short time (Rev. xii. 12). The battle will then be joined. The challenge will be taken up. An angel will cry with a loud voice, "Saying (almost in the words of David in 1 Sam. xvii.) to all the fowls that fly in the midst of heaven, "Come and gather yourselves together unto the supper of the great God; that ye may eat the flesh of kings, and the flesh of captains, and the flesh of mighty men, and the flesh of horses, and of them that sit on them, and the flesh of all men, both free and bond, both small and great. And I saw the beast, and the kings of the earth, and their armies, gathered together to make war against Him that sat on the horse, and against His army. And the beast was taken, and with him the false prophet. . . .

These both were cast alive into a lake of fire burning with brimstone . . . And I saw an angel come down from heaven, having the key of the bottomless pit and a great chain in his hand. And he laid hold on the dragon, that old serpent, which is the Devil, and Satan, and bound him [and kept him bound] a thousand years, and cast him into the bottomless pit, and shut him up, and set a seal upon him" (Rev. xix. 17—xx. 3).

Here, in this final judgment scene on EARTH, we have the full realisation of the eighth Psalm. It will then be said

"THE TIME IS COME."

Then the Son of Man will exercise dominion in the earth; for then will be seen the great final victory, "The Death of the Champion," *Muth-labben*: for the time shall have come to "destroy him that had the power of DEATH, that is, the devil."

"MAHALATH."

(The Great Dancing).

Psalm lii.*

David and Goliath.

Up to the present time this title stands as the *super*-scription of Psalm liii.; but, as we have seen, it is really the *sub*-scription of Psalm lii.

This is another of the Psalms that have to do with David and Goliath.

It consists of three parts:

(1) The *Super*-scription: "Maschil of David: when Doeg the Edomite came and told Saul, and said unto him, David is come to the house of Ahimelech."

(2) The Psalm proper: verses 1-9.

(3) The *sub*-scription: "For the Chief Musician; relating to Mahalath."

The Psalm comes to us, therefore, stamped with a special connection with that memorable turning-point in David's history so intimately linked with the destiny of the nation.

The first question is: What does "Mahalath" mean?

Again we have to discard man's guesses, and seek for some meaning worthy of so great and important a subject.

When the Septuagint Translators came to their task, they could make nothing of the word; and so contented themselves with transliterating it, transferring the Hebrew

* Not Psalm liii. over which this title now stands in the Versions.

in Greek letters "μαελέθ" (*maeleth*): a word which, in Greek, has no meaning.

Of course the Hebrew at that date (250 B.C.) had no vowel-points, so that the Septuagint Translators pointed it with the three vowels *a*, *e*, and *e*.

When *Aquila* made his Greek Translation about 160 A D., he supplied (doubtless for some good reason) other vowels:—*o*, and *o*, and read the word *m'choloth*. This word has a meaning, and Aquila rendered it χορεία (*choreia*) *dancing*.

Symmachus, who make another Greek Version about 170 A.D., follows *Aquila* in the vocalization of the Hebrew word.

This rendering at once connects itself with the historical *super*-scription of the Psalm; and associates it with the dancing, music, and song which celebrated that great event.

When we turn to 1 Sam. xviii. 6, 7, we read, "the women came out of all the cities of Israel, singing and dancing, to meet king Saul, with tabrets, with joy, and with instruments of music. And the women answered one another as they played, and said,

'Saul hath slain his thousands,
And David his ten thousands.'"

It was, for Israel, exactly what it was for England, when the news came of the "relief of Mafeking." So great was the spontaneous outburst of popular feeling, that the event has been indelibly stamped on the nation, and has even given rise to a new word "Mafficking."

For Israel the joy meant much more: for the danger was graver, and the rejoicings were deeper and more sacred.

But the occasion was one ever to be remembered as *M'cholath* "The Great Dancing." *

The immediate consequence, in this case, was Saul's anger; the flight of David; and his coming to the house of Ahimelech.

With Goliath's sword in one hand (it may be), and his pen in the other, David writes this fifty-second Psalm.

Its spirit is the same as that of Psalm viii., which relates to the same event.

All glory is ascribed to God.

"THOU HAST DONE IT,"

is the basis of the praise.

Psalm lii. is simple in its structure.

A | 1-5. David's apostrophe to Goliath and Doeg.

B | 6, 7. The righteous onlookers.

A | 8, 9. David's praise to God.

Read the Psalm again in the light of the true *sub*-scription; and of its structure; and it lives before our eyes.

It is impossible for us to read the first five verses, without seeing the reference to David's challenge to Goliath in 1 Sam. xvii. 45-47. It may be that there is a reference to DOEG's "mischievous and deceitful tongue."

From the first, David took his stand on the fact that "the LORD will deliver thee into my hand" (compare verse 37). And, when he said "all this assembly shall know," he expresses what he afterwards wrote in Ps. lii. 6, 7 (Heb. 8, 9), "The righteous also shall see, and fear." †

---

* Twice afterwards this event was referred to as a great historical epoch in David's life (1 Sam. xxi. 11; xxix. 5.

† And yet Wellhausen says: "the person addressed (in verses 1-5) is not an alien tyrant, but a Jew in high position!"

It seems a *bathos*, to come down to the guesses of lexicographers and commentators.

One of them thinks it is a catchword of a song giving the name to a tune or an instrument. Another thinks it the catchword of "an older hymn." Just so; there is always something "older" with these critics. Another thinks it is the name of a tune called "sickness"; another says it is the name of a musical choir that dwelt in Abel-Meholah.

What if it is? What is there in that for either our minds or our hearts?

Such guesses as these do not treat the Psalms as possessing even common literary merit. Critics only bring down the Scriptures to their own literary level when they deal with them in such a fashion. Their aim seems to be to degrade the Word of God: they treat it, not, as they profess, "like any other book," but with less respect than they bestow upon other books.

No! There is something more than all that in this title When David wrote Psalm lii. under those special circumstances, and afterwards formally handed it over to the Chief Musician for Liturgical use, it was because there was instruction in it for the People of God, for all time, to give God the glory: for, whatever may be the goodness and mercy of God which He has manifested toward us, we too can say to-day:

"I will praise Thee for ever,
Because Thou hast done it:
And I will wait on Thy name;
For it is good before Thy saints."

"MAHALATH-LEANNOTH."

(DANCINGS WITH SHOUTINGS).

Psalm lxxxvii.*

THE BRINGING UP OF THE ARK.

THIS Psalm-Title (lxxxvii.) has another word associated with *Mahalath*: *Leannoth.*

There is no question as to the meaning of this latter word. All are agreed that it is from עָנָה ('*anah*) *to celebrate by responsive shouting.*† Hence *Leannoth* means *with shoutings* as answering other shoutings, in the celebration of an event. (See Ex. xv. 20, 21. Ezra iii. 11. Num. xxi. 17. Exod. xxxii. 17, 18; and 1 Sam. xviii. 6, 7).

---

* Not Psalm lxxxviii. over which this title now stands in the Versions.

† With regard to the two meanings of עָנָה we should not imagine *two* words, but *one* having two principal senses, arising from one root-conception of *answering*. And response may take the form of approval or reproof; sympathy in joy, or compassion in misery; it may be positive or negative. Hence, *to sing* or *to wail; to shout* for *joy*, or *to mourn* by way of giving expression to suffering. These varied senses all come from the one root-idea; and, of course, the *Piel* would be intensive, and include the thought of *repetition*—which, needless to say, is more naturally inherent in singing than in complaining. Hence, Gesenius classes Psalm lxxxviii. 1, Isaiah xxvii. 2, Exodus xxxii. 18, under the first meaning of עָנָה as having the *Piel* sense of *chant, sing* (as in *Kal.*)

As for *Mahalath*, it is no word. The reading of *Aquila* reduces it to a distinct vocable, *M'holoth*. Otherwise, it is suggested to mean "a stringed instrument" or "sickness." Both these cannot be right; and neither can have any association with the other. The reading of *Symmachus* supports that of *Aquila*: for in the day when those versions were made, the Septuagint puzzle (transliterating the word) was solved. Mr. Thirtle recognizes this: and the sense of the Psalms supports it. Moreover, *M'holoth* is a word not only suited for a musical note, but finds a distinct verbal echo in one of the Psalms (lxxxvii. 7).

Mahalath-Leannoth may thus be well Englished by

DANCINGS with SHOUTINGS.

We have not far to seek for the event in David's life which was, of all others, thus characterized.

The Ark of the Testimony had been taken by the Philistines (1 Sam. iv. 1-11); but, after seven months, it was restored to Israel (ch. vi. 1—vii. 2); and it abode in Kirjath-jearim for twenty years.

As soon as David was come to the Throne, his first business was to bring up the Ark of God to Zion: and 2 Sam. vi. gives the account of that great historical event. There, we read in verses 14, 15:—

> "And David DANCED before the LORD with all his might. . . So David and all the house of Israel brought up the Ark of Jehovah with SHOUTING, and with the sound of the trumpet."

Here we have, in the English,* the two words † of the *sub*-scription to Ps. lxxxvii. used in the account of bringing the Ark to Zion.

What was there that made this event so worthy of celebration? First, look at

The Structure of Ps. lxxxvii.

A[1] | 1, 2. Other dwellings spoken of.
  B[1] | 3. Zion spoken to. Selah.
A[2] | 4. Other nations spoken of.
  B[2] | 5. Zion spoken to.
A[3] | 6. Other nations spoken of. Selah.
  B[3] | 7. Zion spoken to.

* Not in the Hebrew, though we have an obvious allusion to such rejoicings as are indicated in the *sub*-scription to Ps. lxxxvii.

† In *v.* 16 it is not the same word for *shouting* in the Hebrew; but, it is included in the more general and comprehensive word *'anah*.

Here, there is a distinct allusion, in verse 2, to the other places in Jacob where the Ark had had a dwelling place: Shiloh (1 Sam. i. 3; ii. 14; iii. 21, Ps. lxxviii. 60), Gibeah (2 Sam. vi. 3, 4), and the house of Obed-edom the Gittite (v. 10-12), Beth-Shemesh (1 Sam. vi. 13), Kirjath-jearim (vii. 1).

But none of these was the dwelling that God had chosen and desired (Ps. cxxxii. 13, 14; lxxviii. 67-69; cxxxii. 1-8).

Zion was the place—"the mount Zion which he loved."

Other places might make their boast, and set forth their claims; men might claim their citizenship of other cities: but there was one city which was yet to be the joy of the whole earth; and the time would come when all other boasts would sink into nothingness beside the claims of being born in, or of belonging to, Zion.

It is this great and blessed fact which is celebrated in the Psalm of "dancings with shoutings" *(Mahalath-Leannoth)* which commemorates the bringing up of the Ark to the Tabernacle of David.

Much has yet to be studied with regard to David's Tabernacle as prior to, and distinct from, the Temple of Solomon.

It is referred to in 2 Sam. vi. 17; vii. 2; and Ps. cxxxii., where the shoutings are mentioned (v. 9). Also in 1 Chron. xvi. 1; 2 Chron. i. 4; Amos ix. 11, 12. It is this "tabernacle of David" which is to be restored, according to Acts xv. 15-18. "After this": *i.e.*, after the taking out of the Gentiles a people for His name (it is written), "I will return, and will build again the tabernacle of David, which is fallen down; and I will build again the ruins thereof, and I will set it up: that the residue of men might seek after the Lord, and all the Gentiles, upon whom my name is called, saith the Lord, who doeth all these things.

Known unto God are all his works from the beginning of the world."

Acts xv. 14 is not yet fulfilled. The Prophecy of Amos ix. 11, 12, which is quoted in Acts xv. 16 and 17, will not be fulfilled till the "taking out" in verse 14 is completed. "Simeon hath declared how God at the first did visit the Gentiles to take out of them a People for His name" (*v.* 14).

This refers to the present dispensation of election, when a People is being "taken out" from among the Gentiles, and a remnant from Israel "according to the election of grace." (Rom. xi. 5).

Then Acts xv. 15 says "After this," *i.e.*, after this double election has been "taken out," "After this I will return, and will build again the tabernacle of David, which is fallen down; and I will build again the ruins thereof, and I will set it up: that the residue of men might seek after the Lord and the Gentiles upon whom my name is called, saith the Lord."

This future blessing of Israel as a nation and "All the Gentiles," are distinguished from the present election of grace. These future blessings are connected with Zion, not Moriah; with the Tabernacle of David, not with the Temple.

David, "being a prophet" (Acts ii. 30), might well foretell of some of these "glorious things" which are* "spoken of" in Psalm lxxxvii:—

* See Cant. viii. 8. As there are cases of *Piel* with בּ so it is not surprising to find the *Pual* form in a like association. And, in view of the intensive sense of these forms, all difficulty vanishes. In the case of the Psalm, the "glorious things" are not only *spoken*, but with the force of Divine assurance, continually *repeated*. In the case of the passage of Canticles, the maid is not only *bespoken*, but asked for with all the urgency of a love which *repeats* its demand: And any other preposition would have failed, in both cases, to give expression to the relations which reside in the ideas employed.

"MAHALATH-LEANNOTH."

New Expository Translation of Ps. lxxxvii. according to the Structure (above).

A[1] | 1. His foundation upon the holy mountains doth Jehovah love. 2. [He loveth] the gates of Zion more than all the dwellings of Jacob.

B[1] | 3. Glorious things are spoken of thee, O thou City of God. *Selah.*

A[2] | 4. I will make mention of Egypt[a] and Babylon to them who know me:—Lo! Philistia, and Tyre, with Ethiopia [say] "This one was born there."

B[2] | 5. But, to Zion it shall be said: "Generation after generation[b] was born in her; and the Most High Himself shall establish her."

A[3] | 6. Jehovah will record, when he enrolleth nations—"This one was born there." *Selah.*

B[3] | 7. Both they that SHOUT and they that DANCE [shall say of Zion] "All my descendants[c] shall be in thee" [O thou City of God].

---

a Heb. *Rahab.* It is the poetical name for Egypt on account of its meaning, *pride.* Compare Ps. lxxxix. 10. Is. xxx. 7; li. 9. In the Hebrew, this name Rahab is differently spelt from that of the woman who, "through faith," sheltered the spies.

b Heb. *Man and man: i.e., one man after another; man after man;* in contrast to the individuals born in other places: and in conformity with the Divine prophecies. See Is. lx. 4; liv. 1-3; lxvi. 7-14.

c Mr. Thirtle suggests this rendering of the word *fountains*, and gives Deut. xxxiii. 28 as suggesting this sense. We may add by comparison Ps. lxviii. 26, margin, with which Isa. xlviii. 1 may be compared. Zion will be the fountain whence all Jehovah's blessings will flow forth for Israel and the nations.

Such are some of the "glorious things" which are and will be spoken of Zion; and they are well worthy of being recounted on such a momentous occasion as the bringing up of the Ark of the Covenant to Jerusalem.

The Critics cannot get beyond the Dispersion! All that Wellhausen has to say is:—

"The text is in so defective a state that in many passages we can only conjecture the meaning. The general sense admits of no doubt: the Jews are scattered all over the world, but Jerusalem continues to be their common home and mother. The significance of the Dispersion and the abiding importance of Jerusalem are distinctly visible."

When Critics see some *defect*, it is always *the Text* that is defective. It never seems to dawn on them that the *defect* is in themselves!

They first settle that the Psalm is *Post-exilic*, and then do their best to read the Exile into it.

It cannot be done. Hence it seems to them to be "defective"! So far from the "Dispersion" being "distinctly visible," we can see nothing of it at all; but, we can see a great event in David's history, commemorated by himself, in words worthy of the great theme, which fills his heart and carries him forward in prophetic vision to future times, when the "glorious things which are spoken of Zion" shall have a glorious accomplishment.

This view of the Psalm takes it right back, at once, to David's own day; and establishes the antiquity and authenticity both of the Text, and of the Canon.

"AIJELETH HASH-SHAHAR."

(The Day-Dawn).

Psalm xxi.*

The Coronation (or National) Anthem.

In the A.V. and R.V. this title stands over Psalm xxii. In the latter it is given as "Aijeleth hash-Shahar." But the meaning is given, in the margin of both versions, as "*The hind of the morning.*"

With this meaning we are quite content. It has been generally accepted since it was given by Aben Ezra.

The more ancient Jewish commentators Rashi and Kimchi, interpreted it as meaning "*a hind fair as the morning*" (the former word "hind" being the same as in Song ii. 7; and the latter word "morning" the same as in Song vi. 10).

In all versions (following the Septuagint) it has stood as the *super*-scription over Psalm xxii.; and, in this position, has greatly puzzled both translators and commentators as to what connection there could possibly be between this title and that Psalm.

Luther tried to adapt the words by rendering them "the hind early chased," referring it to the sufferings of the Messiah.

The Jewish Targum has it as meaning "the morning sacrifice."

But all of them alike were misled by the Septuagint: and it is the use of the key, so wonderfully discovered by Mr. Thirtle, which alone enables us, for the first time since the

* Not Ps. xxii. over which this title now stands in the Versions.

Dispersion, to connect the words with the Psalm to which they properly belong; and to see the beauty of both.

Using this key, we not only solve a difficulty, but gather most blessed instruction, and learn precious truth.

The great point for us to remember is, that the words *Aijeleth Shahar* or *Aijeleth hash-Shahar* are the *sub*-scription belonging to Psalm xxi.; and not the *super*-scription of Psalm xxii.

It is this that makes all the difference.

Psalm xxi.

therefore stands thus: its *three* parts being

(1) The *super*-scription: "A Psalm of David."

(2) The *Psalm* proper: verses 1-13.

(3) The *sub*-scription: "To the Chief Musician, relating to *Aijeleth hash-Shahar*."

What we have now to consider is, first, the meaning of this *sub*-scription; and secondly its teaching as connected with Psalm xxi.

We need not stop to mention the usual explanations which see nothing beyond the name of a tune, or of a musical instrument; or the catchwords of an "older" song.*

We look for something more dignified and worthy of Divine revelation than such puerile guesses.

The words are a Figure of Speech, quite common in the East, and frequently met with in Arabian poetry to-day.

Its use arose from the rays of the sun appearing and

* The Critics deal strangely with the Teaching and the Text of Scripture.

The *Teaching*, which is deep and grand beyond all conception, they fritter down to some commonplace reference; while the *Text*, which is simple and clear, they mystify with their imaginations and manipulations.

shooting up above the horizon like horns, before the sun actually appears: just as the horns of a hind might be seen above the rising ground before his body comes into view.

It denotes therefore *the rays of the rising sun*; the first beams of light mounting up, as is frequently seen in pictures of the rising sun.

The meaning therefore of *Aijeleth hash-Shahar* is clear, and may well be represented in English by

THE DAY-DAWN.

If we desire to know what this refers to, we have no need to go down to Egypt for help; or to turn to Babylonian tradition. The Scriptures contain all that is needful; and will prove our all-sufficient guide.

There we read of the promised dawn of a day that will bring peace and blessing to a sin-distressed and sorrow distracted world.

Now, it is "night": but the same Scripture that tells us it is night, tells us also that it is "far spent."

David's "last words" tell of this coming Day-dawn; and of Him, who, as the Sun, shall cover the whole earth with the glory of His light. He reveals in his prophetic utterance what Isaiah revealed when he said (Is. xxxii. 1):

"Behold, a king shall reign in righteousness,
And princes shall rule in judgment."

"THE LAST WORDS OF DAVID"

refer to this coming glorious Day, as being the complete fulfilment of God's unconditional Covenant, made with him, as to his throne, in 2 Sam. vii. David's "prayers" also end with the same reference to the same glorious events recorded in Psalm lxxii., which ends with the words (*vv.* 18-20):

"Blessed be LORD God, the God of Israel,
Who only doeth wondrous things:

And blessed be his glorious name for ever;
And let the whole earth be filled with his glory;
Amen, and Amen.
The prayers of David the Son of Jesse are ended."

When that prayer is answered, there will be nothing more to pray for.

"The last words of David the Son of Jesse" have the same blessed theme for their subject. They are written in 2 Sam. xxiii. 1-5. He says:

"David the Son of Jesse saith,[1]
And the man who was raised up on high,
The anointed of the God of Jacob,
And the sweet Psalmist of Israel, saith[1]
The Spirit of the LORD spake[2] by me,
And his word[3] was in my tongue.
The God of Israel said,[4]
The Rock of Israel spake[2] to me."

Having thus impressed us with the fact that "these last words" were Divinely inspired, and, therefore, were Divine words, the great revelation is made in verses 3-7.

Their Structure is as follows:

A | -3. The Ruler. The requirement for His rule.
  B | 4, 5. His righteous rule for His People.
  B | 6. His righteous judgment on His enemies.
A | 7. The Ruler. The requirement for His judgments.

We need not translate the whole of this: but we must enlarge on verse 4 and 5, in which we have *the Day-dawn* for Israel and the world.

---

[1] נְאֻם (*na'am*) *to utter* oracularly: *to give an oracular utterance.*

[2] דִּבֵּר (*davar*) *to speak*, referring to the substance of Divine revelation.

[3] מִלָּה (*millah*) referring to the *Divine Decree.*

[4] אָמַר (*'amar*) referring to *the mode* by which the word was imparted.

In verse 4 we have four lines. In the *first* and *third* lines we have a simile, showing the effects of the sun-rising, in the heaven and on the earth. In the *second* and *fourth* lines we have the clearness and beauty of the light itself.

The lines are alternate; for all is in Divine order, proceeding to carry out Jehovah's counsels:

Verse 4. (*The Day-Dawn*).

C | "He shall be as the light of the morning, when the sun riseth.

D | Even a morning without clouds;

C | As the tender grass springing out of the earth

D | By clear shining after rain."

After the long darkness comes the clear and beauteous light, revivifying the heaven and the earth.

Then in verse 5 we have the righteous rule, shedding its light and glory over all; and based on the Covenant made with David in 2 Sam. vii.

Again we have four lines: but, this time, arranged as an introversion because this rule will upset man's rule, and set up the righteous rule of Messiah.

In the Hebrew, each line commences with the same word כִּי (*kī*) *for*. In the A.V. they are rendered "Although," "Yet," "For," and "Although." In the R.V. they are rendered "Verily," "Yet," "For," "Although."

We prefer to keep the same word "For" in all the four lines, and to make our translation conform to the *marginal* renderings of the R.V. We shall thus see that the *first* and *fourth* lines are questions concerning David's house: while in the *second* and *third* lines we have Jehovah's covenant. All is thus seen to be plain and simple. The verse will then read:

Verse 5. (*The Righteous Rule*).

E | "For is not my house thus with God?

F | For He hath made with me an everlasting covenant, ordered in all things and sure.

F | For this is all my salvation and all my desire.

E | For, Shall He not make it to prosper?"

Yes, this is *the Day-dawn* of which David prophesied and sang. This is the Day-dawn for which creation groans, and for which Israel waits. This "waiting for the morning" is beautifully expressed in another Psalm (Ps. cxxx. 5-6):

"I wait for Jehovah, my soul doth wait,
And in his word do I hope.
My soul waiteth for Jehovah
More than they that watch for the morning;
I say, more than they that watch for the morning."

This is *Aijeleth Shahar;* this is "the hind of the morning." This is THE DAY-DAWN! And, this is the subject to which Psalm xxi. relates. It is the "tender mercy" of God; it is the "Day-spring from on high" whose visitation is celebrated in Luke i. 78.

When we compare this Psalm (xxi.) with 2 Sam. xxiii. and the other passages cited above, it will be seen, how wonderful is the relation between the Psalm (xxi.) and its *sub*-scription.

It may have been, in the first instance, written for, or in connection with David's own coronation: but, like all the special Psalms "of David" it refers to David's Son, and David's Lord; it is prophetic of Him. Hence, when it was formally handed over to the Chief Musician for liturgical use, it assumed a new status, and acquired a new application, in which all God's people for all time would henceforth be interested.

In substance, it is on the lines of "the last words of David," as will be seen if it be compared with 2 Sam. xxiii. 3-7.

We cannot do more than give the Structure:

Psalm xxi.

A | 1. The King's rejoicing in Jehovah's power (עז).

B | a | 2-5. Jehovah's gifts to the King.
  b | 6. Jehovah's appointments for the King (R.V. margin).
  c | 7. Reason for the King's establishment.
} Jehovah addressed.

B | *a* | 8-10. The King's judgment on His enemies.
  b | 11. His enemies' devices* against the King.
  c | 12. Reason for His enemies being driven away.
} The King addressed.

A | 13. His People's rejoicing in Jehovah's mighty deeds † (עז).

It will thus be seen that Ps. xxi. is Israel's National Anthem: but no mawkish poet has dealt with it as the English National Anthem has recently been dealt with, when the lines were attempted to be cut out:

"Confound their politics,
Frustrate their knavish tricks."

---

* It should be *plural*, as it is in some Codices, the Septuagint, Aramaic, and Vulgate versions, and four early printed editions. See Ginsburg's Heb. Text and note.

† It should be *plural*, as in some Codices, Septuagint, Vulgate, and one early printed edition. See Ginsburg's Heb. Text and note.

No! The Ruler among men, when He rules in righteousness, will not only bring light, and blessing, and peace, and glory, to His People: but He will do it by first putting down all their *enemies*. For, while they live, there can be no peace: while they rule, there can be no blessing.

And now, we, too, long for this Day-dawn.

We are living in this "dark place"; but we have the Divine prophetic word, which is our only light in it. To this Word we "do well to take heed." Popular teachers tell us we do well not to take heed to it: and they practise, in this case, exactly what they preach.

But we will "take heed to it in our hearts": for these are the words (in 2 Pet. i. 19) which must be connected. It is to be heart-work with us. It is the work of "waiting for God's Son from heaven" (1 Thess. i. 10). Yea, waiting more than they who watch for the morning. We look for this Day-star: we watch for this Day-dawn: and we remember how it is written:—"We have also a more sure word of prophecy: whereunto ye do well that ye take heed in your hearts* until the day dawn, and the day-star arise."

* The words "until the day dawn and the day-star arise" must be put in a parenthesis. For it is not unconverted people who are to take heed until they are converted; but the Lord's People who are to take heed in their hearts till the promised Day shall dawn.

"JONATH-ELEM-RECHOKIM."

(The Dove of the Distant Woods).

Psalm lv.*

David's Flight from Absalom.

There is only one Psalm which bears this title.

At present this title stands as part of the *super*-scription of Psalm lvi. But, using Dr. Thirtle's key,† we note that its original and proper place was, and is, the *sub*-scription to Psalm lv.

With this key, Psalm lv. will consist of the following three parts:—

(1) The *Super*-scription: "Maschil, a Psalm of David."‡

(2) The Psalm Proper: verses 1-23.

(3) The *Sub*-scription: "To the Chief Musician, relating to *Jonath-elem-rechokim*."

The remaining words form no part of this *sub*-scription, but form the Title proper of Psalm lvi. So that the present *super*-scription of Ps. lvi. must be divided, and the first part of it put at the end of Psalm lv.

With regard to the meaning of the words "upon Jonath-elem-rechokim," it is generally agreed that it means

"*Relating to the Dove of the distant Terebinths.*"§

---

* Not Psalm lvi. over which the title now stands in the Versions.

† See pages 1—9.

‡ "To the Chief Musician on Neginoth" belongs, of course, to Psalm liv., of which it is the *sub*-scription.

§ Or, *oak-woods*. Others prefer "*the silent Dove in the far-off regions.*"

David is this Dove. He is far away in the distant woods, bemoaning the trouble that has come upon him, in the rebellion of Absalom recorded in 2 Sam. xv.-xix.

Most commentators and readers have observed that there is nothing "relating to a dove" in Ps. lvi.: but, many *have* noticed that there is in Ps. lv. But even this never awakened the thought that perhaps these words might after all really belong to Ps. lv.

But now, all is clear, even to a child. It is only those who will not see who remain blind to this wonderful discovery.

The "higher" critics of course have treated it with a conspiracy of silence. The gravamen is voiced in *The Times* review (May 20, 1904). That review does not point out any error, it exposes no fault, but Mr. Thirtle is held up to execration because "he deliberately refuses to accept the recognized methods of modern literary criticism."

This is the unpardonable sin! But we say,—all praise to Mr. Thirtle, who by this discovery of the lost key, has established the fact that the Psalter, as we have it to-day in our Hebrew manuscripts and Bibles, is the same, line for line, as it was 2,500 years ago. This, of course, writes folly on the speculations of men who have been only too eager to make the Psalms a human composition by bringing them down to post-exilic dates.

This is the Title under which we may well pause and consider this aspect of the question. For many have been puzzled by the fact that the Title in question *does* suit Ps. lv. and does *not* suit Ps. lvi. over which it at present stands. And yet the Critics refuse to accept this simple explanation which removes the difficulty.

And why do they refuse? Just because it *does* remove it! Just because it proves that Psalm lv. is David's

Psalm; that it is the outpouring of David's own heart in a trial that was his, and his alone! But this is what the Critics do not want. They begin with the desire to do away with the authorship claimed in the Scriptures for these Psalms, and hence they may well be first alarmed, then silent, and then angry with those who refuse to accept "the recognized methods of modern literary criticism"!

And yet, when we come to apply the ordinary methods of *genuine* criticism, we are struck with the internal evidence and beauty of Psalm lv. as we see how wonderfully it accords with the circumstances in David's life, and with the experiences of him who alone could have been the writer.

The Psalm, as we have said, relates to, perhaps, the greatest trial of David's life. We have only to read 2 Sam. xv.-xix. and Psalm lv., to see how beautiful and appropriate are the words.

We read of David's flight from Jerusalem to the "distant woods" (those woods in which Absalom was afterwards entangled and slain): how "he went up by the ascent of Mount Olivet, and wept as he went up, and had his head covered, and he went barefoot; and all the people that was with him, covered every man his head, and they went up, weeping as they went. And one told David, saying, Ahithophel is among the conspirators with Absalom. And David said, O Jehovah, I pray thee, turn the counsel of Ahithophel into foolishness" (2 Sam. xv. 30, 31).

His hope in God was expressed to Zadok, when Zadok wished to bring the Ark of God with him. "Carry back the Ark of God unto the city; if I shall find favour in the eyes of Jehovah, he will bring me again, and show me both it, and his habitation"(*v.* 25).

Now turn to Psalm lv., and there we find David saying (*v.* 2).:

"I mourn in my complaint and moan" (R.V.) . . .

Here we have the moaning of "the Dove." Hezekiah in later days knew this experience, in a trial equally great, when he said (Isa. xxxviii. 14).

"I did mourn* as a dove."

David goes on to tell of his "weeping (*vv.* 4-8).

"My heart is sore pained within me:
And the terrors of death are fallen upon me.
Fearfulness and trembling are come upon me.
And horror hath overwhelmed me.
And I said, Oh that I had wings like a dove!
For then would I fly away, and be at rest.
Lo, then would I wander far off,
And remain in the wilderness.
I would hasten my escape from the stormy wind and tempest."

And again in *vv.* 16, 17, he turns to Jehovah in his trouble:

"As for me, I will call upon God:
And Jehovah shall save me.
Evening, morning, and at noon, will I pray, and moan† (R.V.)
And he shall hear my voice."

The desertion of Ahithophel is also alluded to in verses 12-14.

"For it was not an enemy that reproached me;
Then I could have borne it:
Neither was it he that hated me that did magnify himself against me;
Then I would have hid myself from him.
But it was thou, a man mine equal,

---

* The very word used by David of himself in Ps. lv. 17. See Ezek. vii. 16, where we have it again.

† Compare Is. xxxviii. 14, and Ezek. vii. 16.

My guide and my familiar friend (R.V.).
We took sweet counsel together,
And walked unto the house of God in company."

Thus does David "moan like a Dove in the distant woods." None but he could have written this Psalm.

Truly does its *super*-scription declare it to be "Of David."

All Psalms so headed have a reference to David's Son, and David's Lord. This Psalm refers especially to the trials of Messiah, and *vv.* 12-14 to His betrayal by Judas of whom Ahithophel reminds us, and who, in like manner "hanged himself."*

Whatever may have been the original circumstances out of which such Psalms arose, and to which their *interpretation* belongs, there is an application in them to the true David, the Messiah.

Hence, when such a Psalm was formally handed over to "the Chief Musician," for liturgical use, it was because it was capable of a wider application. It at once assumed a new position; and could be used for all time, and long after the fulfilment in the experience of Him who, in like trouble, "offered up prayers and supplications with strong crying and tears unto him that was able to save him" (Heb. v. 7).

Such Psalms can be applied to and used by the Lord's people in all their times of trial and desertion.

David was a prophet (Acts ii. 30); and he spake of Christ. Hence, his inspired words stand for all time, for the comfort and instruction of the people of God.

* 2 Sam. xvii. 23. Matt. xxvii. 5-8, Acts i. 16-19.

"AL-TASCHITH."

(Destroy Not).

Psalms lvi., lvii., lviii., and lxxiv.*

The Cry at a Crisis.

There are four Psalms that bear this title. Not Psalms lvii., lviii., lix., and lxxv., over which it now stands as the *super*-scription; but Psalms lvi., lvii., lviii., and lxxiv., at the end of which it should stand as the *sub*-scription.

In three of these Psalms (lvii., lviii., and lix.), the *sub*-scription of one Psalm has been mixed up with the *super*-scription of the following Psalm. These titles must, therefore, be divided: the former part belonging to the preceding Psalm, and the latter part to the Psalm over which they now already stand.

It will thus be seen that the first three (lvi., lvii., lviii.) are all Psalms of David, while the fourth (lxxiv.) is a Psalm of Asaph.

Two of those by David are stated to be connected with some special event in his life.

Psalm lvi.: "When the Philistines took him in Gath."

Psalm lvii.: "When he fled from Saul in the cave."

But all three are connected with a peculiar time of trouble; and consist of complaint to God, and trust in Him.

There is no dispute as to the meaning of *Al-taschith* (or as it is in the R.V., *Al-tashheth*). Both versions give it as meaning

* Not Psalms lvii., lviii., lix. and lxxv., over which it now stands in the Versions.

"AL-TASCHITH."

"DESTROY NOT!"

We need not go outside the covers of the Bible to find the signification of this exclamation.

It had been made by Moses at a great crisis, in Exod. xxxii. 11-14; and it was made at a great crisis, by David, in 2 Sam. xxiv. 16, where we have the same Hebrew word שָׁחַת (*shachath*).

These Psalms, written originally as a special appeal for Divine mercy, and for justice to sheath its sword, became afterwards equally appropriate and applicable for use at any similar time when at some such crisis a similar appeal was called for.

Hence, they were handed over to "the Chief Musician" as suitable for liturgical use in times of trouble, when the same appeal "Destroy not!" would voice the inward cry.

In the Wilderness God had threatened to destroy the whole nation, and make another nation of Moses (Exod. xxxii. 10).

And the reply of Moses was an expansion of these words "Destroy not!" (*vv.* 11, 12).

In Deut. ix. 25 Moses reminds the people of this, and said, "I fell down at the first, because the LORD had said he would destroy you. I prayed, therefore, unto Jehovah, and said, O Adonay Jehovah DESTROY NOT thy people and thine inheritance."

David, in like manner, in a similar time of trouble, makes the same appeal. When the angel "stretched out his hand upon Jerusalem to destroy it," he prayed in the spirit of these same words, "Destroy not!" (2 Sam. xxiv. 16, 17.

Indeed, both Moses and David acted on the injunction of Jehovah in Deut. iv. 30, 31.

> "When thou art in tribulation, and all these things are come upon thee, even in the latter days, if thou turn to the Lord thy God, and shall be obedient unto His voice (for the Lord thy God is a MERCIFUL God), he will NOT forsake thee, neither DESTROY thee, nor forget the covenant of thy fathers which he sware unto them."

This is why the first two of these Psalms commence with the words, "Be merciful unto me, O God" (Psalms lvi. 1; lvii. 1).

We have not space to quote these four Psalms in full, but would ask our readers to study them carefully in this new light thrown upon them by *Al-taschith*, "Destroy not!"

Read especially Psalm lvi. 1, 9, 10, 11.
Psalm lvii. 1-3, 6, 7;
Psalm lviii. 3, 6, 7, 11, and
Psalm lxxiv. 1-3, 10, 11, 18-20, 22, 23.

Psalm lxxiv. is distinctly prophetic, and refers to a yet future time of trouble, even "the latter days" spoken of in Deut. iv. 30. For in Asaph's days Zion was not in the hands of the enemy.

A day is coming—"the day of Jacob's trouble"—when the same appeal to Divine mercy will have to be made; and "Destroy not!" will be the suited appeal.

And why not prophetic? David was a prophet (Acts ii. 30). He speaks of Millennial days in Psalms xciii. xcvii. xcix. ci., &c., and "spake of the resurrection of Christ." But no one has suggested that Psalm xvi. is a Post-resurrection Psalm. These and other Psalms were not written after the Millennium; why then should Psalms which refer to the Exile be considered as having been written after the Exile, and dubbed "Post-Exilic"?

"AL-TASCHITH."

Why should not Psalm lxxiv. and other Psalms, as they were written in the Land when as yet no enemy had devastated it, be prophetic, and refer to the future, when their language would be suited for those who should live in "the latter days"?

Meanwhile their application is universal, for they are Psalms of humiliation, and appeals to the mercy of God, based on his everlasting Covenant. They may well be used, therefore, by His people in their times of trouble and in their times of national judgment.

"NEHILOTH."

(INHERITANCES).

Psalm iv.

AGAIN we have to show how far the Commentators have been led astray by following a false scent. Having started with the hypothesis that all or most of these Psalm-Titles have to do with *music*, or *musical instruments*, they are tethered by this assumption, and naturally think they find what they so carefully look for. But Dr. Thirtle has shown how and why this is.

They have taken נְחִילוֹת (*nechīlōth*), as being derived from חָלַל (*chalal*), *to bore*, because it was an easy transition from that idea to *flutes*. But it is a very forced and unnatural derivation.

Wellhausen has *wind instruments*. Perowne, *with stringed instruments*.

The Ancient Versions suggest quite another derivation of the word; and by the use of Mr. Thirtle's wonderful key we are able to proceed, as with other Titles, and find something more worthy of the Word of God.

The Septuagint has *concerning her that inherits* (which Perowne dismisses by saying "which is clearly wrong"). Aquila's revision of the Septuagint has *Divisions of inheritance*. Symmachus (another revision) has *Allotments*. The old Latin Versions have similar renderings.

This shows that the Hebrew word they had before them was simply נחלת (*n-h-l-th*); and these four letters being without vowel points, they took the letter *cheth* ח,

as having an "*a*" (חָ). The later Massorites took it as having or needing an "*i*" (חִ). But we are not bound to follow this latter idea, and make the word *Nehiloth*, which has no sense, and leads only to an insoluble puzzle, when the other word, *Nehaloth*, gives us an intelligible meaning, and one which we can test for ourselves.

We have therefore to see whether this is "clearly wrong": and to see this, we have to do only two things: First, to take the first part of the *super*-scription of Psalm v. and read it as the subscription of Psalm iv., and then read Psalm iv. in the light of it, and see if there is any connection between the word "inheritances" and that Psalm.

When we do this, we at once see the connection, and the beauty of it; especially when we remember what is the essence of the Divine thought about *inheritances*.

The Scripture speaks of *two* inheritances. It was with Israel as it is now with the Church of God.

Jehovah's inheritance was His People, and their inheritance was Jehovah.

So with the Church: we have God's inheritance in the Saints, in Eph. i. 18; and our inheritance in Him, in Eph. i. 11.

So, of Israel, it is written (Deut. xxxii. 9):—

"Jehovah's portion is his people,
Jacob is the lot of his inheritance."

And all Godly Israelites could say with David: "Jehovah is the portion of mine inheritance and of my cup." (Psalm xvi. 5, compare lxxiii. 26; cxix. 57; cxlii. 5; Jer. x. 16. Lam. iii. 24.)

These are the great truths brought out and declared in this Psalm, v. 3, and it is heralded forth as a matter of supreme knowledge (as it is in Eph. i. 18).

> **"But know that Jehovah hath set apart one that he favoureth, for himself."***

"If Jehovah hath taken delight in us, he will bring us into this land, and give it us" (Num. xiv. 8). All was owing to Jehovah's favour.

This is put in contrast with the "vanity" and "falsehood" of men; and their estimate as to what is real possession and true inheritance. Man does not know the meaning of the word "good": he cannot tell us what is real "good."

Hence, verse 6 asks the question

> **"Many there be that say, 'Who will show us good?'"**

And this question gets a Divine answer in the words that immediately follow:—

> **"Jehovah, lift THOU up the light of THY countenance upon us.**
> **THOU hast put a gladness in my heart**
> **Greater than [they have], when their corn and their wine are increased."**

Joy in Jehovah is more than the joy of harvest or vintage (Isa. viii. 3, Jer. xlviii. 33). And Jehovah's "favour" is better than any earthly inheritance.

With this Psalm should be read Psalm cxliv., where the same precious teaching is found "*concerning inheritances*."

We have the same "vanity" and the same "falsehood" of the "strange children"; and the same false estimate of

---

* *See* R.V. margin.

those who are strangers to Jehovah's covenant (*vv.* 8, 11).* In verses 12-14 we have their estimate of what is true happiness and true inheritance. But we must note that the word אֲשֶׁר (*'asher*) is the relative Pronoun *that*, or *who*, and not the Conjunction, *that*: This being so, the nominative "who" requires a verb, and this Ellipsis must be supplied by the word *say*.† Then all is clear; and we can dispense with the multitude of *italics* which are otherwise required to make any sense. Verses -11-15 will then read:

"Who [say]: 'Our sons are as plants grown up in their youth;
'Our daughters are as corner-stones polished after the similitude of a palace;
'Our sheep bring forth thousands and ten thousands in our streets;
'Our oxen are strong to labour.
'There is no breaking in or going out
'There is no complaining in our streets,
'Happy people that are in such a case'"

---

* This is shown by the Structure of Psalm cxliv.

A[1] | 1-7. David's words (Praise and Prayer).

B[1] | 8. The vain and false words of the "strange children."

A[2] | 9-11-. David's words (Praise and Prayer).

B[2] | -11-15-. The vain and false words of the "strange children."

A[3] | -15. David's words. (The truth as to happiness, in opposition to the vanity and falsehood spoken by the "strange children").

† As is so frequently the case, see Gen. xxvi. 7. 1 Kings xx. 34. Psalms ii. 2; cix. 5 (where in verses 6-20 we have the imprecation words of David's enemies, and not the words of David). Isa. v. 9; xiv. 8; xviii. 2; xxii. 13; xxiv. 14, 15; xxviii. 9 (Whom [say they] shall he teach, &c.). Jer. ix. 19 ([saying] How are we spoiled). Jer. l. 5 (thitherward [saying]). Hos. xiv. 8 (Ephraim [shall say]). Acts. x. 15; xiv. 22, 2 Cor. xii. 16, &c.

The Structure requires us to supply the word "Nay" instead of the "*Yea*" of the A.V.

> "[**Nay!**] **Happy is the People whose God is Jehovah.**"

This alone is true happiness and real "good." This is the only source of abiding joy and gladness for any People. It is not any increase in our earthly *inheritance;* it is not the increase of corn and wine; but it is the light of Jehovah's countenance.

It is not the multiplying of sheep and oxen. It is not the store which men put into their garners, but it is the "gladness" which God puts into their hearts.

How beautifully therefore this Psalm iv. opens its treasure to us when the proper key is applied.

"Concerning inheritances," indeed! Yes, the true inheritances of Jehovah and His People; in the knowledge of which all who possess it may well say

> "In peace will I both lay me down and sleep!
> For THOU, Jehovah, alone makest me to dwell in safety" (Ps. iv. 8).

(3) WORDS RELATING TO SPECIAL CHOIRS.

We have spoken of those Titles which relate entirely to the *subject-matter* of the Psalms and have shown how their misplacement which makes them stand at the beginning of a Psalm instead of at the end of the previous Psalm, has caused the loss of their meaning for so many centuries.

It is the same with words in the other Titles in which we have to do, not so much with the *subject*, as with other matters.

There are three words which are connected with special singers: *'Alamoth*, *Sheminith*, and *Jeduthun*. We will deal with these in order.

"'AL 'ALAMOTH."

(Relating to the Maidens' Choir).

Psalm xlv.

'Al 'Alamoth (עַל עֲלָמוֹת) is one of these words; which relates not so much to the subject-matter of the Psalm itself, but to the manner of its use.

'Alamoth is found only once; and in all the Versions it is placed over Psalm xlvi. But, when it is removed from its present position as part of the *super*-scription of Psalm xlvi., and put in its proper place, as part of the *sub*-scription of Psalm xlv., it will stand connected with, and related to, this latter Psalm, xlv.

We must again call attention to the preposition עַל (*'al*). It greatly obscures its meaning if we limit it to the sense of "after the manner of," "upon" or "set to," "to" or "for," as it is variously rendered.

It is a word in very common use; and its range of meanings is of wide extent. Its primitive meaning is (1) *on* or *upon*: from which we have (2) the sense of *over*, (3) *at*, *near*, or *by*, and (4) *relating to*, or *connected with*.

As to '*Alamoth*, there is a consensus of opinion that it means *maidens*. We have '*Almah* in the singular and plural seven times,* and it is always used in this sense.

It appears, therefore, that the plural '*Alamoth* must mean *maidens*.

If Psalm xlv. were the only occurrence of the word, then its use would be sufficiently satisfied by the subject-matter of the Psalm; for we have references to "king's daughters" and "honourable women" (*v.* 9); "Hearken, O daughter" (*v.* 10); "the daughter of Tyre" (*v.* 12); "the king's daughter" (*v.* 13); "the virgins her companions" (*v.* 14).

But the word does occur in one other passage (1 Chron. xv. 20); and here it relates to the singing of maidens, as distinct from men's voices.

There is no need to associate such singing with the Temple or its services. There was singing in other places beside Jerusalem and the Temple. There was *processional* singing, and that in the open air.

In 1 Chron. xv. the order of the procession is prescribed for bringing up the ark from the house of Obed-edom to Zion. There were three bodies appointed:

(1) First came the *Levites*, the singers with instruments of music (psalteries, harps and cymbals) (*vv.* 16-19), and the names are given of those who were set over them.

* It is rendered *virgin*, Gen. xxiv. 43, Song i. 3, vi. 8, Isa. vii. 14; *maid*, Ex. ii. 8, Prov. xxx. 19; and *damsel*, Ps. lxviii. 25. But the proper word for *virgin* is *Bethulah*. Every *Bethulah* is an *Almah*; but not every *Almah* is necessarily a *Bethulah*.

(2) Then came another body of singers, *the maidens*, with timbrels; and the names of those who were over the '*Alamoth* are given (*v.* 20).

(3) Then the *Sheminith* closed the procession. These, again, were men* singers, with harps, and those who were "over the *Sheminith*" (*v.* 21) are mentioned by name as in the former two divisions.

This order corresponds exactly with that given in Psalm lxviii., a Psalm of David, and in connection, not with the celebration of some victory, but referring specially to the bringing up of the Ark (after its wanderings) to Zion.†

Num. x. 35 gives us the words with which the Ark always moved:

> "Rise up, Jehovah,
> And let thine enemies be scattered.
> And let them that hate Thee flee before Thee."

Ps. lxviii. 1, opens with almost the very same words

> "Let God arise,
> Let His enemies be scattered.
> Let them also that hate Him flee before Him."

What words could be more appropriately used "when the Ark set forward" from the house of Obed-edom?

That Psalm lxviii. relates to this very event in David's life is further shown by his disposition of the procession, as given in 1 Chron. xv.: for it is closely followed, and accurately described, in Ps. lxviii. 24, 25:

† See on *Sheminith* in the next chapter.

‡ Though Psalm lxviii. was written originally and specially for this great occasion, yet there was in it that which made it most suitable for use at the Passover Festival. The word JAH of Ex. xv. 13 reappears in Ps. lxviii. 4, and is the link that unites the two. Hence it was handed afterwards "to the Chief Musician relating to Shoshannim."

"They have seen thy goings, O God;
The goings of my God, my King, into the Sanctuary.
The Singers went before, (1 Ch. xv., 16-19)
The Players on instruments followed after, (*v.* 21)
In the midst were damsels (the '*Alamoth*) playing with timbrels." (*v.* 20).

We find the same reference to the words of Num. x. 35 in Psalm cxxxii. 8, where the going up of the Ark is celebrated:—

"Arise, O Jehovah, into Thy rest
Thou, and the Ark of Thy strength."

The "goings" here spoken of in Ps. lxviii. 24, refer to the going up of the Ark of God into the Sanctuary, as described in 1 Chron. xv. and celebrated in Chron. xvi., Ps. lxviii., xlvii., lxxxvii. and other Psalms. If we compare Ps. lxviii. 18 with xlvii. 5 we see this connection at once.

To what can Psalm lxviii. 11 refer, but to 1 Chron. xv. 20. The R.V. have rightly translated the feminine participle,

"The LORD giveth the Word.
The women that publish the tidings are a great host."

But they give the wrong reference, "Ex. xv. 20 and 1 Sam. xviii. 6," instead of 1 Chron. xv. 20.

And, at so low an ebb is Biblical study that Psalm lxviii. 11 is wrenched from its context and used as an excuse for disobeying the Divine precepts concerning the preaching of women in this Gospel Dispensation.

Surely there can be no doubt as to the meaning of the word '*Alamoth*, or to the beauty and perfection, of the close connection between 1 Chron. xv., and Psalm lxviii.

There is no profit to our souls in knowing what different

commentators have said about the word *Alamoth*,* or about its two occurrences; or about the presence of *'Almah* in Ps. lxviii. 5.

Psalm lxviii. is no mere "celebration of a victory," as some think; but it is a Psalm of thanksgiving by David on the occasion of bringing the Ark of God into the Sanctuary which he had prepared for it on Mount Zion.

Yet, in the face of these plain Scriptures, all that Wellhausen has to say is: "The position of affairs is that of 1 Maccabees v. (167 B.C.): there is nothing to remind us of the deliverance from Babylon (537 B.C.)"†; and he gives a plate of an "Assyrian Triumphal Procession."

Not even as early a date as B.C. 537 will the "higher critics" allow as the date of Psalm lxviii.: and yet no other date will suit it, and no other event, but that of David's bringing up the Ark of God to Zion, which was at least 1040 B.C.!

We write not, however, for these Critics. Nothing will convince them that the hypotheses on which they base their criticisms is false: but we write for those who "believe God"; feeling sure that they will rejoice in that which makes His Word more clear, more beautiful, and more precious.

---

* Gesenius gives it as "*to* (the voice of) *young women*." Kirkpatrick "*in the manner of maidens*." Perowne "*after the manner of maidens*." Wellhausen "*with Elamite instruments*." Fuerst "*a choir dwelling in Alemeth*." Others interpret both *upon 'Alamoth* and *upon Sheminith* as meaning *melodies*. But this cannot be; because they are united in the same procession, and this would cause two melodies at the same time for the same Psalm. Neither can they mean *instruments*; inasmuch as they are in each case associated with, and accompanied by, instruments. Several commentators render Alamoth, *trebles*, and Sheminith, *basses*, in 1 Ch. xv. 20.

† Wellhausen, *Psalms*, page 191 (Dr. Paul Haupt's *Polychrome Bible*).

"SHEMINITH."

THE EIGHTH DIVISION.

Psalms v. and xi.

THIS word, at present stands in all the Versions as part of the *super*-scription over Psalms vi. and xii. But, from our preceding Papers we have seen that we must regard it, and place it, as part of the *sub*-scription to Psalms v. and xi.; with which Psalms *Shemînith* must henceforth stand connected.

Again : there is a fair consent of authority that it means *the eighth*; but there is a great divergence of opinion as to what *the eighth* refers to. The word occurs thirty-one times; and is always rendered *eighth*, except in 1 Ch. xv. 21, and in these two Psalm-Titles, where it is transliterated—"Sheminith." The A.V. puts *the eighth* in the margin in all three cases; the R.V. only in the latter two. The Septuagint transliterates the word in 1 Ch. xv. 21, referring us, in the margin, to Ps. vi. 1: and it translates the word in the Psalm-Titles.* Wellhausen says *the eighth mode*. Gesenius and Delitzsch, *the bass* or lower *octave*. Perowne and others, *upon the octave*. Kirkpatrick *tenor* or *bass*. Others take it to refer to the *eighth day*; which was a day of special solemnity; or to the *eighth year*. Others refer it to an instrument with *eight strings*. But, in 1 Ch. xv. 21, those with harps were set "over the *Shemînith*" (as others with psalteries were set "over the '*Alamoth*.'") This shows that it cannot mean an instrument; as certain instruments could not be "set over" other instruments

* In the Septuagint the Psalms are vi. and xi.

(1 Ch. xv. 21): and the *Shemînith* are additional to *Neginoth* in the *sub*-scription to Psalm v.

It is this passage (1 Ch. xv. 21) which helps to determine the meaning for us. For, if the singers in verse 20 were *'Alamoth* or *maidens*, it would seem obvious that those in verse 21, called *Shemînith*, were men.

But what class of males or "singing men" are meant by the special term "*Shemînith*"?

The answer suggested by the Talmud* is that *Shemînith* is explained as referring to circumcision and is used to designate a certain class of men, those who had been circumcised on *the eighth day*, and therefore true Israelites as distinguished from all other circumcised or uncircumcised: because, in Israel, it *was* the special rite of the *eighth* day. It was this that distinguished circumcision as the sign of God's Covenant with Israel, from the circumcision of Ishmael and his descendants, which was in the thirteenth year. Circumcision was practised not only by Ishmaelites but by other nations, but it was always later in life† and *never on the eighth day.* But this hardly satisfies the context: for the other males, the Priests and the Levites, were all thus similarly circumcised men. *The Shemînith* are distinguished not merely from the *'Alamōth*, but from all others in the procession which is so minutely described in 1 Chron. xv.

We come back to the point therefore that *Shemînith* means the *eighth*: but the question remains: the eighth *what?*

---

* *Yebamoth* 43b compare 53b. *Yeb.* is the first of *seven* treatises in the third book called *Nashim*, which treats of the distinctive rights of men and women. *Yeb.* consists of sixteen chapters, and treats of the marrying of a deceased brother's wife, etc.

† Josephus, Ant. i. 12. ‡ 2.

Dr. Thirtle, after discussing the various suggested solutions says: "Possibly, however, the Male Choir may have been described as *Shemīnith* on other grounds" (p. 112); and it "may point in one of several directions. A *time* might be intended; but the passage in 1 Chron. 15 is against that. A *place* might be intended; but here again the way is barred. A *class* seems the inevitable intention." (p. 111).

Dr. Thirtle thus points to the true solution.

A *class* is intended; but not necessarily the class suggested by the Talmud: for, though that class of circumcised men would agree with the scope of the preceding verse, it is not in perfect harmony with the context of the chapter as a whole: because, though a class as distinct from the maidens, this would not mark them as a class as distinct from the other males, mentioned in verses 14-19: for these also were circumcised.

Substitute another word for "class," and we have the answer to our question:—the eighth *division* in the procession.

The whole chapter points to a procession. The Ark was to be carried up with great solemnity to the place which David had prepared for it. It was not going up in the midst of a crowd of people. It was not going up in unseemly disorder. Everything in this important chapter shows that the greatest possible care was taken with a view to order. The places of the Priests, and the Levites, were designated. Those who were to carry the Ark were duly appointed according to Ex. xxv. 14; Num. iv. 15; vii. 9, "as Moses commanded according to the word of Jehovah" (*v.* 15).

"And David spake to the chief of the Levites *to appoint* their brethren," &c. (*v.* 16, compare *v.* 19).

Everything, and every one, occupied an appointed place in the goings of the Ark of God into the Sanctuary (Ps. lxviii. 24, R.V.)

In 1 Ch. xxiv. 1, we read of "The divisions of the sons Aaron:" and in *v.* 5 we read "thus were they divided."

In 1 Ch. xxvi. 1, we find that even the porters had *divisions*; and in *v.* 12 we read of "the *divisions* of the porters, . . . having wards one against another, to minister in the house of Jehovah."

It seems impossible for us to get away from the conclusion that 1 Ch. xv. 21 refers to the *the eighth division.*

The definite article is emphatic, and points to the last division of the procession, that immediately preceding the Ark of the Covenant, and therefore the nearest to it.

The subject of verse 21 is the appointing of this eighth division. "Mattithiah, and Elipheleh, and Mikneiah, and Obed-edom, and Jeiel, and Azaziah, with harps over *the Sheminith* to lead."

"To excel" is hardly the suitable word. The R.V. renders it *to lead*; and this is its general meaning. In 1 Ch. xxiii. 4, 2 Ch. xxxiv. 12, Ezra iii. 8, 9, it is rendered *set forward*, either work or workmen. So here, these men who are named, were appointed *to lead* this eighth division, in its setting forward; the eighth division itself being appointed specially *to lead* the actual Ark-bearers.

But, was everything ordered except the Psalms which were to be sung in the procession? Were the "singers" appointed, and no words appointed for them to sing? Surely not. The next verse tells us that "Chenaniah chief of the Levites was over the song; he instructed about the song, because he was skilful" (*v.* 22).

Then comes the Ark itself (*v.* 23), with its doorkeepers and others "before the ark of God."

This closes up the grand procession, and completes its description.

It would appear that three Psalms were specially prepared. One is given in the next chapter (1 Ch. xvi. 7-36); the other two would be Psalms v. and xi.

The first appears again: parts of it being included later in Psalms, Ps. cv., xcvi., cvi., cvii., cxviii., cxxxvi.

The other two (Pss. v. and xi.) were suitable for more general use; and hence, were formally handed over "to the Chief Musician," for subsequent use in the Temple service. They are "relating to *the Shemīnith*"; and Ps. v. was "with stringed instruments," *viz.*, the "harps" of 1 Ch. xv. 21.

We naturally turn to these two Psalms and look for some reference to the great event. We find such reference, both in the Structure, and in the words.

The Structure of both the Psalms specially contrasts *the righteous worshippers* of Jehovah with the wicked.

PSALM V.

A | 1-3. Prayer to Jehovah.
  B | 4. Reason ("For"): Character of Jehovah.
    C | 5, 6. The wicked, and their wickedness.
      D | 7. The righteous worshippers contrasted. ("But"). The *Shemīnith*.

A | 8. Prayer to Jehovah.
  B | 9. Reason ("For"). Character of the Wicked.
    C | 10. The wicked, and their destruction.
      D | 11, 12. The righteous worshippers contrasted. ("But"). The *Shemīnith*.

"SHEMINITH."

PSALM XI.

A | 1. Trust in Jehovah, the Defender of the righteous.
  B | 2. The wicked. Their violence manifested.
    C | 3. The righteous tried.
      D | 4-. Jehovah's throne in heaven.
      D | -4. Jehovah's eyes on earth.
    C | 5-. The righteous tried.
  B | -5, 6. The wicked. Their violence revenged.
A | 7. Trust in Jehovah, the Lover of the righteous.

In both these Structures we see the set contrast between the righteous worshippers and the wicked: while in the words we find special reference and allusion to those who alone are worthy to go up unto the house of Jehovah.

PSALM V. 4-8.

4. "Thou art not a God that hath pleasure in wickedness:
   Evil (men) will not sojourn with thee.
5. The arrogant shall not stand before Thine eyes:
   Thou hatest* all workers of iniquity.
6. **Thou wilt destroy them that speak falsehood:**
   Jehovah will abhor a bloodthirsty and deceitful man.
7. **But, as for me, in the multitude of Thy loving-kindness shall I come into Thy house:**
   In Thy fear shall I worship toward Thy holy temple.
8. **Lead me, O Jehovah, in Thy righteousness, because of mine enemies;**
   Make Thy way plain before my face."

---

* *i.e.*, hast always hated.

So Ps. xi. 2-5 (R.V.):

2. " For, lo, the wicked bend the bow,
They make ready the arrow upon the string,
That they may shoot in darkness at the upright in heart.

3. If the foundations be destroyed,
What can the righteous do?

4. **Jehovah is in His holy temple,
Jehovah, His throne is in heaven** :
His eyes behold, His eyelids try, the children of men.

5. **Jehovah trieth the righteous:
But the wicked and him that loveth violence His soul hateth."**

These two Psalms (Pss. v. and xi.), having been originally written with reference to their use in the procession which took up the Ark of God to Zion, were afterwards formally handed over to " the Chief Musician " for use in the Temple worship, because their teaching was of general application to the worship of Jehovah and to those who alone could worship Him in His holy Temple.

The word *Sheminith*, left in their *sub*-scriptions, retained and recorded the memory of their original reference to that important event.

When we thus compare Scripture with Scripture, we find it to be its own best expositor: explaining and expounding itself; bringing in light where all was darkness; producing order where all was confusion: and substituting the verities and beauties of the words of God for the vain guesses and imaginations of men.

"JEDUTHUN."

Psalms xxxviii., lxi., lxxvi.

CONNECTED with the Divisions of "singing men and singing women" was the special choir associated with the name of *Jeduthun*.

Jeduthun was one of the three Directors of the Temple Worship. 1 Ch. xvi. 41, 42; xxv. 1-6. 2 Ch. v. 12. He was a descendant of Merari (1 Ch. xxvi. 10), who was one of the three sons of Levi. Asaph was a descendant of Gershom, while Heman was a descendant of Kohath.

It would appear that Jeduthun had also the name of Ethan (1 Ch. xv. 17, 19); (compare xvi. 41, 42; xxv. 1, 3, 6; and 2 Ch. xxxv. 15).*

Since he is mentioned in connection with those two other *men*, it seems to be going out of our way to create a difficulty to suppose Jeduthun to be *a musical instrument*,† or *the name of a tune* (R.V. margin), or *of a measure* (Perowne).

In 2 Chron. xxxv. 15 he is called "the king's seer"; and in 1 Chron. xxv. 1 the duty of these three was "to prophesy," and "to give thanks and praise Jehovah" (*v.* 3), and this was "according to the king's order" (*v.* 6).

His name, *Jeduthun*, comes from יָדָה *(yādāh) to confess, to give thanks*, and *to praise*.

If we read these three Psalms (xxxviii., lxi. and lxxvi.) we shall find that they have this note.

---

* That there was an Ethan a Merarite we learn from 1 Ch. xv. 17; vi. 44 (29).

† Hastings's *Dictionary of the Bible*, Vol. II., page 555.

The use of Dr. Thirtle's discovery removes a difficulty arising from the confusion of the *super*-scriptions and the *sub*-scriptions. Psalms xxxix. and lxii. as they stand in the Versions appear to have two authors, Jeduthun and David.* While Psalm lxxvii. is ascribed to Jeduthun and Asaph.

By dividing these "Titles," and putting the former part of them as the *sub*-scription of Psalms xxxviii., lxi. and lxxvi., and leaving the latter part as the *super*-scription of Psalms xxxix., lxii., and lxxvii., all this confusion is removed.

These three Psalms will then stand thus :—

Ps. xxxviii.

Super-scription. A Psalm of David : to bring to remembrance.†

The Psalm itself. Verses 1-22.

Sub-scription. To the chief Musician—Jeduthun.‡

Psalm lxi.

The *Super*-scription begins with the words A Psalm of David.§

The Psalm itself. Verses 1-8.

The *Sub*-scription. The the chief Musician—Jeduthun.||

---

* As Ps. lxxxviii. in the Versions is ascribed to two authors : the sons of Korah and to Heman.

† See under section "Psalms relating to Purpose and Object."

‡ The remaining words ("A Psalm of David") belong, of course, to Ps. xxxix., of which they form the *super*-scription.

§ The former part of this *super*-scription ("To the chief Musician, belongs, of course, to Psalm lx., of which it is the *sub*-scription.

|| The remaining words ("A Psalm of David") belong, of course, to Psalm lxii., of which they form the *super*-scription.

"JEDUTHUN."

Psalm lxxvi.

The *Super*-scription begins with the words: "A Psalm or Song of Asaph."*

The Psalm itself. Verses 1-12.

The *Sub*-scription. "To the chief Musician — Jeduthun."†

* The former part of this title ("To the chief Musician on *Neginoth*") belongs to Psalm lxxv., of which it is the *sub*-scription.

† The remaining words ("A Psalm of Asaph") belong to Ps. lxxvii., of which they form the *super*-scription.

(4) WORDS CONNECTED WITH LITERARY FORM.

HITHERTO, all the Titles we have considered have formed part of, and belonged to, the *sub*-scription of the preceding Psalms. Although, in the Versions, we find them to-day as the *super*-scription of the following Psalm, their proper place, according to Mr. Thirtle's discovery, is in the *sub*-scription of the previous Psalm.

Moreover, none of them, with the one exception of *Neginōth*, has anything to do with musical instruments; so that the common view, which is only an hypothetical assumption, must be given up.

We come now to a class of words whose proper place in a typical Psalm (Hab. iii.) is in the *super*-scription, or in the body of the Psalm itself. This at once marks these words off as a distinct and separate class; and it may be that the Psalms were originally known by their classes, rather than by numbers.

The Literary Class stands by itself, and designates certain Psalms as being *Michtam*, *Maschil*, *Shiggaion* or *Higgaion*; and Psalms so specialised may be Songs, Prayers, Praise, &c.

Our own modern classification contains Hymns, Songs, Canticles, Anthems, &c.: but we use these words with reference only to literary form and character; whereas these Scripture terms have reference to the *subject-matter*, and to the sense of the words. This is much weightier in principle, and more dignified, and more worthy of the Sacred Text.

Enough has been said to show us that we are to look, not

for musical instruments, which are only for the mouth or the hands, but for matter and for instruction which shall be for the heart and for the mind.

"MICHTAM" (ENGRAVEN).

Psalms xvi., lvi., lvii., lviii., lix., lx.

IMPRESSIVE DAVIDIC TRUTH.

The *Michtam* Psalms are six in number, and are all David's. They are Psalms xvi., lvi., lvii., lviii., lix., lx. With the exception of the first (xvi.) they thus form a group or class by themselves (lvi.— lx.)

We need not go through all the fanciful views which have been put forth as to the meaning of the word. The A.V. suggests "A Golden Psalm" (from כֶּתֶם, *Kethem, gold*) on account of its being *hidden away* in treasuries; or, on account of some precious or *treasured* teaching contained in it.

We derive it from כָּתַם (*Kātam*) to *cut in, engrave*, as in Jer. ii. 22; "Though thou wash thee with nitre, and take thee much soap, yet thine iniquity is *graven* before me." It is rendered *marked* in A.V. and R.V. It means *written*, but written in a permanent form which cannot be erased. The Septuagint renders *Michtam* στηλογραφία (*stēlographia*) *a sculptured writing*; hence, στήλη (*stēlē*) was the word for *a grave-stone*, or sepulchral monument, because of the inscription written or graven upon it.

The word *Michtam* thus points to *a graven* (and therefore a permanent) *writing*: graven on account of its importance.

What that importance is can be gathered, not from Lexicons or Commentaries, but only by a close and consecutive study of the Michtam Psalms, and from the *scope* of the Psalms with which it stands associated. None of us has any advantage over another in this. All that any of us can do is to "open the book," and carefully read these Psalms again and again, and note their predominant note and special feature.

If we do this, we shall find that they are pervaded by the common fact that they are all *Personal*, *Direct*, and more or less *Private*.

One of them (Ps. lx.) seems to associate the word with a special object "*to teach*."

May it not be that, as all are David's, there may be some special teaching concerning the true David; David's Son, and David's Lord (Matt. xxii. 41-45); even Him who is, at once, "the root" (from whence David sprang), and "the offspring" (who sprang from David). (Rev. xxii. 16).

Being private, personal and direct, the reference passes from the original circumstances to teach concerning truths of more general application.

But there seems to be a special reference to Resurrection in all these *Micktam* Psalms: to a Deliverance from imminent danger or death, even from the grave itself. With this the Septuagint rendering seems to agree. See Psalms xvi. 10, 11; lvi. 13; lvii. 8; lviii. 10, 11; lix. 16; lx. 5, 12.

It is David as a "Prophet" whom we have in these Psalms (Acts ii. 25-31). And he, "being a prophet," knew that God "would raise up Christ to sit on his throne;" and hence this is the great *engraven* truth of Psalm xvi., which stands out by itself as the first of these *Michtam* Psalms.

In this special, private and personal character, these Psalms stand in contrast to the *Maschil* Psalms.

"MASCHIL" (UNDERSTANDING).

Psalms xxxii., xlii., xliv., xlv., lii., liii., liv., lv., lxxiv., lxxviii., lxxxviii., lxxxix., cxlii.

PUBLIC HOMILIES.

The *Maschil* Psalms are thirteen in number, and are found scattered in four out of the five Books of the Psalms. They are xxxii., xlii., xliv., xlv., lii., liii., liv., lv., lxxiv., lxxviii., lxxxviii., lxxxix., cxlii.

Unlike the *Michtam* Psalms, they are not all by one author, but are by various writers.

Six are by DAVID (xxxii., lii., liii., liv., lv., and cxlii.)
Three are by the sons of KORAH (xlii., xliv. and xlv.)
Two are by ASAPH (lxxiv. and lxxviii.)
One by HEMAN, the Ezrahite (lxxxviii.)
One by ETHAN, the Ezrahite (lxxxix.)

Unlike the six Michtam Psalms, these thirteen Maschil Psalms seem to be *Public* rather than Private. That is to say, they are specially characterised as being for Public instruction, after the character of the "Homilies" of the Church of England.

The word is from שָׂכַל (*sākal*), *to look at, scrutinise, to look well into* any thing (1 Sam. xviii. 30). Hence the noun will mean *understanding* arising from deep *consideration, discernment* (Prov. xiii. 15. Neh. viii. 8). Hence the Septuagint rendering συνέσεως (*suneseōs*), *understanding*, or εἰς σύνεσιν (*eis sunesin*), *for understanding*. It is our old verb *to skill*.

In view of this, the general idea that it means to *play skilfully* seems trivial in the extreme. But the commentators, being tethered by tradition, cannot get beyond the length of their tether, and can see nothing but *music*.

But the moment we look at the Psalms themselves our attention is fixed upon the very first of these (Psalm xxxii.), and, on looking more closely into it, shall soon see that we have the basis of all true *instruction* in the knowledge of how sin is to be put away and forgiveness enjoyed.

In verse 8 we have the scope expressed :—

"I will **instruct** thee,
And **teach** thee in the way that thou shouldest go . . ."

"Be not as the horse or as the mule, which have no **understanding**.

And Psalm xlv. 10 :—

"Hearken, O daughter, and consider, and incline thine ear."

Here we have meaning and *sense*, which accords well with the word *Maschil*, which appears in the title ; but has no connection whatever with music or a musical instrument.

"SHIGGAION" (A CRYING ALOUD).

Psalm vii. and Hab. iii. 1.

A LOUD CRY IN DANGER OR JOY.

This word occurs only in the *super*-scription of Psalm vii. (Shiggaion); and in the plural in Hab. iii. 1 *(Shigionōth)*.

It has been derived from שָׁגָה *(shāgah), to wander, to go astray* ; and is then referred to what is called the erratic character of the words or music.

But we have already seen and learnt enough for us to discard at once such an interpretation as unworthy of God's Word, and destitute of even human literary merit.

"SHIGGAION."

The meaning of the word must be sought, not in doubtful etymology, but in the *scope* of the sure Word of God.

When we notice that this Psalm is marked as a special Psalm, which "David sang to Jehovah concerning the words of Cush the Benjamite," we see at once that there must be something deeper than mere literary or musical form.

In the first place, its *sub*-scription (which is at present found as part of the *super*-scription of Psalm viii), shows that, whatever may have been the special circumstance which suggested Psalm vii., it was afterwards formally handed over for liturgical use to the Chief Musician, as being specially suited for the Feast of Tabernacles. It is marked "relating to Gittith."*

The Feast of Tabernacles tells of *safety in Jehovah's keeping*; and connects the blessed facts that He who is Israel's Deliverer is also Israel's Keeper.

Now, read Psalm vii. in the light of these facts and we see at once its solemnity; and, if we look at the Structure, we shall see its *scope*.

PSALM VII.

A | 1-. Trust in Jehovah for Defence.
  B | -1. Prayer for Deliverance.
    C | 2. The Evil to be delivered from.
      D | 3, 4-. Our demerit.
      D | -4. Our merit.
    C | 5. The Evil to be delivered from.
  B | 6-9. Prayer for Deliverance.
A—10-17. Trust in God.

We notice, in A and *A*, that we have the expression of *Trust* in Jehovah; in A it is briefly stated; in *A* it is declared at length.

---

*See under this Title, above pages 10-15.

Then in B and *B* we have the *prayer* for Deliverance ; in C and *C*, the *Evil* to be delivered from ; while in D and *D* we have the character of the speaker.

With this before us as the *Scope* of the Psalm, we look for an etymology which shall give us a more intelligent understanding of the word *Shiggaion* ; and we find it in שָׁאַג (*Shāag*)* *to cry out* as in trouble, danger or pain ; and also *to cry out* in praise ; *to cry aloud*.

We have both these meanings in Psalm vii. and still more markedly in Hab. iii.

In Psalm vii., we have the loud cry of David when in danger of being torn in pieces ; and in Hab. iii. (plural, *loud cries*), we have the same expression of trust, and of Jehovah's power in delivering His People, and a more intensified *crying aloud* in praise :

"I will rejoice in Jehovah,
I will joy in the God of my Salvation."

A closer study of these Psalms as the words of God, will more and more firmly convince us of the very real connection between them and their Titles, and the Divine themes which form their subject-matter.

*It occurs twenty-one times and is always translated *roar*.

(5). WORDS RELATING TO PURPOSE AND OBJECT.

THERE are *five* Psalms of which the *Purpose* or *object* is stated in the Title: which purpose is quite independent of Literary, Historical, Musical, or other feature.

Two of them are David's: the first two: Psalms xxxviii. and lxx.: and both are

"To bring to remembrance."

The other three are anonymous:—

Ps. xcii. "For the Sabbath day,"

Ps. c. "A Psalm of Praise" (marg. *thanksgiving*).

Ps. cii. "A Prayer of the afflicted, when he is overwhelmed, and poureth out his complaint before the LORD.

In these, as in all other Psalms, we must always bear in mind, that it is not the *Title*, or any particular *word*, which can give us the *scope* of the Psalm; but it is from a careful study of the Psalm itself that we can gather the meaning of the words of the Title.

When we find the correspondence that links them together, then we have the key to their true meaning, and to the spiritual instruction which they contain.

(6) THE ONE WORD CLAIMED FOR MUSIC.

"NEGINOTH."

SMITINGS.

Psalms iii., v., liii., liv,, lx. (sing.), lxvi., lxxv., and Hab. iii.

THESE are the *Neginoth* Psalms according to the law and key discovered and recovered by Dr. Thirtle.

In the Versions they are of course Psalms iv., vi., liv., lv., lxi. (sing. with עַל (*al*) instead of בּ) lxvii. and lxxvi.

It is the only title which may be connected with musical instruments.

We know that instruments of some kind were used under certain circumstances, but these only for an accompaniment; and certain Psalms may have been specially designated to have such accompaniment.

Neginoth is from נָגַן (*nāgan*), *to strike.* Hence it has been associated with *striking* the strings of a musical instrument.

But supposing that this may have been the primary significance of the word, Why should this *striking* be limited to strings? Why may it not have reference also to Him who was indeed the Stricken One? Why may it not refer to *the stroke* of an affliction, or to the *smiting* with words, as well as to *striking* an instrument with a plectrum?

Indeed, it is associated with the stroke of affliction in Lam. iii. 63, "I am their music," or their song: *i.e.*, My sufferings are the subject of their song. I am their instrument (as it were) which they strike. (Compare Job xxx. 9; Lam. iii. 14.)

The use of the word may well be thus extended, even if the primary reference to music be admitted. "I am he whom they smite with their words."

There is a reference to these smitings with words and deliverance from personal afflictions in the *Neginoth* Psalms. (See Ps. iii. 2 ; v. 6 ; liii. 1 ; liv. 3 ; lx. 1, 11, 12 ; lxvi. 10-12 ; lxxv. 4-6).

We have the verb again in Psalms lxxvii. 7. "I call to remembrance my song," which may well be the remembrance of his affliction.

So in Isaiah xxxviii. 20, "We will sing, or make songs, of my afflictions," which were, in fact, the subject and burden of Hezekiah's song. He concludes his prayer and thanksgivings after his recovery with the promise that he would cause his deliverance from his afflictions to be remembered by making them the subject of his songs, even as Asaph had said before, "I call to remembrance my song" (or my affliction).

In Hab. iii. the Prophet is calling to remembrance his smitings and affliction ; his deliverance from all that he feared ; and his trust in Jehovah. In *v.* 16 he tells how his belly trembled, his lips quivered, and rottenness entered into his bones, when he thought of Jehovah's coming to avenge himself on His enemies.

In any case, what we insist on is that, it is needless to limit the word *neginoth* to the striking of a musical instrument ; and that it may have reference to a further and deeper smiting more in harmony with, and more worthy of, the subject matter of the *Neginoth* Psalms.

(7). THE HISTORICAL TITLES.

THIRTEEN Psalms have Historical Titles, or Titles which relate to some event in David's life.

They all stand in connection with some particular incident which called forth the Psalm, and was the immediate cause that led to the Psalms being written.

Moreover they are all associated with David. This fact takes them all back to at least 1040 B.C., and links them all on to special scenes in David's life.

They are as follows :—

Ps. iii. "When he fled from Absalom his son." (2 Sam. xv.-xviii.). 1023 B.C.

Ps. vii. "Concerning the words (marg., *business*) of Cush the Benjamite." (2 Sam. xvi.). 1062 B.C.

Ps. xviii. Relating to "the day that Jehovah delivered him from the hand of all his enemies, and from the hand of Saul" (2 Sam. xxii.). 1018 B.C.

Ps. xxx. "At the dedication of the house of David" (2 Sam. v. 11, 12 ; vi. 20). 1042 B.C.

Ps. xxxiv. "When he changed his conduct before Abimelech ;* who drove him away, and he departed." (1 Sam. xxi. 13). 1062 B.C.

Ps. li. "When Nathan the prophet came unto him, after he had gone in to Bathsheba." (2 Sam. xii. 1. Compare xi. 2, 4). 1034 B.C.

Ps. lii. "When Doeg the Edomite came and told Saul, and said unto him, David is come to the house of Ahimelech." (1 Sam. xxii. 9). 1062 B.C.

---

* His other name was Achish. See 1 Sam. xxi. 13.

Ps. liv. "When the Ziphims came and said to Saul, Doth not David hide himself with us?" (1 Sam. xxiii. 19; xxvi. 1). 1061 B.C.

Ps. lvi. "When the Philistines took him in Gath." (1 Sam. xxi. 11). 1062 B.C.

Ps. lvii. "When he fled from Saul in the Cave." (1 Sam. xxii. 1; xxiv. 3). 1062 B.C.

Ps. lix. "When Saul sent, and they watched the house to kill him." (1 Sam. xix. 11). 1062 B.C.

Ps. lx. "When he strove with Aram-Naharaim and with Aram-Zobah, when Joab returned, and smote of Edom in the valley of salt twelve thousand."* (2 Sam. viii. 3, 13. 1 Chron. xviii. 3, 12). 1040 B.C.

Ps. cxlii. "When he was in the cave" (1 Sam. xxii. 1; xxiv. 3). 1062 B.C.

In all these Psalms the reference to the events is not a mere historical reference. But we have to look for some special feature in the event which furnishes us with the link which connects it with instruction or with its spiritual teaching. The Psalm itself is not meant to *repeat* the history itself, but to reflect some special circumstance in connection with it.

---

* In 2 Sam. viii. 13, 14, it is of course DAVID's exploit that is referred to. In 1 Chron. xviii. 3, 12, it is ABISHAI's command; while in the title of Psalm lx. it is specially confined to JOAB's share in the campaign. The total losses of the enemy were 18,000, of which Joab's share was 12,000, as he took six months longer in finishing his task (1 Kings xi. 15, 16).

(8). THE DOMINANT WORD.

LAMENATZEACH.

"The Chief Musician."

In the foregoing pages the word לַמְנַצֵּחַ (*Lamenatzeach*), which is usually rendered "*To the chief musician*," has been explained (pp. 8, 9) in connection with the literary requirements of the Text, the Facts, and the History; and its connection with historical Titles shows that this interpretation must be correct, if only as the foundation for other applications.

But this is not to say that the meaning is exhausted by the primary *interpretation*; or that there is no further lesson conveyed in the word by way of *application*.

And if it can be shown to have a further and deeper reference to spiritual truths, that is not to say that our literary interpretation is wrong. Both may be, and we believe are, true. Our danger and temptation is to see only a part, and then to put the part for the whole; thus setting one Scripture at variance with another, and using one truth to upset another truth.

Let it be granted then that Dr. Thirtle's interpretation of *Lamenatzeach* is correct; bringing it into harmony with the literary setting, as well as with the circumstances and requirements of the historical setting of the Psalms.

Then, while we may grant that there is this, we may hold that there is something more than this; and something beyond the mere surface of the Word; yea, that there is spirit as well as letter.

We may thus be able to explain some of the other renderings which the word has received, and which cannot be ignored

It is remarkable that none of the Ancient Versions seem to know anything about this "Chief Musician": and vary much in their renderings of the word.

In the Septuagint it is rendered εἰς τὸ τέλος (*eis to telos*) *unto* or *for the end.* The Arabic, Ethiopic and Vulgate, *in* or *at the end.* The Chaldee Paraphrast renders it at Psalm xlv. *to the Praise* (explainable, perhaps, by Psalm xxii. 3). The Talmudists say it relates to Him who is to come. Aquila gives it as τῷ νικοποιῷ, *to the giver of victory*, or *to the One who maketh us to conquer.*

In all this variety of renderings there is one thing clear, and that is that a person is meant. They thus agree with the other rendering, which refers it to a person also; *i.e.*, to the Director of the Temple worship. But there can be no reason, as we have said, why the interpretation should be limited to him; or why he may not be a type of Him who is the Leader of the Heavenly Worship, who is at the same time the object and end of all worship, even of Him who "inhabiteth the praises of Israel" (Psalm xxii. 3).

We know that Christ is the life-giving *pneuma* or spirit of the Word of God. And as the title of the Psalms is *Sepher Tehilīm*, a *Book of Praises*, in which the glories of Christ shine forth, are manifested, and displayed, we must surely look beyond all mere historical references, and see Christ pervading the Psalms as He does the rest of the Old Testament.

Hence in *Lamenatzeach* we can see not merely the Temple Director, but Christ also. He alone harmonises all the other renderings. In them all we can see Christ (Luke xxiv. 44). He is *the End.* It is He who *maketh to conquer.* It is He who *giveth the victory.* It is He who is *the coming One.*

The first appearance of the word is in the *sub*-scription

of Psalm iii., and surely in David's experiences here we have a type of Christ's experiences as the true David.

Its association with *Neginoth* here, in its first occurrence, is not without significance, and points to something more than a musical instrument.

(See above, under *Neginoth*, *pp.* 90, 91).

In the word *Lamenatzeach*, therefore, we may see the key to unlock the deeper application, and the spiritual teaching of the Psalms; and, we are thus directed to Christ, who is indeed their great object and subject; even to Him who is "the root and the offspring of David" (Rev. xxii. 16), David's son, and David's Lord, even the true David

PART II.

SPECIAL WORDS IN THE TEXT.

(THE DOVE OF THE DISTANT WOODS).

SPECIAL WORDS OCCURRING IN THE TEXT.

WE come now to two words which are not connected with any Titles, but which occur in the body or text of the Psalm itself.

They thus form a special class by themselves, and must be treated separately, in a special part.

They are "HIGGAION" and "SELAH."

"HIGGAION" (SOLILOQUY).

Psalms ix. 16, xix. 14, xcii. 3.

WORTHY OF MEMORY.

In this word, again, we see no trace of any reference to music : or to a musical instrument.

It shares, with other words, the common idea : which is nothing but mere assumption.

We find it in three Psalms, viz., Ps. ix. 16, xix. 14, and xcii. 3.

In ix. 16 it is transliterated "Higgaion."

In xix. 14, it is translated "Meditation," and

In xcii. 3, it is rendered "solemn sound."

The word occurs also in Lam. iii. 62, where it is rendered in the A.V. "device"; and in the R.V. "imagination."

It is derived from הָגָה (*hāgāh*), and means, *to soliloquise, to speak to one's self*, hence, to meditate, Josh. i. 8, "thou shalt meditate therein." So Ps. lxxvii. 12 and cxliii. 5.

As a noun, it would mean *a Meditation*, or a speaking in *premeditated* words, and therefore, worthy of *memory* or *repetition*.

If we now read the three passages associated with the word *Higgaiōn*, we shall see the importance of the statement, and understand how worthy it is to be thought upon, remembered and spoken of.

In Ps. ix. 16, it is the judgment of Jehovah in the excision of the wicked man (16), and wicked men (17).

In Ps. xix. 14, it is the words concerning the heavens, and the word of God.

In xcii. 2, 3, it is the loving-kindness and faithfulness of Jehovah, with profound meditation.

"SELAH."

No word in the book of Psalms has received a greater variety of interpretations than this. And the determination to look upon all Titles, and all such words as being connected with music, musical "rendering," or musical instruments, has prevented or hindered research in any other direction.

There are two classes of interpreters: (1) Those which regard the word as being derived from סָלָה (*sālāh*) *to pause*, and take it as meaning that the voices are to pause while the instruments play an interlude: and (2) those who derive it from סָלַל (*sālal*) *to lift up*, and understand it as meaning that the voices are to be lifted up, while the instruments are subdued. But we may ask, What then? What is there "for our learning" in either or both of these interpretations? What is there for intellect, heart, or conscience in this? How much the better are we for knowing whether the musical instruments played or not? What is there for doctrine or practice, teaching or instruction for our life and walk in all this?

Suppose the word *Selah* does mean *to pause*: Why should we limit the pause to *music*? Suppose it means *to lift up*, Why should we limit it to lifting up the *voice*?

All that we have at present seen in our studies of the Psalm-Titles connects these words with the *subject-matter*, and not with music; with truth, not with *tunes*.

If it means *to pause*, why should it not refer to our minds and thoughts? Why should not *we* pause and reflect on what is "written for our learning?"

If it means *to lift up*, why should it not refer to the lifting up of our *hearts*?* Why should we not lift up our *thoughts*, and look up to God, who is speaking to us in these Psalms?

We may well believe the late Bishop Perowne, who says of "Selah"† "it is almost hopeless to attempt to give a satisfactory explanation of the word."

Yes, it is not only "almost," but *quite* hopeless so long as we are tied and bound by the tether of tradition; and it will be hopeless so long as our thoughts cannot rise above a musical performance: quite hopeless while we think of the setting rather than the jewel; the frame rather than the picture; the means rather than the end; the music rather than the words.

But, thank God, it it not hopeless when we break the tether of tradition, and search and see how the Holy Spirit has used the word, rather than how man would guess at its etymology.

It is not only "hopeless" to seek for a satisfactory explanation; but it is profitless also, unless, and until, we approach the Scripture as a Divine Revelation, and receive it as being not the word of men, but as it is in truth the Word of God, which effectually worketh in them that believe (1 Thess. ii. 13).

The profit, and blessing, and teaching will come when we study the *usage* of the word *Selah*; and seek to find out all about it from the way in which the Holy Spirit has employed it. Not till then shall we be in a position to consider its derivation.

The *scope* of its use will give the meaning of the *word*. And in studying the scope we are all equal before the

---

* We believe that someone has suggested "*Sursum corda*."

† Psalms, Introduction, page c.

Divine Word. For this study depends, not on the critical acumen of the brain, but on the accurate reading of the text; not on the possession of human wisdom, but on the gift of the "spiritual mind;" not on the power of natural understanding, but on having that understanding "opened" by the Spirit of God.

Our first duty, therefore, is to gather all the data concerning the use of the word *Selah*, and to observe all the facts connected with it, before we attempt any conclusion.

As to these facts, we note that,

1. The word *Selah* occurs 74 times in the Bible, and all in the Old Testament. Of these, 71 are in the Book of Psalms; and 3 are in the model Psalm—"the Prayer of Habakkuk" (chap. iii.).

2. The use of the word is confined to only 39 Psalms out of the 150. And it is distributed among the five books of the Psalms as follows:—

Book I. (i-xli.), 17 times in 9 Psalms.
Book II. (xlii.-lxxii.), 30 times in 17 Psalms.
Book III. (lxxii.-lxxxix.), 20 times in 11 Psalms.
Book IV. (xc.-cvi.), not once.
Book V. (cvii.-cl.), 4 times in 2 Psalms.

3. In the 39 Psalms which contain *Selah*, we notice that 31 of them have לַמְנַצֵּחַ (*lam'natseach*) "For the chief musician," in the *sub*-scription: which tells us that these 31 Psalms were formally handed over to the Director of the liturgical worship of the Tabernacle and the Temple.

4. In 16 of these 39 Psalms, *Selah* occurs *once* (*viz.*, vii., xx., xxi., xliv., xlvii., xlviii., l., liv., lx., lxi., lxxv., lxxxi., lxxxii., lxxxiii., lxxxv., cxliii.

In 15 Psalms it occurs *twice* (*viz.*, iv., ix., xxiv., xxxix., xlix., lii., lv., lvii., lix., lxii., lxvii., lxxvi., lxxxiv., lxxxvii., lxxxviii.).

In 7 Psalms it occurs *three times* (*viz.*, iii., xxxii., xlvi., lxvi., lxviii., lxxvii., cxl.).

In one Psalm it occurs *four times* (*viz.*, Ps. lxxxix.).

5. As to its position: some speak of it as being always "at the end of a poem or of a strophe."*

But this statement begs the whole question at the very outset: for this is the very point we are seeking to find out. We are enquiring as to the manner in which it is used, and we are met with a conclusion before we set out.

Is it, we ask, always "at the end"? This is the very point we are considering; and the very question we are seeking to answer.

After Dr. Thirtle's great discovery of the Key to these Psalm-Titles in Hakbakuk iii., we shall not too readily accept any conclusions drawn from the apparent position, of a *super*-script, or of a *sub*-script line.

What is true of those lines, may be true of this word. It may quite as well belong to what follows it, as to what precedes it; and this is the very point we wish to find out.

True, there are *four* Psalms where *Selah* does occur at the close of a Psalm (*viz.*, iii., ix., xxiv., and xlvi.). But it does not follow from this, nor must we conclude from this fact, that its proper place is always "at the end of a Psalm or Strophe."

It might just as well be taken as referring to the beginning of what follows, after what we have seen (in our first chapter) as to the confusion of the *super* and *sub*-script lines.

Dr. Thirtle himself suggests that its usage is similar to

* Briggs. Article "Selah," Hastings' *Dictionary of the Bible.*

that of the use of the printer's sign ¶, which is the arbitrary mark for a paragraph.*

There is, however, another fact: it is that no less than *four* times we find *Selah* so closely connected with the context that, when the Hebrew Text came to be divided by the Massorites into verses, *Selah* was included so as to come *in the middle of the verse* (*viz.* Psalms lv. 19., lvii. 3; Hab. iii. 3, 9).

This fact seems fatal to both the theories: that *Selah* always comes at the *end* of a Psalm or Strophe; or that it always marks the *beginning* of a new paragraph.

Neither of these can be the case, in the face of this fact. Yet *both are true.* Each is a part of the truth, but when a part is put for the whole, we get error instead of truth.

Selah does always come at the end; but it always comes at the beginning also: for, it comes *in the middle*, closely connecting the end of one subject with the beginning of another, because of some wonderful inter-relation between them. This association of the two members is "for our learning." Either to mark an *expansion* of what has been said, or a *contrast* with it; or to give an explanation of it; or to call our attention to the latter, as being the cause or the effect of the former, or as being the reason, or the consequence of it.

When we find, in the case of all the Psalm-Titles, that *subject-matter* is the one great and all-important consideration, we should naturally look for the same in the case of the word *Selah*; and, instead of labouring to find some trivial explanation in some musical expression or instrument, we

* The word *paragraph* means, *something written at the side*: especially a mark or stroke in the margin, to indicate the commencement of a new subject, or a break in a subject: hence, it came to mean the *paragraph* itself. It is now represented by a "P" printed backward, ¶, and standing for the word "paragraph."

should look for something worthy of the revelation by which God would impart to us Divine and spiritual teaching.

The Word of God is made up of words; and words are thus, necessarily, the vehicle of Divine thoughts and truths. Surely then, these should take precedence of all other phenomena in connection with the Sacred Text.

If we make a careful study of each of the seventy-four passages where *Selah* occurs, we shall find that it neither *ends*, nor *begins* a passage; but that it CONNECTS two passages, in order to emphasise both, and to link together their important truths and teaching.

Selah would thus, as Dr. Thirtle suggests, act as a Paragraph mark, ¶; not, however, as a mere literary paragraph, but as a Divine subject-connector or thought-link. Not the mere *passing away* or onward to a new subject, but the *connecting* of something new with the old, either by way of contrast, or development. Sometimes what has been said is shown, thus, to be the basis of a prayer. Sometimes a cause is connected with the effect; or vice-versa.

In every case, it answers to our "N.B." (*nota bene*), *note well*. It bids us to look back at what has been said, and mark its connection with what is to follow; to look forward, and mark some additional truth that arises out of what has been said, or some additional teaching, consequent thereon.

This additional matter to which our attention is thus transferred may be, as we have said, synthetic, or antithetic; it may be by way of contrast or amplification; but it is always "*for our learning*," and not merely for our singing or our playing.

Perhaps the best representation of the word *Selah*, and

that which would convey its meaning, in many cases would be to regard it as saying,

"*That being so, note well what follows.*"

The one point to be borne in mind is that it is neither the beginning nor the end of one paragraph; but it is the

CONNECTING-LINK

of *two* thoughts, statements, or subjects.*

From what has been said, it will be seen that the word *Selah* must be closely bound up with the "Structure" of the Scriptures. Its importance will be shown, in the fact that, being the key to the Structure, it is the key to the Scope.

So far is this the case, that, on more careful study of the Structures, with the use of this key, several of them have had to be revised. Outward literary form may easily mislead us in forming the structure, if we see not the internal spiritual truths, which alone can rightly guide us.

We may easily mistake mere verbal correspondence between the different members of a Psalm, and be misled, if we see not the real correspondence of Divine truth.

In our consideration of the occurrences of *Selah*, we shall have to note the Structures in certain Psalms, and a careful study of the 74 passages will show how far they bear out what we have now said.

* When *Selah* comes at the end of a Psalm, it is the connecting link between the two Psalms, either as a whole, or as connecting the end of one with the beginning of another.

THE OCCURRENCES OF "SELAH."

PSALM iii. 2, 4.

In this Psalm we have *three Selahs.*

(1) Between verses 2 and 3.
(2) Between verses 4 and 5.
(3) Between verse 8 and iv. 1.

The *first* occurrence of *Selah* must necessarily be full of instruction, as being the key to the whole. It presents us with a *contrast*; and connects, what man falsely says, with what is the real fact.

2. "**Many there be that say of me***
'There is no help for him in God.'

SELAH.

3. **But Thou, O Jehovah, art a Shield about me,**
My glory, and the lifter up of my head."

Here the contrast stands out sharply and clearly. Man, being a creature of God, knows God (*Elohim*) only as the Creator: he knows not Jehovah.

But David knew God as his Covenant Lord: and turns to Him as Jehovah, as did Jehoshaphat in a later day (2 Chron. xviii. 31). This Psalm has a historical title. "When he fled from Absalom his son." The history is recorded in 2 Sam. xv.—xviii.; and this is exactly what his many adversaries did say:—"The Lord hath returned

* Heb., *my soul.*

upon thee all the blood of the house of Saul, in whose stead thou hast reigned; and Jehovah hath delivered the kingdom into the hand of Absalom thy son" (2 Sam. xvi. 8).

The Selah, here, contrasts the *Jehovah* of verse 3 with the *Elohim* of verse 2.

"**But Thou**" emphasizes the blessed fact that, in spite of all they might say, Jehovah was his Shield, and would restore him and his kingdom, and in due time lift up his head.

This would not have been half so impressive without the Selah, which bids us connect and contrast the true fact with the false assertion.

The *second* Selah occurs between verses 4 and 5, and is meant to convey the same precious truth as is contained in Phil. iv. 6, viz., that when we have made known our requests to God, His peace will be enjoyed in our heart, and will "keep" us from being full of care.

"Be careful for nothing; but in everything, by prayer and supplication with thanksgiving, let your requests be made known unto God. And God's peace (which passeth all understanding) shall keep your hearts and minds, through Jesus Christ."

The peace that must reign in the presence of Him who seeth the end from the beginning must be wonderful indeed, and perfect. It is just this very fact, that we do not see beyond the present moment, which fills us with care, and prevents us from enjoying the keeping power of that Divine and perfect peace.

Now, see how we are called to learn this same lesson as it is taught in David's experience.

4. "I cried unto Jehovah with my voice,
And He heard me out of His holy mountain.

SELAH.

5. I laid me down and slept;
I awaked; for Jehovah sustained me."

Yes, in that terrible night of his flight from Jerusalem, David could lay him down and sleep. True he was awoke out of it by the tidings sent from Hushai by Jonathan and Ahimaaz, the sons of Abiather, who said, "Arise, and pass quickly over the water (Jordan). . . . Then David arose, and all the people that were with him, and they passed over Jordan, and by the morning light there lacked not one of them that was not gone over Jordan" (2 Sam. xvii. 21, 22).

David's trust in Jehovah is seen in 2 Sam. xv. 25; xvi. 12. It was all the affair of a night (2 Sam. xvii. 1), but David slept in peace, his heart and mind "kept by the peace of God," to whom he had cried; and by whom he was answered and sustained.

The *third* Selah occurs at the end of the Psalm, between verse 8 and Ps. iv. 1. It thus *connects* the two Psalms, and tells us that they both refer to the same circumstances, viz., to the time "when David fled from Absalom his son."

It gives us, in Ps. iv. 1, the words of the cry in Ps. iii. 4; and (in iv. 2) it connects the lies of the adversaries in iii. 1, 2.

Selah here, at the end of Psalm iii., gives us the first example of this usage.

Indeed, in this first Psalm in which the word occurs, we have the three chief uses to which it is put (1) *contrast*, (2) *additional* and consequent truth and teaching, and (3) a literary *connecting link*.

This literary connection is again seen in iv. 8, where we have the same reference to that terrible *night* in David's experience (2 Sam. xvii. 1). It is not merely "an evening Psalm," as it has been called. It is far more than that. It finds its place in David's history, and is linked on to that night when he fled from Absalom, and Absalom said, "I will arise and pursue after David this night." It is thus connected with events which took place at least 1020 years B.C. These events, and these alone, satisfy it and explain it.

It is "concerning Inheritances" (*Nehiloth*[1]): or *the Great Inheritance.*[2] David's Inheritance was in jeopardy. His "glory" was in danger of ceasing; his "crown" of being profaned; and his "throne" of being cast down to the ground (Ps. lxxxix. 39, 44).

This leads us up to

PSALM iv.

in which we have *two Selahs.*

(1) The first between verses 2 and 3.

(2) The second between verses 4 and 5.

The *first Selah* of Ps. iv. shows that, in spite of all the vain lies of those who would turn David's glory into shame (*v.* 2), and cast his crown and his throne to the ground, Jehovah, his God, would hear him when he called unto Him, because he had found favour in the eyes of Jehovah. All depended on His grace and favour. This was his support in that time of trouble. See 2 Sam. xv. 25: "Carry back the ark of God into the city: if I shall find favour in the eyes of Jehovah, He will bring me again, and shew me both it and His habitation." This was the note of

---

[1] See under this title, page 62 above.

[2] If we take this as the plural of majesty.

praise also in another deliverance, "He delivered me, because He had a favour unto me" (2 Sam. xxii. 20); "He delivered me because He delighted in me" (Ps. xviii. 19).

This is exactly what is emphasized by this *Selah.*

2\. **"O ye sons of men, how long will ye turn my glory into shame?**
[How long] **will ye love vanity,**
[How long will ye] **seek after lies.**

SELAH.

3\. **But know ye, that Jehovah hath set apart him that is godly unto Himself:**
Jehovah will hear when I call unto Him."

When he heard the cursing of Shimei, as he fled from the city, he said: "Let him curse; for Jehovah hath bidden him. It may be that Jehovah will look on my affliction, and that Jehovah will requite me good for his cursing this day" (2 Sam. xvi. 11, 12).

The second *Selah* of Ps. iv. occurs between verses 4 and 5: and, coming here, it points to the true structure of this Psalm. In verse 1, and again in verses 6-8, we have *Prayer*, or David's address to Jehovah. The four verses which form the middle part of the Psalm are addressed specifically to the "sons of men." The former two are at once seen to be *Expostulation*; and the latter two *Exhortation.*

This may be better exhibited by the Structure:

THE STRUCTURE OF PSALM IV.

A | 1. Prayer.
  B | 2, 3. Expostulation. *Selah.*
  B | 4, 5. Exhortation. *Selah.*
A | 6-8. Prayer.

Now we are in a position to note that the first *Selah* occurs in the middle of B, connecting verses 2 and 3. And that the second *Selah* occurs in the middle of *B*, connecting verses 4 and 5.

We have already considered the force of the first *Selah*, and seen that it is meant to emphasize the *Expostulation*, by *contrasting* Jehovah's favour with man's disfavour.

The second *Selah* is now seen to be *Synthetic*, and is used to emphasize the *Exhortation*.

The first part of the Exhortation which precedes the *Selah* is directed to the sin of "the sons of men" against David. These "sons of men" were (1) to "tremble," and (2) to consider themselves, and (3) to hold their tongues.

The *Selah* conducts us to a much more important part of the Exhortation, viz., their *duty* to God. The putting away of their sin by offering the sacrifices required by a righteous law, which would give them also a title to trust in Jehovah.

Now look at the two verses, and see the force of the *Selah* which connects them and teaches this important lesson.

4. "**Stand in awe, and sin not:**
Reflect [on Jehovah's favour to me] **in your heart,**
upon your bed, and be silent.
SELAH.
5. **Offer the sacrifices of righteousness,**
And put your trust in Jehovah."

Thus these two *Selahs* of Psalm iv. point us to the true structure of the Psalm; and the Structure, in turn, gives us the scope and the correct meaning and interpretation of the words.

We have already considered a further lesson conveyed by this fourth Psalm, in the *sub*-scription, which in our Bibles stand at present as part of the *super*-scription of

Psalm v. We have seen under the word *Nehiloth* that it is "*concerning Inheritances*;" or, *the Great Inheritance*.

PSALM vii.

THIS Psalm has one *Selah*; between verses 5 and 6.

The Psalm has a historical title. It is headed:

"*Shiggaion* of David, which he sang unto Jehovah concerning the words of Cush, a* Benjamite."

We have seen under "SHIGGAION" (page 86), that this word means *a loud cry* in danger or joy: and this Psalm is indeed *a loud cry* of David to Jehovah his God, in whom he ever found refuge.

Who "Cush the Benjamite" was we do not know; but, being of the same tribe as Saul, he was probably one of Saul's adherents. If so, the date of the Psalm would be many years prior to the rebellion of Absalom, when we have the cursing of Shimei.

What the words of Cush were, we can gather only from David's words in this Psalm. They were evidently false accusations, mixed up with threats of destruction: hence this *loud cry of distress* to Jehovah, his Refuge, his Deliverer, and his Judge.

The *Selah* connects verses 5 and 6; and, as before, it marks the end of one member and the beginning of the next.† Our attention is called to the strong *contrast*, in which the thought passes from the *treading down* of the enemy, to "the loud cry" to Jehovah for Him *to rise up* in His anger, to lift Himself up, and awake for David's deliverance:

5. **"Let the foe pursue me,‡ and overtake me;§**

* There is no article in the Hebrew.

† See pp. 106-7. Also the Structure of the Psalm, given under *Shiggaion* (p. 87.)

‡ Heb., *my soul*. § Heb., *it*.

Yea let him tread my life down to the earth,
And lay mine honour in the dust.

SELAH.

6. **Arise, O Jehovah, in thine anger,**
Lift up thyself against the rage of mine adversaries:
Yea, awake for me!—Thou hast commanded judgment."

The contrast is clear and sharp. The circumstances were special and peculiar. The danger was great and imminent. The cry was loud. The need of a deliverer was urgent. In verse 2 (Heb. *v.* 3) the danger is shown:

2. "Save me from all my pursuers,
And deliver me;
3. Lest he* tear† me like a lion,‡
Rending me in pieces,§
And there be no sign|| of a Rescuer."¶

But Jehovah was his Refuge, his Rescuer, and his Judge. This is the contrast which is emphasised by the connecting *Selah.*

The true *sub*-scription of this Psalm vii. (which in the Versions now stands as the *super*-scription of Psalm viii.) assigns it as having been formally handed to the

* While "pursuers" in *v.* 2 is plural, the verb and participle in *v.* 3 is singular, referring probably to Saul, Cush, or one of his pursuers.

† טָרַף (*tāraph*), *to prey* on living victims.

‡ Heb., *my soul.*

§ According to the Aramaic and Syriac Versions (see Ginsburg's Hebrew Text, and note) this middle line of verse 3 should be omitted.

|| While אַיִן in the absolute means *none at all*, אֵין in the Construct, as here, means *no sign of.*

¶ Implying a personal interest in the one Rescued, which *Deliverer* does not.

Chief Musician as appropriate for use at the Feast of Tabernacles.*

Tabernacles told of Jehovah's goodness in having made His people to *dwell safely* in the midst of enemies and danger. This Psalm, therefore, had that in it which made it appropriate for that Feast; as commemorating Jehovah's goodness, and praising Jehovah for His protecting care.

PSALM ix.

In Psalm ix. we have two *Selahs*—

(1) Between verses 16 and 17.

(2) Between Ps. ix. 20 and Ps. x 1.

It is a Psalm of David,† and is a Psalm of triumphant thanksgiving for the excision of the wicked. It refers to the "times of trouble," and therefore looks forward to the future, even to "the Great Tribulation" (Jer. xxx. 6-8; Matt. xxiv.).

It corresponds with the song of praise in Isa. xii.: which relates to "that day"; (referring back to Isa. ii. 11, 17).

Its great subject is shown in

The Structure of Psalm ix.

A | 1, 2. Thanksgiving.

B | 3-10. Excision of the wicked.

A | 11. Thanksgiving.

B | 12-20. Excision of the wicked.

It will be seen from this that the great bulk of the Psalm has for its subject-matter *Deliverance from*, and *Judgment of, the wicked.*

The *Selah* sets its seal upon this theme by connecting

* See under "*Gittith*," page 10.

† The *super*-scription—"To the Chief Musician relating to *Muthlabben*" (the Death of the Champion)—belongs, of course, to Psalm viii., to which it is the *sub*-scription. See under "*Muthlabben*," (page 25.)

verses 16 and 17; emphasising this judgment, by marking the contrast, and pointing to a necessary discrimination.

This is further marked by the word "*Higgaion*" being associated with "*Selah.*"

We have already seen that *Higgaion* denotes *something worthy of memory.** Something that we can, and are to meditate upon for our instruction.

In verse 16 (Heb. *v.* 17) we have רָשָׁע (*rāshā'*), *the wicked man* (Singular). In verse 17 (Heb. *v.* 18) we have רְשָׁעִים (*reshā'im*), *wicked ones.* (Plural. No art.)

Thus the contrast marked by this Selah is, between the *Singular* and the *Plural*: "the wicked man," "the man of the earth" (Ps. x. 18), the antichrist (Singular), and "*wicked men*," his followers (Plural).

16. **"Jehovah hath made Himself known; He hath executed judgment:**
The wicked [one] is snared in the work of his own hands.

HIGGAION. SELAH.

17. **The wicked** (pl.) **must be returned unto Sheōl.**
[Even] all [the] nations that forget God."

Here, then, we see the force of our *Higgaion*: here is something for us to think about, and meditate upon. Here we see the force of the *Selah*: here are two solemn truths for us to connect and contrast.

These two, the Singular and the Plural, are connected for us again in Rev. xix. 19-21 (the first of the final five Judgments†).

In Rev. xix. 20 we have the Singular (Individuals), the

* See above, under *Higgaion* (page 99).

† See Editor's work on *The Apocalypse* (Pages 606, 607).

Beast and the False Prophet, cast alive into the lake of fire burning with brimstone, corresponding with Ps. ix. 16.

Then, in verse 21, we have the Plural, the rest of the wicked, his followers, slain with the sword of Him that sat upon the white horse. This corresponds with Ps. ix. 17.

The *Selah* accords with this, and tells us that we are not to confuse these *two parts* of the first of these final five judgments, either as to the subjects of it, or as to the manner of its execution.

In obeying the *Higgaion* we further *meditate* on this, and notice that the word (in Ps. ix. 17) rendered "*turn*" in A.V. and "*turned backward*" in R.V., is שׁוּב (*shūv*), and means *to re-turn*. It is a word of frequent occurrence, and is nearly always so translated. There can be no dispute as to its meaning. Its first occurrence furnishes the key to its interpretation, Gen. iii. 19.*

"Till thou **return** unto the ground; for out of it wast thou taken: for dust thou art, and unto dust shalt thou **return**."

It is thus clear that this "return" must be to that which was their former condition, "dust."

And the word "*Sheōl*" confirms this.† It occurs 65 times, and is, in the A.V., rendered *grave* 35 times (31 times in the Text, and 4 times in the Margin, instead of *hell*). It is rendered *pit* 3 times (Num. xvi. 30, 33, and Job xvii. 16, where it evidently means the *grave*). So that we have the meaning *grave* 38 times out of 65 occurrences.

---

* Compare the next occurrences, Gen. viii. 3, xv. 16, xxvii. 44, and Ps. xc. 3.

† See *Things to Come*, Dec., 1902, Vol. IX., pp. 67-69; published by Messrs. Horace Marshall & Son, 125 Fleet Street, E.C.; or the pamphlet entitled *Sheol and Hades*, published by Eyre & Spottiswoode, 33 Paternoster Row, London, E.C.

This, combined with the word RE-turn, confirms the Divine statement: "dust thou art, and unto dust shalt thou return." This is a truth frequently stated. (See Job xxi. 26; xxxiv. 15. Ps. civ. 29. Ecc. iii. 20; xii. 7.)

This is the destiny of wicked men (Plural). It is not the destiny of the Beast and the False Prophet. These are super-human, and are cast alive into the lake of fire "Jehovah is known by the judgment which he executeth" (Ps. ix. 16). And if we would *know* what that judgment is to be, we must *meditate* upon it, and connect, while we discriminate, what He has revealed.

THE SECOND SELAH occurs at the end of this Psalm ix., and thus connects it with the next, Psalm x.

That this connection of these two Psalms is no mere fancy is shown, further, by the fact that there is an irregular acrostic running through the two Psalms, beginning with the first letter of the alphabet at Ps. ix. 1, and ending with the last letter at Ps. x. 17.

Then there is also a repetition of similar words and phrases occuring in a remarkable way in the two Psalms. This is clearer in the Hebrew than in the English. We give the comparison in the literal meaning of the words:—

Words and Phrases.	Ps. ix. verses.	Ps. x. verses.
"the wicked (or lawless) one"	5, 16	3, 4, 13, 15
"times of trouble"	9	1
"the oppressed"	9	18*
"mortal men"	19, 20	18
"forget," etc. שָׁכַח, *shākach*)	13, 17, 18	12
"humble"	12, 18	12, 17

* Or *crushed.* דָּךְ (*dāk*), *to crush to dust:* it occurs only here, and Ps. lxxiv. 21.

Words and Phrases.	Ps. ix. verses.	Ps. x. verses.
"not alway" (ix. 18); "never" (x. 11) (לָנֶצַח, *lānetzach*)	18	11
"which" (ix. 15); "that" (x. 2) (זוּ, *zū*)	15	2
"for ever and ever"	5	16
"Arise, Jehovah!"	19	12

The *Selah* not only thus *connects* these two Psalms, but it tells us that we are to *discriminate* also between them.

The first *Selah* has taught us to discriminate between the judgments of the *wicked man* (sing.) and wicked *men* (pl.).

The *second Selah* teaches us to discriminate also between the two Psalms. For Ps. ix. has "*men*" for its subject, while Ps. x. has the "man of the earth." Note how our thought is again transferred by the *Selah* from the plural to the singular—

ix. 20. **Put them in fear, O Jehovah;**
Let the nations know that they are but men.
SELAH.

x. 1. **Why, O Jehovah, standest Thou afar off?**
Why hidest Thou Thyself in times of trouble?
2. **Through the pride of THE LAWLESS ONE he hotly pursueth the humble;**
Let them be caught in the devices which they have devised,
3. **For THE LAWLESS ONE hath boasted of his soul's desire,**
And the covetous one hath blasphemed, yea, hath abhorred Jehovah.*

* This is the primitive reading of the Hebrew Text. It is one of the eighteen passages in which the *Sopherim*, or Scribes, altered the primitive reading out of a mistaken sense of reverence due to God.

And so the Psalm goes on to speak of the words and deeds of "the lawless one." If we ask what blasphemies are here referred to, we shall find further particulars concerning them in other Scriptures :—

He shall "boast of his inmost desires," and do "according to his own will" (Dan. xi. 3, 16, 36). Hence, he is called "the wilful king." (Compare Hab. i. 11-16.)

He shall "exalt himself and magnify himself against every god, and speak marvellous things against the God of gods" (Dan. xi. 36).

We have further details concerning this "lawless one" in 2 Thess. ii. 3, 4, and Rev. xiii. 5, 6.

Truly is it foretold in this Psalm, by David the prophet (Acts ii. 30), that this Lawless one should boast of his inmost desire, and blaspheme Jehovah.

We thus see the force of these two *Selahs* of Psalm ix. The *first* transfers our thoughts from the lawless one to his followers, and teaches us to discriminate between their respective judgments.

The *second* transfers our thoughts from Psalm ix. to Psalm x. : from lawless "*men*" to "the lawless *man*," "the man of the earth."

The *Scope* of the two Psalms as thus revealed by these two *Selahs* enables us to revise the Structure of Psalm x. :—

The idea of "blaspheming Jehovah" was so repugnant to them that, to avoid pronouncing it with their lips, they give (in the Massorah) a list of passages in which they changed קָלַל (*chalal*), *to curse*, and גָּדַף (*gadaph*), *to blaspheme*, *for* בָּרַךְ (*bārach*), *to bless:* viz., 1 Kings xxi. 10, 13. Job i. 5, 11 ; ii. 5, 9 ; and Ps. x. 3.

From not knowing this fact which has been made known in recent years in Dr. Ginsburg's *Massorah*, and in his *Introduction to the Hebrew Bible* (p. 365), Commentators have struggled to show that בָּרַךְ (*bārach*), which now stands in the printed Heb. Text, can mean *curse* as well as *bless*. (See a Pamphlet on the *Massorah* by the same Author and Publisher, price 1/-)

The Structure of Psalm X.

A | 1. Appeal to Jehovah. (Interrogative.)

  B | 2-6. The Lawless one. His acts (*vv.* 3-5). His thoughts (*v.* 6).

  B | 7-11. The Lawless one. His acts (*vv.* 7-10). His thoughts (*v.* 11).

A | 12-18. Appeal to Jehovah. (Positive.)

It will be noted that as the first *Selah* in Ps. ix. contrasts "the wicked (or lawless) one" (singular) with the wicked men, his followers; so, the second *Selah*, at the end, contrasts Ps. x. with Ps. ix. pointing us on, as it does, to the doings and the thoughts of the Lawless one in greater detail, connecting him with "the times of trouble," or the Great Tribulation: and contrasting him, a second time with his followers; Ps. ix. 20 being in the plural, and Ps. x. referring to the singular.

PSALM XX.

There is one *Selah* between verses 3 and 4.

It is a Psalm of David; and therefore he, being a prophet, speaks of David's Son and David's Lord, the Lord's anointed.

It immediately precedes the National Anthem of Psalm xxi., which relates to the Day-Dawn* of the Millennial Kingdom.

It is not closely linked to it by a *Selah* at the end: but its great subject is the same; it is the King, Jehovah's Anointed, the Messiah.

In Ps. xx. 4 we have the point of the Psalm in the prayer:

> **"Grant thee according to thine heart,**
> **And fulfil all thy counsel."**†

---

* See under *Aijeleth-Shahar*.

† Compare Ps. xxxiii. 11 and the contrast in *v.* 10.

In Psalm xxi. 2 we have the answer to the prayer:

> **"Thou hast given him his heart's desire;**
> **And hast not withholden the request of his lips."**

Thus the two Psalms (xx. and xxi.) are linked together: for the *Selah* precedes the prayer in Ps. xx. 4, and it follows the answer to it in Ps. xxi. 2.

In Ps. xx. 4, the Selah shows that peace with God and acceptance with Him in virtue of atoning sacrifice is the basis of prayer: and that true prayer springs out of true worship. This worship in this prayer is addressed to Jacob's God (*v.* 1); the God who met Jacob when he had nothing and deserved nothing, and yet promised him everything. In New Testament language, therefore, "the God of Jacob" is "the God of all grace" (1 Pet. v. 10).

Not only do we learn trust in Jacob's God, but the acceptance of the burnt sacrifice by turning it to ashes (*see* A.V. margin).

That is how a sacrifice was accepted. That is how God "had respect" to Abel's offering (Gen. iv. 4). That is how "God testified of his gifts" (Heb. xi. 4). That is how Abel "obtained witness that he was righteous." No sacrifice which God accepted was ever consumed by fire emanating from this earth. It was always "fire from heaven" (Lev. ix. 24). And, when sacrifices were offered away from the place which God had chosen, and where He had set His name, then the fire had to fall specially from heaven (*see* Judges vi. 21;* 1 Kings xviii. 38; 1 Chron. xxi. 26, and 2 Chron. vii. 1).†

---

* This is remarkable, for here "fire" (Heb. "the fire") "ascended out of the rock."

† This is in no way affected by the question of the lad Isaac to Abraham, "Behold the fire and the wood, but where is the lamb for

The fire which had consumed the sacrifice was carried into "the holy place," and there used to kindle the incense which was then burnt on "the Golden Altar" (Lev. xvi. 12; Num. xvi. 46). Incense is ever the symbol of prayer: and the lesson of this Selah is to *connect* the two things; and teach us that *there can be no true prayer apart from an accepted sacrifice;* that the *accepted sacrifice* is the basis of the prayer, and the *prayer* is the outcome of the accepted sacrifice.

All other fire was "strange fire" (Lev. x. 1, 2). It was not from heaven, "from before the LORD"; and hence it could not be used to kindle the incense upon the Golden Altar.

In this Dispensation of Grace, our sacrifice (Christ) has been *accepted:* and the High Priest is gone, "not into the holy places made with hands, . . . but into heaven itself." Heaven, therefore, is now our only "place of worship," the place of "the prayers of the saints" (Rev. viii. 1-4).

The fire is "from before the Lord," and must come from thence. Only the New nature "born from above" (John iii. 3, 7) can pray. True worship must be truly in spirit (John iv. 24). True prayer is the "vital breath" of the New nature; for, "that which is born of the Spirit is spirit;

---

a burnt offering?" (Gen. xxii. 7). The fire which Isaac spoke of was in Abraham's hand (*v.* 6), "he took the fire in his hand." What Abraham had in his hand could not be alight or burning, and so carried for three days. What Abraham thus carried must have been the "kindling," which God would light at the moment of His acceptance of it. Just as when we say "Light the fire," or speak of a fire's being lit, we do not mean that we set light to the fire, but to the wood, or to what we call the "firing." So here, that which Abraham carried in his hand was "the firing" which God would light, or set fire to.

and that which is born of the flesh is flesh" (John iii. 6). The flesh cannot pray. It can "say prayers" or "offer prayer," but "it profiteth nothing" (John vi. 63). For the flesh to pray is like the offering of "strange fire."

This is the teaching to which this *Selah* points, between the third and fourth verses of Ps. xx.

3. "**Remember all thy offerings, and accept** (by turning to ashes) **thy burnt sacrifice.**

SELAH.

4. **Grant thee according to thine heart,**
And fulfil all thy counsel."*

PSALM xxi.

The *Selah* between verses 2 and 3 leads us forward; and shows us what these "heart's desires," which had been mentioned in Psalm xx. 4, were.

Hence, the *Selah* follows the answer to the prayer (*v.* 2); and, in giving the reason for the answer, reveals the petitions of the prayer.

2. "**Thou hast given him his heart's desire,**
And hast not withholden the request of his lips.

SELAH.

3. **For Thou wilt meet him with the blessings of goodness** (or, good things);
Thou wilt set a crown of pure gold upon his head.

4. **He asked life of Thee;—Thou gavest it him;**
Even length of days for ever and ever.†

* See note above.

† Or, filling up the *Complex Ellipsis*:—
"Life asked he, of Thee;
Thou gavest it him:
Length of days [asked he]
[Thou gavest it Him] for ever and ever."

5. **His glory is great in Thy salvation;**
Honour and majesty wilt Thou lay upon him.
6. **For Thou wilt make him most blessed for ever:**
Thou wilt make him glad with joy in Thy presence," etc.

This *Selah*, then, connects the desires of the king's heart (Ps. xx. 4) with the answer to those desires in Ps. xxi. 3; and adds the reason for this granting, and the nature of the gifts given.

PSALM xxiv.

This Psalm has two *Selahs*.

The first between verses 6 and 7.

The second at the end, connecting Ps. xxiv. 10 with Ps. xxv. 1.

THE FIRST SELAH marks off the first of the three great (threefold) members of which the Psalm consists.

The subject of the Psalm is, without doubt, the bringing up the Ark of Jehovah to the "Tabernacle of David," which he had prepared for it on Mount Zion.

For many years it had wandered about. In the days of Eli it had been removed from Shiloh, and taken in battle by the Philistines.

For seven months it remained in the hands of the Philistines, and it had been brought back to Beth-shemesh (1 Sam. vi.). From thence it was taken to Kirjath-jearim, where it remained for twenty years (1 Sam. vii. 1, 2) in the house of Abinadab in the hill Gibeah (2 Sam. vi. 3); Eleazar, his son, being its guardian.

As soon as David became the king of "all Israel," his first act had been to take Jebus; and his second act was to bring up "the Ark of God whose name is called by the name of Jehovah of hosts that dwelleth between the cherubim" (2 Sam. vi. 2).

In the manner of doing this they (in the first instance) followed the practice of the idolatrous Philistines (1 Sam. vi. 10, 11), and put it on *a cart* (2 Sam. vi. 3); instead of obeying the law of God (as written in Numbers vii. 9; iv. 2, 15. Deut. x. 8; xxxi. 9), which commanded that the Ark should be borne upon the shoulders of the Kohathites.

God showed His displeasure at this; and David turned aside, and chose the house of Obed-Edom for the Ark to rest in for three months. This was no chance act of David's. He doubtless chose Obed-Edom's house because he was a Gittite: *i.e.*, a dweller in Gath. For Gath was one of the cities of the Levites (Josh. xxi. 24) in which the special family of the Kohathites lived (Josh. xxi. 20). Obed-Edom therefore was a Kohathite, and was thus specially qualified, and charged with the custody of the Ark; and when, after three months, the work of taking the Ark to Zion was undertaken, it is carefully mentioned that it was carried in the manner prescribed in the Law. (*See* 2 Sam. vi. 13; 1 Chron. xv. 2.)

It was a joyous moment in David's life; and he celebrated it by "*dancings with shoutings*," as is shown by the title of Psalm lxxxvii. "*Mahalath Leannoth*" (*see* above (page 39) under that title; and compare 2 Sam. vi. 14, 15, and 1 Chron. xv. 27, 28).

The more detailed account of the bringing up of the Ark is that given in 1 Chron. xv.: where the order of the procession* is described, and Obed-Edom holds a position of honour in being set over the *Sheminith*† (*v.* 21), besides being one of the special doorkeepers.

Psalm lxviii. was another Psalm which was written specially for this procession.*

---

* See under *Alamoth* above, p. 67.

† See under *Sheminith* above, p. 72.

Putting all this information together, and noting the remarkable words of 2 Sam. vi., which speak of "the Ark of God whose name is called by the name of the LORD of hosts" (*i.e.*, Jehovah Sabaioth), we read in Ps. xxiv. the entering into Zion of "the King of glory," "the LORD strong and mighty," "the LORD mighty in battle," "the LORD of hosts." How can we understand this of anything except "the Ark of the LORD," which was the symbol and token of His presence; and where, between the Cherubim, the Shechinah marked His dwelling?

Psalm xxiv. is now seen to describe *the actual entry of the Ark into Zion*, and into "the Tabernacle of David which he had prepared for it" (1 Chron. xv. 1; xvi. 1).

We have several Psalms connected with the celebration of this great event.

Ps. lxviii., the processional Psalm for the setting-out and for the journey;

Ps. xxiv., for the entrance into Zion;

Ps. lxxxvii., the joy of the entrance. *Mahalath Leannoth, the dancings with shoutings.*

Ps. cv., for the subsequent worship (*see* 1 Chron. xvi.).

As to Psalm xxiv., the first *Selah*, as we have said, marks off the first great threefold member, as will be seen from the Structure, and thus gives the key to the other two. Each triad of members consists of (1) a Claim, (2) a Question, (3) the Answer.

The first triad, thus marked off by the *Selah*, is the fullest and most comprehensive. The claim is not merely, as in the other two cases, to the right of the Ark as representative of Jehovah to the Tabernacle of David in Zion; but (1) to the *right* of Jehovah, the King Himself, to the whole earth: (2) the *question*, as to who is entitled to ascend Mount Zion (*v.* 3); and (3) the *answer* to the question.

In other words, in the first triad we have the king, and who is worthy to carry the Ark to Mount Zion. *Selah* marks the answer: viz., the Kohathites, and not the "new cart"; and transfers our thoughts to the Ark, which is in question through the rest of the Psalm. This is thus shewn by the Structure of

Psalm XXIV.

A[1] | 1, 2. Jehovah Himself the King.
  B[1] | 3. Question. Who is worthy to ascend and enter His holy place?
    C[1] | 4-6. Answer. *Selah.*
A[2] | 7. The Ark of the glorious King.
  B[2] | 8-. Question. Who is the glorious King?
    C[2] | -8. Answer. The LORD of hosts.
A[3] | 9. The Ark of the glorious King.
  B[3] | 10-. Question. Who is the glorious King?
    C[3] | -10. Answer. The LORD of hosts.

Now look at the two verses and two subjects indicated.

6. "**Such are they that worship Him,**
That seek thy face O [God of*] Jacob.

SELAH.

7. **Lift up your heads, O ye gates:**
And lift up yourselves* ye everlasting† doors,
That the King of glory may come in."

Having described the worthiness of the Ark-bearers, and their qualification to enter, the *Selah transfers our thoughts* to, and connects them with the entrance of the Ark itself, even Jehovah the King whom it represented.

---

* So it should be, with Septuagint and Syriac Versions. (*See* Ginsburg's Hebrew Text, and note.)

† Or, ancient.

THE SECOND SELAH, at the end of the Psalm, is designed not so much to connect the two verses, Ps. xxiv. 10 and Ps. xxv. 1, as to connect the tw Psalms as such.

Ps. xxiv. has for its subject the constituting of the place of worship; and Ps. xxv. the worship itself, which was to be, and could now be, offered there.

In other words, Ps. xxiv. corresponds with 1 Chron. xv.; and Ps. xxv. with 1 Chron. xvi. In this chapter (1 Chron. xvi.) we have a full description of the worship referred to in Ps. xxiv. 6, for which elaborate preparation had been made, immediately consequent on the entrance of the Ark (*see* 1 Chron. xvi. 1, 2, 4, 37-42); while Obed-Edom the Kohathite, and his brethren, are again specially mentioned in connection with their ministry "to bring to remembrance, and thank and praise Jehovah, the God of Israel."

Ps. xxv. is marked off by the second *Selah* as being closely connected with Psalm xxiv. It is also marked as special by being one of the Acrostic Psalms.

The unworthiness of the worshippers is emphasised, and stands out in strong contrast with the greatness of Jehovah, the object of their worship. The following is the structure of

Psalm XXV.

A[1] | 1-7. Supplicatory.
  B[1] | 8-10. Didactic.
A[2] | 11. Supplicatory.
  B[2] | 12-14. Didactic.
A[3] | 15-22. Supplicatory.

It is thus seen to consist of three members, whose common subject is Supplication; and these are separated by two members, in which David declares the goodness of Jehovah in thus teaching sinners His way, and showing them His covenant.

PSALM xxxii.

IN this Psalm there are three *Selahs:*

(1) Between verses 4 and 5.
(2) Between verses 5 and 6.
(3) Between verses 7 and 8.

The first connects verses 4 and 5; and shows how David's trouble of mind and body in verses 3 and 4 led to his confession of sin in verse 5.

By this connection are we taught the use of trouble. As long as "silence" was maintained, so long was there "the heavy hand." As long as there is no acknowledgment of sin, so long must the trouble endure. But, when it has had its perfect work it produces conviction of sin, and a contrite heart, as evidenced by confession; as indicated and emphasised by the *Selah.*

3. **"For, because I kept silence my bones grew old**
Through my groaning all the day long.
4. **For day and night Thy hand was heavy upon me,**
My moisture was turned to summer's drought.

SELAH.

5-. **My sin I would* acknowledge unto Thee,**
And mine iniquity I did not hide."

Thus are we taught and shown how "the heavy hand" of trouble leads to repentance and conviction of sin.

It was Nathan's parable that convicted David in this case (2 Sam. xii. 1-13). That did for him what a famine did for Joseph's brethren (Gen. xliv. 16); what Job's trouble did for him (Job xlii. 5, 6); what a glorious vision did for Isaiah (Isa. vi. 1-5); and for Daniel (Dan. x. 1-8);

* When we find the Future in such a position as this, can it mean "I [made up my mind that I] **would?**"

what a wondrous miracle did for Peter (Luke v. 1-8), and what another famine did for the lost son (Luke xv.).

This is the lesson to which the first *Selah* points.

THE SECOND SELAH.

The *second* takes up the Confession which follows in the latter part of verse 5; and connects the Divine forgiveness, which follows immediately upon that confession, with the fact that it is only forgiven and justified sinners who are able truly to pray. None others are in a fit position and condition for praying. None others have such cause. Note how this cause is shown:

5. **"I said, 'I will confess concerning my transgression* unto Jehovah,'**
And Thou, Thou didst forgive the iniquity of my sin.

SELAH.

6. **For this cause let every godly man pray to Thee,**
In a time when Thou mayest be found.
Surely in the overflow of many waters,
They will not reach unto him."

THE THIRD SELAH.

The third *Selah* carries us a step further; and shows us that not only are such forgiven ones able to pray, and have a place of safety, and are able to rejoice, but that Jehovah answers their prayer, and promises them guidance and protection.

7. **"Thou art my hiding-place;**
Thou wilt preserve me from trouble,
Thou wilt compass me about with songs of deliverance.

* Some Codices, with the Septuagint and Vulgate Versions, read *transgression* (singular instead of plural). See Ginsburg's Heb. Text, and note. This would be David's sin for which Nathan was sent to convict him (2 Sam. xii.).

SELAH.

8. **Let Me instruct thee, and teach thee in the way thou shouldest go;**
Let Me guide thee with Mine eye."

Then follows (in *v*. 9) an exhortation as to this Divine guidance. Jehovah gees on to say:

"Be ye not like a horse or a mule without understanding:
Whose mouth must be held with bit and bridle.
[Else] he will not come near [to help*] thee."

The guidance of Jehovah is chiefly of two kinds. (1) The guidance of the eye, and of the hand (Ps. cxxiii. 2): *i.e.*, by signs which only those who are in close communion can understand and interpret: for, in long intercourse with God, we get used to indications of His will which cannot be explained to, or appreciated by, another.

(2) If such guidance is not seen, then we need the painful "bit and bridle" of adverse circumstances to bring us near to God, that we may serve and worship Him.†

PSALM xxxix.

There are two *Selahs* in this Psalm of David:

(1) One between verses 5 and 6.
(2) The other between verses 11 and 12.

To understand the exquisite teaching emphasised by these two *Selahs* we must see their own inter-relation in the Structure of the Psalm:

---

* Heb. קָרַב (*kārav*), *to draw near* in the sense of being able to help. (See Deut. iv. 7. Ps. xxxiv. 18; cxix. 151; cxlv. 18. Neh. xiii. 4.)

†This is another application of the word קָרַב (*kārav*), *to draw near* in worship. (Lev. xvi. 1. 1 Sam. xiv. 36. Ezek. xl. 46; xliv. 15.)

The Structure of Psalm xxxix.

A | 1-3. Silent meditation.
  B | 4. Prayer.
    C | 5-. The Fading of life.
      D | -5, 6. The Vanity of man. Selah.
        E | 7, 8. Prayer.
A | 9. Silent meditation.
  B | 10. Prayer.
    C | 11-. The Fading of beauty.
      D | -11. The Vanity of man. Selah.
        E | 12, 13. Prayer.

We see at once that the two *Selahs* occur in the corresponding members D and *D*, the subjects of each being *The Vanity of Man.*

If we look closer at these two, we notice that one comes in the middle of the member D, synthetically expanding and emphasising the vanity itself; while the other occurs at the end of the member *D*, leading us to the only and right conclusion arising from the fact of man's being vanity: viz.: Hope in, and Prayer to, God, as expressed in the corresponding members E and *E* (verses 7 and 12).

The thoughtful reader will require no further help in gathering the full instruction contained in, and conveyed by, these two *Selahs*.

-5. "**Surely, every man, at his best estate, is nothing but a breath.**

SELAH.

6. **Surely every man walketh in a vain show;**
Surely they are disquieted in vain:
He heapeth things up, and knoweth not who shall gather them!"

Thus forcibly is the vanity that is mentioned as a fact in verse 5 expanded, expounded, explained, and emphasised in verse 6.

THE SECOND SELAH

takes up the thought of *vanity* at the end of verse 11; but this time it does not ask us to dwell upon that vanity. It takes us on to a more happy and abiding reality; it sets this frality and vanity of man in vivid contrast with Hope in and prayer to Jehovah, and makes it the very basis of all dependence on Him.

11. "**Surely, every man is but a breath.**

SELAH.

12. **Hear Thou my prayer, O Jehovah,**
And unto my cry give ear;
Hold not Thy peace at my tears.
For I am a stranger with Thee,
And a sojourner, as all my fathers were."

This is the blessed outcome of rightly connecting the two thoughts: the vanity of man, and the reality of Jehovah.

If man be but a "breath," then let that breath breathe forth in prayer, in dependence on Jehovah.

If man be but a "stranger" and a "sojourner," then let it be "with Thee"—with Jehovah.

PSALM xliv.

THIS Psalm contains one *Selah*. It occurs between verses 8 and 9.

It points us to the Structure, and indicates the first break; or the close of the first member, and the beginning of the second. With this key, we read on from verse 9 (of the trouble which had come on the nation) to the end of verse 22, when we return to the first theme, *God our help*, with which the Psalm commenced (*vv.* 1-8). So that it really connects the two members A and *A*, thus treating B and *B* as parenthetical.

A | 1-8. God our help. *Selah.*
  B | a | 9-14. Us.
      b | 15. Me. Thy reproach
  B | *b* | 16. Me. The reason   } Trouble
      a | 17-22. Us.
A | 23-26. Jehovah our help.

The *Sub*-scription (which at present, in the Versions, stands over Psalm xlv.) appoints it for use at the Passover,* showing that, whatever might have been the occasion of the composition of the Psalm, or of the circumstances out of which it arose, or to which it originally referred, it was specially suitable for use at a Festival which celebrated Jehovah's goodness in delivering the People from their oppression in Egypt.

From the internal evidence of the Psalm, furnished by the nature of its subject-matter, it is necessary that we should find a time for it when the Temple-worship was being conducted in due order; and when there was opportunity and occasion for this Psalm to be handed over formally to the Director of the Temple worship, for definite liturgical use.

But it is difficult to find a time in the reigns or history of either David or Solomon, when verses 9-22 would be truly in accordance with the facts of the history. Verse 9 assumes that the People were in the land as a nation, and possessed armies which could go forth.

---

* See under the title, *Soshannim*, above, Part I., page 10.

Prof. Kirkpatrick has entirely disposed of the arguments of those who would place it in the days of the Exile.

Hengstenberg, Kiel, and Dilitzsch assign it to the invasion of the Edomites in the days of David.

De Wette and Moluck assign it to the time of Josiah immediately preceding the Exile.

Calom says: "If anything is clear, it is that the Psalm was written by anyone rather than David!" and refers it without hesitation to the tyranny of Antiochus.

But we need not go so far as this.

The invasion of Sennacherib furnishes us with all the conditions required by the language of this Psalm.

Israel had been "cast off," as verse 9 declares, on account of the idolatry which had been introduced by Jezebel. Judah had been threatened with a similar judgment on account of similar apostasy, led astray by her daughter Athaliah.

But this judgment had been arrested by the great Reformation of the Temple and of its worship in the reign of Hezekiah. This of itself would fully justify the language of verses 17 and 18:—

17. . . . We have not forgotten Thee,
Neither have we been false to Thy Covenant.

18. Our heart is not turned back,
Neither have our steps declined from Thy way.

Israel had gone astray, and been false to Jehovah's Covenant; but Judah, though it had turned back from His way, had returned to Him.

There were no circumstances till then in which it could be said that God had "cast off His People" and "put them to shame" (*v.* 9); when he had "not gone forth with their armies;" when they had been "scattered among the heathen" (*v.* 11); when they had been "made a reproach to their neighbours, and a scorn and derision to them that were round about them" (*v.* 13).

Nothing but the reproaches of Sennacherib and Rab-shakeh could be so well described as "the voice of him that reproacheth and blasphemeth" (*v.* 16).

We look, in vain, through the reigns of David and Solomon for any circumstances which could call forth the expressions used in verses 14—22.

We need not search the times of the Maccabees; for we have, in the history of Sennacherib's invasion, all that we need to explain and describe the exact condition of things in 2 Kings xviii.

If anything is needed to complete those details we have them succinctly recounted on the six-sided cylinder now to be seen in British Museum,* London. It contains the annals of Sennacherib, king of Assyria, about B.C. 705—681, and contains a record of this siege of Jerusalem. He says in the following lines:—

11\. . . . . And of Hezekiah [King of the]
12\. Jews, who had not submitted to my yoke,
13\. forty-six of his fenced cities, and the strongholds, and the smaller cities
14\. which were round about them and which were without number,
15\. by the battering of rams, and by the attack of engines,
16\. and by the assault of foot-soldiers, and†

---

* British Museum 55—10—3, i. We have two photographs of it to give, below, in Part iii.

† The three words which end this line are the names of military engines.

17. I besieged, I captured, 200,150 people, small and great, male and female,
18. horses, and mules, and asses, and camels, and oxen,
19. and sheep innumerable from their midst I brought out and
20. I reckoned them as spoil."

Sennacherib goes on to tell us how he devastated the land and spoiled it, and to describe how Judah's king was "overwhelmed" with fear.

All this exactly suits the language of this Psalm, and accords with the history as given in 2 Kings xviii., 2 Chron. xxxii., and Isa. xxxvi.

Without going further into this now, our purpose will be served by accepting this as a reasonable suggestion, against which no serious objection can be urged.

On the face of the subject it is much more worthy, even as a hypothesis, than that of the "higher" critics, which would bring it down to times later than the return from Babylon. For it succeeds in putting it into immediate connection with the history with which it so perfectly and beautifully accords; and to which it so plainly refers.

But, this being so, it at once brings the Psalm into B.C. 705—681.

Looking then at this Ps. xliv., and reading it over again in the light of Hezekiah's history, it shines forth with new beauty and with new force. We can fit in many of the very expressions and references with the actual circumstances of the time, when Sennacherib and the forces of Assyria were devastating the land; when efforts had been made in vain to buy him off by stripping the temple of its gold.

What more suitable words of prayer could be found to give expression to the actual condition of things than those contained in the first eight verses, which mark off the first great member of the Structure, and correspond so perfectly with the Prayer resumed in the last three verses.

God's past deliverances of His People are called to mind; His goodness and grace vouchsafed to them are remembered; and His power put forth on their behalf is celebrated.

After this outburst of thankful remembrance, the *Selah* suddenly arrests us. The subject is broken off abruptly, and we are bidden, by it, to connect the sad condition of their then present calamities. This new subject is at once the consequence of that remembrance of former favours; and those favours are the cause of the painful contrast.

This sad picture of their condition is continued down to the end of verse 22, when it is suddenly made the ground of prayer, and there is a return to the subject with which the Psalm commenced—God our help.

Jehoshaphat had, before this, under similar circumstances, done exactly the same; and in his prayer, in 2 Chron. xx. 7 and 12 made Jehovah's past deliverances the plea for His future help.

It is the same here with Hezekiah; and, the *Selah*, between the eighth and ninth verses, is put there to call our attention to the fact; to show us the contrast; and to point us to the solemn circumstances which called forth the Psalm itself:

8. "In God have we made our boast* all the day long.

* Compare Ps. lvi. 4, 10, 11.

And to Thy Name will we ever give thanks.

SELAH.

9. **But* Thou has cast us off, and put us to shame : and goest not forth with our armies. . . .**
10. **They who hate us have plundered us† at their will."**

It is needless to quote more of the Psalm. It must be read as a whole to get the full value of the *Selah*, and to note the full contrast between verses 7 and 10.

We must also turn again to the Structure of the Psalm which is given above, and note how the two pleas are marked off and distinguished, at the beginning and at the end. We shall also note how the "us" of verses 9-14 and 17-22 is in contrast with the "me" of verses 15 and 16.

There is a keen sense of the reproaches and blasphemies of Rab-shakeh and Sennacherib, which were keenly felt both by Hezekiah and his people.

On reading Ps. xliv. again throughout, in connection with the history, it will be exactly what we should expect to find; and the more closely we study it in the light of its historical setting the more shall we see the accuracy of its historical references, and the beauty of its earnest prayers.

PSALMS xlvi., xlvii. and xlviii.

These three Psalms are so closely connected that they must be considered together.

---

* אַף (*aph*), introducing a very strong contrast, as in Ps. lviii. 2; lxviii. 16.

† So some Codices, with the Aramaic and Syriac Versions. See Ginsburg's Hebrew Text and note.

There are five *Selahs* distributed between them.

(1). Between verses 3 and 4 of Psalm xlvi.

(2). Between verses 7 and 8 of Psalm xlvi.

(3). Between the two Psalms xlvi. and xlvii.

(4). Between verses 4 and 5 of Psalm xlvii.

(5). Between verses 8 and 9 of Psalm xlviii.

These three Psalms form a triology of praise for some special deliverance of Jerusalem from a formidable foreign invasion.

In Psalm xlvi. the subject is Jehovah, the only help and resource of His people.

Psalm xlvii. is a Song of Praise based on Psalm xlvi. 10, expanding the subject that Zion's King is the true great King over all the earth (compare Psalm xlviii. 2).

Psalm xlviii. is a Song and Psalm celebrating the power and favour of God as being Zion's joy; the joy being the result flowing from the fact of the presence of God in the midst of Zion, which is the subject of Psalm xlvi.

As we have said, there can be little or no doubt but that these three Psalms celebrate the great deliverance which had been so earnestly prayed for in Psalm xliv.

They do not celebrate the close of a momentous struggle.

They do not commemorate a great victory or triumph after conflict between opposing hosts.

They do not commemorate a campaign, or a successful assault upon a fortified enemy; but rather a wonderful deliverance from the hand and power of a beseiging force, wrought by its sudden and complete destruction.

There is wonderful unanimity among commentators

in agreeing that that deliverance can be none other than the sudden and miraculous destruction of the army of Sennacherib under the walls of Jerusalem in the reign of Hezekiah! [1]

Delitzsch stands almost alone in referring these Psalms to the victory of Jehoshaphat over the allied forces of the Moabites, Ammonites, and Edomites in 2 Ch. xx.[2]

But, as we have said, the Psalm celebrates not so much victory over foes as deliverance from them: not so much a triumphant battle as a successful defence; not so much the delivery of a great assault as a deliverance from an overwhelming siege.

No event in Jewish history fits these circumstances so well as Sennacherib's siege of Jerusalem. We have seen above, under Psalm xliv., that Sennacherib records, in his account of that campaign, how he had swept the land, city after city falling into his

---

[1] Of course, the Higher Critics are voiced by Professor Cheyne, who says:—"To suppose from this Psalm that Zion's situation was that which existed during the siege by the Assyrians (701 B.C.) is an utter mistake." Nothing (he says) satisfies the Psalm but the revolution occasioned by Alexander the Great, 330 B.C.

[2] Indeed, the whole group (Psalms xliv.--xlviii.) belong to the same period, and may well have the same authorship. Dr. J. J. Blunt (*Undesigned Coincidences*, pp. 225-6) emphasises the marriage of Hezekiah by the reference to his wife's name *Hephzi-bah* in Isa. lxii. 4, and 2 Kings xxi. 1. He uses it as an evidence as to Isa. lxii. being the work of Isaiah. He might have extended his reference to Psalm xlv., the circumstances of Hezekiah's marriage being rendered of such importance on account of his sickness and threatened death at a time when he was without an heir to his throne. It was a crisis thus marked by Hezekiah's Sickness, Sign, Recovery, Marriage, Siege, Deliverance, and the Birth of his heir in third of the fifteen added years.

hands. Judah seemed about to share the same fate, for his armies were encamped about Israel.

We know how both king and people had been encouraged by Isaiah to trust wholly in Jehovah as their only defence; how he had caused them to put their trust in the Lord of Hosts; how Sennacherib and Rabshakeh bade the people not to heed the advice of Hezekiah to trust in Jehovah, but to trust in him and his god (2 Chron. xxxii. 6-15. 2 Kings xviii. 29-36).

If this Psalm be the expression of Hezekiah's trust and confidence in God, then we can read it in the light of his history as written in the Books of Kings, Chronicles and Isaiah.

No succour was to be expected; and no deliverance was possible unless God should interpose.

Isaiah had assured them that God was in the midst of Zion, and would assuredly deliver the city out of the hands of the King of Assyria (2 Kings xix. 20-34), and Jehovah had said:—"I will defend this city, to save it, for Mine own sake, and for My servant David's sake."

Zion, the "city of God," we now know, stood on the south side of Moriah, and not on the west side as on the ordinary traditional maps.

This is proved by recent discoveries, as may be seen from the publications of the Palestine Exploration Fund.

But Scripture is sufficient of itself. There is no question that Jebus was the mount immediately South of Moriah; and that it was bordered on the East by the Valley of the Kedron. This was the city which David took as soon as he was proclaimed king over Israel.

He was stoutly resisted by the Jebusites; but it is written, "Nevertheless, David took the stronghold of Zion, the same is the city of David" (2 Sam. v. 7-9. 1 Chron. xi. 5-8). Two other passages identify Zion with the city of David (1 Kings viii. 1. 2 Chron. v. 2).[1]

When David had taken Jebus, he "dwelt in the fort, and called it the city of David, and David built round about from Millo and inward" (2 Sam. v. 8).[2]

The wall was continued by Solomon (1 Kings ix. 15, 24; xi. 27); and afterward by Hezekiah (2 Chron. xxxii. 5).[3]

We are carefully informed in the history how Hezekiah, on the approach of the Assyrian hosts, "took counsel with his princes and his mighty men to stop the waters of the fountains which were without the city; and they did help him. So there was gathered much people together, who stopped all the fountains, and the brook that ran through the midst of the land [*i.e.*, the Kedron Valley] saying, Why should the kings of

---

[1] We learn also that, coming out of the Dung Gate at the S.W. corner of the Temple area, Nehemiah first turned East, and then South, following the walls to "the Gate of the Fountain;" this fountain being (the lower) Gihon Spring, known to-day as "the Virgin's Fount" (Neh. ii. 14; iii. 15; xii. 37). The Water Gate was also on the East side of Ophel, which was another name for the ancient Jebus. A careful study of these Scriptures, with the most recent maps, is all that is needed to show that the traditional site of Zion (like most other traditions) is quite wrong; that it originally occupied the hill of Ophel, and that its wall enclosed the Pool of Siloam at the extreme South-East corner.

[2] Millo means *a filling up*, and refers to the filling up of the valley which separated Moriah from Jebus.

[3] Manasseh extended this wall, which was on the West of Ophel, of Gihon, and of the city of David (2 Chron. xxxiii. 14).

Assyria come and find much water?" (2 Chron. xxxii. 3, 4).

Among these must have been the Great Fountain which gave its name to the gate, on the East side of the hill of Ophel, near En-Rogel, and on the West side of the Valley of the Kedron. This fountain of Gihon must originally have had an outlet forming a stream flowing down the midst of the land, *i.e.*, the Kedron Valley[1] (2 Chron. xxxii. 4), and at times flooding it.[2]

After stopping up this fountain, its waters, having no further outlet into the Kedron Valley, would be diverted into the rock-cut channels under Ophel. There is still existing an underground channel running southward from this fountain for some 1,800ft., and ending in the Pools of Siloam, at the South extremity of Ophel.[3] This was from 3ft. 6in. to 4ft. wide, by 6ft. in height.

Then, there was another rock-cut channel discovered in 1880, older than the above, running westward from this Fountain of En-Rogel (Gihon) right under Ophel, and coming out on "the west side of the city of David" (2 Chron. xxxii. 30). A slab, discovered in this tunnel, describes its formation, and how the workmen working from either end met each other "pick to pick," and the waters flowed "for a distance of 1,000 cubits." The letters are in the most ancient Hebrew characters yet

---

[1] The Kedron was formerly much deeper, and more to the West than it now runs.

[2] See Thompson's *Land and the Book*, p. 658, 659.

[3] This channel was discovered by Sir Charles Warren in 1867. See his *Recovery of Jerusalem*, pp. 107, 109, 124, 238-255. London, Richard Bentley. Also Harper's *Bible and Modern Discoveries*, pp. 514-525.

discovered; older than those of the Moabite stone.[1]

Isaiah viii. 6 refers to those rock-cut channels.

Hezekiah availed himself of a still older Jebusite work, now lately discovered by Sir Charles Warren. Sir Charles found that, from the spring or fountain on the East side of Ophel, a channel had been cut, running due west, until it was well under Zion.[2] Then a shaft was found, sunk from the Jebusite citadel, immediately over the top of this channel, with a hollow made at the bottom, from which the collected water could be drawn up by buckets. We give a view taken (by kind permission) from Sir Charles Warren's book.

---

[1] See Harper, quoted above, pp. 522, 523. Prof. Sayce, *Fresh Light*, pp. 87, 88. Rev. W. F. Birch's papers in *Quarterly Statement*, Pal. Expl. Fund. Jan. 1889. Herr Schick, in *Quarterly Statement*, 1886, p. 197, for Report.

[2] There can be no doubt but that some of these channels are of much more ancient date than Hezekiah. It is almost certain that they formed part of the ancient defence of Jebus; and that it was this secret water supply, combined with the natural and then precipitous situation of the citadel, which made the Jebusites so confident in their challenge to David; as shown by their scorn, in saying that the blind and the lame would be sufficient to keep David out by merely saying, "Thou shalt not come in hither." This secret rock-cut passage or channel, called צִנּוֹר (*tsinnōr*), is rendered "gutter," in 2 Sam. v. 8 (R.V., "watercourse"). It was doubtless known to Araunah, who, though a Jebusite, was spared; and is seen shortly after possessing property close by. Josephus tells us of the relations existing between Araunah and David. He says, "I shall now make mention of Araunah, who was a wealthy man among the Jebusites, but was not slain by David in the siege of Jerusalem because of the good-will he bore to the Hebrews, and a particular benignity and affection which he had to the king himself; which I shall take a more seasonable opportunity to speak of a little afterwards" (Josephus, *Ant.* Book vii. iii. 3).

Josephus fulfils his promise by adding, further on: "Araunah was by his lineage a Jebusite, but a particular friend of David's; and for

It is a section from E. to W. of the hill of Ophel, formerly 300ft. high, with a steep slope of 30°. Steps now lead down to the fountain from the East side, the Kedron Valley; but nothing was known of any passage beyond it until it was discovered by Sir Charles Warren by a mere accident. In creeping along another rock-cut channel leading N. from the Pools of Siloam, he and Sergeant Birtles came suddenly into this channel, running E. and W. Following this new channel they found the Eastern end was the Gihon spring, and the Western end ran up into Zion. In the vaulted roof, at the point marked C, there is, to-day, an iron ring which had been used for letting the buckets up and down the shaft marked D.

The sides of the upper and more horizontal portion of the passage (B) were lined with loose stones, apparently ready to be cast down the shaft. On these they found three glass lamps of curious construction, placed at intervals, as if to light up the passage; also a

---

that cause when he overthrew the city he did him no harm, as we informed the reader a little before" (Josephus, *Ant.* Book vii. xiii. 4).

It was this affection, which existed before Jebus was taken by David, which doubtless led to Araunah's disclosure of this "*Tsinnor*," or secret passage from the spring to the citadel.

This explains David's proclamation that "Whoever getteth up by the *Tsinnor* and smiteth the Jebusites, and the lame and the blind who hate David's soul, *he shall be chief or captain*; because they (*i.e.*, the blind and the lame) had said of David, 'He shall not come unto the citadel.'"

The translation of this is confused in the A.V., and is not clear in the R.V., as may be seen by comparing the two with their italics and marginal suggestions. (Compare 2 Sam. v. 6-8 and 1 Chron. xi. 6).

The better knowledge of Sir Charles Warren's discoveries makes it all clear.

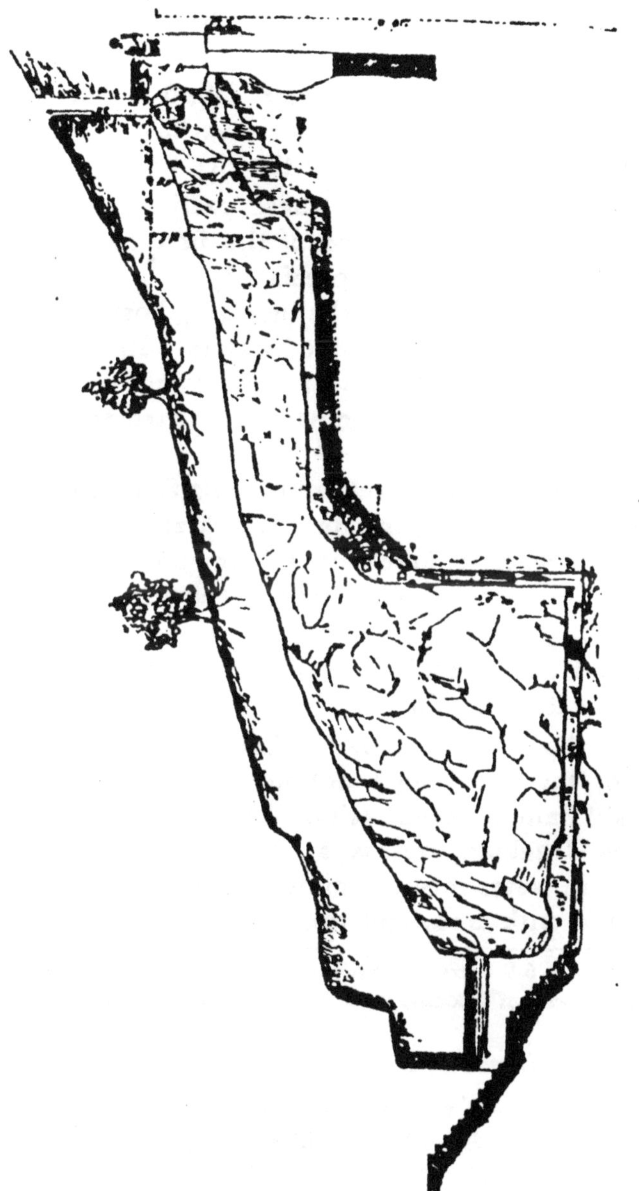

ROCK-CUT PASSAGE ABOVE VIRGIN'S FOUNT.

pile of charcoal as if for cooking; besides a cooking dish and water jar.

Other rock-cut channels were found under Zion: one, 1,800ft. long, by which the overflow water was carried south to Siloam within the city walls.

It is necessary to give all these particulars in order that the meaning and force of the first *Selah* in this Psalm may be seen and appreciated.

In verse 3 the raging of the beseiging hosts was compared to the roaring of troubled waters. In verse 4 the secret purpose of God, by which He would bring about their ruin, is beautifully compared to the secret channels of water "which go softly."[1]

These are the waters referred to in 2 Chron. xxxii. 30, where we read: "This same Hezekiah also stopped the upper water-course[2] of Gihon and brought it straight down to the West side of the city of David."

In 2 Kings xx. 20 we are told that Hezekiah with "all his might . . . . made a pool and a conduit,[3] and brought water into the city."

In the Apocryphal book of Ecclesiasticus (which is good for history though not for doctrine) the writer praises "Famous Men" (xliv.—l.), and in a long list he includes Hezekiah, and says, "he fortified his city and brought in water into the midst thereof: he digged the hard rock with iron, and made wells for waters."

---

[1] In Isa. viii. 6-8 there is the same contrast between these still running waters of Siloam, and the overwhelming flood of the Assyrian host.

[2] Heb. מַיִם (*mayim*) *waters* (pl.)

[3] תְּעָלָה *te'ālāh*, *a trench, or artificial aqueduct*, by which water is conveyed. See 1 Kings xviii. 32, 35, 38; 2 Kings xviii. 17; xx. 20. Isa. vii. 3, 36. Ezek. xxxi. 4. Job xxxviii. 25.

This is the "river" and these are the "streams" of Ps. xlvi. 4. נָהָר (*nāchār*) is used of a constant flow of water.[1]

These waters beneath Zion could be called *nāchār*, being fed as they were by constant springs. The word rendered "streams" is פֶּלֶג (*peleg*) *the small channels* by which water was distributed.[2]

Now we are in a position to understand the first *Selah* in this Psalm, because its purpose is to point out to us the contrast between the rage of the enemy, which is compared to an overwhelming flood, and the silent and secret purposes of God which were working to overthrow them. These secret purposes are compared to the silent, secret, underground rock-cut channels of water, which were ministering comfort and joy to the beseiged, while they were hidden (as God's purposes were) from the beseigers outside the city.

But we must first look at the Structure of the Psalm, and see how it bears out all we have said.

The Psalm consists of *seven* members, which correspond as follows:—

Psalm xlvi.

A[1] | 1. God our help.
    B[1] | 2, 3. The enemy not to be feared. *Selah.*
A[2] | 4. 5. God, Zion's help.
    B[2] | 6. The enemy's raging quelled.
A[3] | 7. Jehovah of hosts, our help. *Selah.*
    B[3] | 8-10. The enemy's destruction.
A[4] | 11. Jehovah our help. *Selah.*

[1] In contrast with נַחַל (*nāchal*), which means a *wady*, or *summer stream* dependent on rains.

[2] And because these, when used in a garden for purposes of irrigation, *divided* it up into *divisions*, they were so called from פָּלַג (*pālag*) *to divide*. Gen. x. 25. Ps. i. 3. Prov. xxi. 1. See *Figures of Speech* by the same author and publisher, pp. 97, 98.

We need not give the whole Psalm, but only the verses that are specially connected, when the contrast will be at once seen:

THE FIRST SELAH.

2. **Therefore will not we fear, though the earth do quake,[1]**
And though the mountains be carried into the midst of the sea;
3. **Though the waters thereof roar,[2] and be troubled;**
Though the mountains shake with the swelling thereof.[3]

SELAH.

4. **There is a river[4] whose channels make glad the city of God.**
The holy dwelling-place of the Most High.
5. **God is in the midst of her; she shall not be moved.**
God shall help her when the morning appeareth[5]
6. **The nations roared,[6] kingdoms were moved.[7]**
He uttered His voice; the earth melted.

---

[1] The same word as in verse 6 (A.V. moved).

[2] The same word as in verse 6 (A.V. uttered his voice).

[3] Prof. Kirkpatrick, not seeing the reason for this *Selah* here, thinks it "probable" that there was originally a refrain here (like that in *vv.* 7 and 11), but that it has dropped out!

[4] Heb. נָהָר (*nāchār*). See above and note on p. 151.

[5] Or, *when the morning draweth nigh*. A.V. margin, *when the morning appeareth*. R.V. margin, *at the dawn of morning*. Lit., *at the turning of the morning*. The reference is to Isa. xxxvii. 6.

[6] The same word as in verse 3 (A.V. "raged").

[7] Corresponding with the same word in *v.* 5. Zion "shall not be moved."

We cannot fail to connect the confident words of assured trust: "God shall help her when the morning appeareth;" with the promise which had been given by Jehovah through Isaiah, "the zeal of the Lord of Hosts shall do this . . . for I will defend this city, to save it, for Mine own sake, and for My servant David's sake.[1] And it came to pass that night that the angel of Jehovah went out and smote in the camp of the Assyrians 185,100; and when they arose **early in the morning**, behold they were all dead corpses" (compare 2 Kings xix. 31-35. Isa. xxxvii. 35, 36). We have the same phrase in Ex. xiv. 27, where there is a similar reference: "And the sea returned to his strength **when the morning appeared**."

This brings us to

THE SECOND SELAH,

which comes between verses 7 and 8, and tells us to connect together the *promised* deliverance (in *v.* 5), and the assured *trust* in that promise (*v.* 7) with the actual fulfilment of that promise, and the *accomplishment* of that deliverance in the destruction of the Assyrian host.

7. **Jehovah of hosts is with us:**
The God of Jacob is our Refuge.

SELAH.

8. **Come, behold the works of Jehovah,**
What terrible things He hath done in the Land.
9. **He maketh wars to cease unto the end of the earth,**

---

1 This refers to the special name of Zion as "the city of David." (See above.)

And breaketh the bow and cutteth the spear in sunder,
He burneth the chariots in the fire."

The *Selah*, here, invites us to reflect upon this marvellous deliverance, and to learn its lessons. It emphasises the deliverance, and bids us note how, by means small, secret, and silent, as those rock-cut channels, He can still the roarings and ragings of the nations even unto the ends of the earth.

That past deliverance has its lessons for the present and for the future; and this second *Selah* exhorts us to learn them.

THE THIRD SELAH

comes at the end of the Psalm, connecting not merely the last verse of Psalm xlvi. with the first verse of Psalm xlvii., but connecting *the whole of the two Psalms as such*, in order to show us that the subject of both is one and the same.

While Psalm xlvi. commemorates the history and records the trust reposed in Jehovah's promised help, and its realisation, Psalm xlvii. goes on to sing the praises of Jehovah Himself for the deliverance which is the subject of Psalm xlvi.

The exaltation of God is their common theme, as we may see by comparing Psalm xlvi. 10 with xlvii. 9.

The title "Most High," in Psalm xlvi. 4 and xlvii. 2 is another connecting link: for it is the Divine Title specially associated with God's sovereignty in the earth.

That the Third Selah is a real connecting link may be easily seen:—

xlvi. 10. **Be still, and know that I am God;**
I will be exalted among the nations;
I will be exalted in the earth.

11. **Jehovah [God] of hosts is with us,**
The God of Jacob is our refuge.

SELAH.

xlvii. 1. **O, all ye peoples, clap your hands:**
Shout unto God with the voice of triumph.
2. **For Jehovah, Most High, is terrible,**
A great King over all the earth.

PSALM xlvii.

Several of the modern Commentators agree in connecting this Psalm (xlvii.), with the wonderful deliverance of Zion from the siege of Sennacherib.

Perowne thus associates it, as he does also Psalms xlvi. and xlviii.; and Hupfeld, he says, is right in calling it "a lyrical expansion of the idea prominent in verse 10, that Jehovah is high exalted above the nations, and the great King over all the earth."[1]

It is called "a Psalm" or Song, and its Structure is as follows:—

Psalm xlvii.

A | 1. A call to Praise.
  B | 2-4. The Reasons. *Selah.*
    C | 5. God exalted.
A | 6. A call to Praise.
  B | 7-9. The Reasons.
    C | 9. God exalted.

---

1 Prof. Kirkpatrick also thus connects it, but suggests Isaiah as the author, or one of his disciples.

The older expositors connect this Psalm with David's removal of the Ark to Zion, after the taking of Jebus (2 Sam. vi.).

Hengstenberg and Delitzsch refer it to the victory of Jehoshaphat (2 Chron. xx.).

Eichorn, who connects Psalm xlvi. and xlviii. with Sennacherib's Invasion and Siege, yet considers Ps. xlvii. as belonging to David: and the "Higher" Critics, of course, end by bringing it down to Post-Exilic days. Prof. Cheyne connects it with a date subsequent to that of Alexander the Great!

The *Selah* at the close of verse 4 connects it with verse 5, and had its purpose been observed and noted, the verb עָלָה (*'ālah*) in verse 5 would never have been meaninglessly translated "gone up:" but *exalted* as in the corresponding member C, verse 9. The exaltation of Jehovah is the burden of the Psalm, as it was of Psalm xlvi. In Psalm xlvi. 10 Jehovah had said:—

> "**Be still and know that I am God:**
> **I will be EXALTED among the nations,**
> **I will be EXALTED[1] in the earth.**"

This is exactly what Psalm xlvi. carries out. Hezekiah and His people do extol and exalt Jehovah in accordance with this expression of His will.

The *Selah* points to this; and connects this exaltation of God with the consideration of what He is in Himself with what He had done.

In the members C. and *C.* (verses 5 and 9), the same word is used.

A | **O, all ye peoples, clap your hands;**
| **Shout unto God with the voice of triumph** (*v.* 1).

B | **For Jehovah is Most High** [and] **terrible,**
| **A great King[2] over all the earth** (*v.* 2).
| **He hath subdued the peoples under us,**
| **And the nation under our feet** (*v.* 3).
| **He hath chosen our inheritance for us;**
| **The glory of Jacob whom He loved** (*v.* 4).

---

[1] The Hebrew here is רוּם (*rūm*) *to be exalted*, and is so translated oftener than by any other rendering.

[2] He is not merely the King of Israel, ("our King" *v.* 6), but "the King of all the earth" (*v.* 7).

The title "great king" has a special reference to Sennacherib, who had arrogated to himself this very title. See Isaiah xxxvi. 4.

This verse 2 links together the three Psalms. See Psalm xlvi. 4 and xlviii. 2.

SELAH.

C | **God is EXALTED[1] with a shout,**
| **Jehovah with the sound of the trumpet** (*v.* 5).

A | **Sing praises to our God[2], sing praises,**
| **Sing praises to our King, sing praises** (*v.* 6).

B | **For God is the King over[3] all the earth.[4]**
| **Sing praises with understanding** (*v.* 7).

The *Selah* shows that the word עָלָה ('*ālah*) must be rendered *exalted*, as it is in the last line; for this is the great subject of the Psalm.

PSALM xlviii.

There is one *Selah* in this Psalm, between verses 8 and 9.

Many commentators agree in connecting this Psalm with Psalms xlvi. and xlvii. as continuing the praises of Jehovah for His great deliverance from the armies of Sennacherib; and the *Selah* at the end of verse 8 shows this connection; while, as it gives the scope of the Psalm, so it suggests the true meaning of the word "thought" in *v.* 9.

But to see these points it is necessary for us to see the structure of Psalm xlviii. It is an extended alternation (as in Ps. xlvii.) consisting of three members, the subjects being repeated in the same order.

---

[1] This is the same as the last line of the Psalm :—"He is greatly exalted"; and should be so rendered here.

[2] Some Codices, with Sept. and Vulg. read "our God." See Ginsburg's Hebrew Text, and Note.

[3] Some Codices, with 2 early printed Editions, read "over" instead of "of." See Ginsburg's Hebrew Text and Note.

[4] This is the burden of the whole Psalm. Compare *v.* 2 and Psalm xlvi. 10.

The Structure of Psalm xlviii.

A | 1. Praise ascribed.

  B | 2, 3. Zion a joy; and God her refuge.

    C | 4-8. The reason ("For.") The *power* of God shown in the deliverance of Zion. *Selah.*

A | 9, 10. Praise ascribed.

  B | 11-13. Zion to rejoice; and to survey her strength and glory.

    C | 14. The reason ("For.") The *favour* of God shown in His goodness to Zion.

This structure shows us that we have a continuation of the same praises; and, for the same reasons, viz., the favour of God as shown in God's deliverance of Zion from her beseiging enemies.

In Psalm xlvi. 10 Jehovah had said

> **"Be still* and know that I am God:**
> **I will be exalted among the nations,**
> **I will be exalted in the earth."**

Psalm xlvii. is the answer to the latter part of xlvi. 10: His demand *to be exalted and extolled.*

Psalm xlviii. is the answer to the command for them *to be still.*

The object of the *Selah* in Psalm xlviii., between verses 8 and 9, is to call our attention to that demand as made in Psalm xlvi. 10. Here in xlvii. 9 the word is דָּמָה (*dāmah*), *to be still, quiet, silent, at rest:* then, because this stillness is the time for thinking, it is used of the *stillness* of thinking. This is its meaning here.

---

* Heb. רָפָה (*rāphah*) *desist, cease your efforts.*

C | As we have heard, so have we seen,[1]
In the city of Jehovah of hosts,
In the city of our God; (*v.* 8).
God will establish it for ever.

SELAH.

A | We have rested O God, in the thought of Thy lovingkindness
In the midst of Thy Temple. (*v.* 9.)
According to Thy name, O God, so is Thy praise unto the ends of the earth. (*v.* 10.)

B | Thy right hand is full of righteousness.
Let Mount Zion be glad,
Let the cities[2] of Judah be glad,
Because of Thy judgments." (*v.* 11.)
Walk about Zion,[3] and count[4] the towers thereof; (*v.* 12.)
Mark ye well her bulwarks; consider her palaces;
That ye may tell it to the generations following. (*v.* 13.)

C | For this God is our God for ever and ever,
He, even He, will be our guide for evermore.[5] (*v.* 14.)

---

[1] This was the beginning of this series of Psalms in Psalm xliv. 1.

[2] Heb. *daughters*. This was the common name for towns and villages which were regarded as daughters of the metropolis, which was the *mother* city. See Num. xxi. 25; Josh. xvii. 11, 16.

These would have special reason to rejoice with Zion, for they had been captured by Sennacherib, and were now delivered (Isa. xxxvi. 1).

[3] This they were now free to do, for the besieging enemies had been destroyed.

[4] Compare Psalm xxii. 17; Gen. xv. 5. The enemies had been counting them before. Now the besieged were at liberty to do so. The Assyrians had counted them for destruction (Isa. xxxiii. 18).

[5] The Parallelism requires this ending, which agrees with the R.V. margin; also with some Codices 5 early printed editions, Aramaic, Sept., and Vulg. Versions. The Massorah by dividing the one word into two makes it mean "unto death," instead of evermore. See Ginsburg's Heb. Text and note.

Jehovah had said: Be still: Cease from your own efforts (Psalm xlvi. 10); and, encouraged by the exhortations of Isaiah they did so cease; and put their whole trust in Jehovah.

Jehovah's power had been put forth; His favour had been manifested; His deliverance had been enjoyed. Hence, this trilogy of Psalms ends with a Psalm of praise and thanksgiving, in which God is exalted and Zion is admired.

The end is reached in the ecstatic words:

"This God is our God for ever and ever;
He, even He, will be our guide for evermore."

PSALM xlix.

In this Psalm *Selah* occurs twice.

(1) Between verses 13 and 14.

(2) Between verses 15 and 16.

In this Psalm, again, if we would see the full force of these *Selahs*, we must study the Structure; because the corresponding members have to be read on from one to the other in order to connect the corresponding subjects. What intervenes between any two corresponding members is thus practically, for the moment, put into, and must be considered as being in a parenthesis.

For example, in the case of the first *Selah*, the verse before it (*v.* 13) begins: "This their way." What does the "this" refer to? and what is "their way"? We can find out only by looking at the corresponding member "d" (*vv.* 10, 11).

The Structure of this Psalm is one of most exquisite and wonderful beauty; perhaps the most beautiful in the whole Bible.

"Selah." Psalm xlix.

(1). It is one of the few Psalms which have a separate introduction.

(2). It is a simple alternation of four members. The second and fourth consist of nearly the same words, while

(3). The first and third members, taken together, are broken up into an introversion of alternating couplets and quatrains; the couplets in the one being answered by a quatrain in the other.

(4). The Introduction consists of two members; each consisting of an alternation *and* an introversion; thus briefly anticipating the form of the Psalm itself.

I.		II.	
Hear	**Low**	**Mouth**	**Ear**
People	**High**	**Wisdom**	**Parable**
Give ear	**Rich**	**Heart**	**Dark saying**
Inhabitants	**Poor**	**Understanding**	**Harp**

The Structure of Psalm xlix.

Theme { I. | 1, 2. All to hear.
Theme { II. | 3, 4. I will speak.

A | a | 5. Why fear? (Couplet.)
  b | 6-9. No redemption for man. (Quatrain, alternate.)
   c | 10-. Death. (Couplet.)
    d | -10, 11. Worldly wisdom. (Quatrain, introverted.)
     B | 12. Man compared to beasts. (Couplet.)

A | *d* | 13. Worldly wisdom. (Couplet.) Selah.
   c | 14. Death. (Quatrain, introverted).
  b | 15. Redemption for Psalmist. (Couplet.) Selah.
 a | 16-19. **Fear not!** (Quatrain, alternate.)
     B | 20. Man compared to beasts. (Couplet.)

It will be seen from this that both the two *Selahs* occur in the second of the two larger members; and, in presenting each verse we must connect it with the verse with which it stands in correspondence.

THE FIRST SELAH

is between verses 13 and 14. The subject of verse 13 must be read on from verse 11, which describes their vain wordly wisdom.

d | **Their inward thought is that their houses** [shall continue] **for ever,**
And their dwelling-places from generation to generation.
They call their lands after their own names.

* * * * (*v.* 11.)

d | **This their way is their folly:**
And [the folly of] **those who, after them, praise their sayings.** (*v.* 13.)

SELAH.

Like sheep, into Sheol are they driven;
Death shall shepherd them;
(And the righteous shall have dominion over them in the morning);
And their outward show shall be for Sheol to consume, that it have no more a dwelling place. (*v.* 14).

The Selah expands and explains the "folly" of *v.* 13; and we are thus shown the end of their worldy wisdom. The *Selah* is intended to emphasise the fact that in spite of all they may say:—They are buried in Sheol, and are turned to dust. Death is their shepherd; and they have no part in the "resurrection of the just" when that glorious morning shall dawn.

THE SECOND SELAH

is between verses 15 and 16. Here, as above, verse 15 must be read as the continuation of verses 6-9:

b | **"None of them can by any means redeem his brother,**
Nor can he[1] give to God a ransom for him (*v*. 7)
(For the redemption of their soul[2] is costly,
And it ceaseth for ever)[3] (*v*. 8).
That he should still live for ever,
And not see corruption" (*v*. 9).

* * * *

b | **"But God will redeem my soul[4] from the power of Sheol,**
For He will receive me (*v*. 15).

SELAH.

Be not thou afraid when a man is made rich,
When the glory of his house is increased." (*v* 16.)

Thus, the second *Selah* is to show us the blessed end of true wisdom. The first shows that the end of *worldly wisdom* is Death, and the fear of death.

The second shows us that the end of *true wisdom* is to take away that fear.[6] It points us to this great con.

---

1 So some Codices read, with one early printed edition. See Ginsburg's Hebrew Text and Note.

2 *i.e.*, them or *their life*.

3 *i.e.*, unless it be redeemed and has a resurrection. Note the parenthesis, and read on from verse 7 to verse 9 for the sense:—

(-7.) "Nor give to God a ransom for him
(9-.) That he should still live for ever."

4 Heb. *my soul*, put by *Metonomy* for the person *me*.

5 Heb. *hand*, put by *Metonomy* for *power* or *grasp*.

6 This is the scope of the Psalm, wisdom and folly: The Wise Man and the Fool. They are characteristic of the Book of Proverbs. The former occurs twice in the Psalms and 46 times in Proverbs. The latter occurs twice in the Psalter and 49 times in Proverbs.

clusion, for which the opening question had prepared us:

a | "**Wherefore should I fear?**" (*v.* 5), and conducts us to the blessed answer,

a | "**Be not thou afraid**" (*v.* 16).

The two *Selahs* together give us the scope of the Psalm.

The whole burden of the Psalm consists of *Divine Information* and teaching concerning Death and the blessed hope of Resurrection.

By nature "Man is like a beast" (B. & *B. vv.* 12 and 20).

His end is the grave (b *v.* 10).

No man can redeem him from it (b *vv.* 6-9).

But "what is impossible with men is possible with God."

HE can redeem; and He will redeem His people from the grave (*b. v.* 15), and

HE will give them the blessedness of those who shall have part in the first resurrection (*v.* 14).

"The rest of the dead" will not have part in it, or "live again" until the thousand years are finished. Then they will be raised for the judgment of "the great white throne," and be "cast into the lake of fire, which is the second death" (*v.* 14).

PSALM l.

There is one *Selah* in this Psalm, between verses 6 and 7.

It connects the two parts of the one great subject of

the Psalm: rather than any two special verses. This is a new usage of the word *Selah*.

A | 1-6. God's call to judgment.

SELAH.

B | 7-23. The grounds of His judgment.

The "call" to hear what God hath spoken is thus separated from the words He actually speaks.

The two Structures are therefore thus marked off by the Selah as being quite distinct. They are as distinct in their scope as they are in their character: for the first part is an Introversion, and the second is an Alternation.

The first part of Psalm l. (vv. 1-6).

A | a | 1. God's call. (General).
  b | 2. God's appearing. (General.)
  b | 3. God's appearing. (Particular.)
 a | 4-6. God's call. (Particular.) Selah.

This call is to judgment, and the particular *words* which are thus connected by Selah are these.

-6. **"For God is about to judge.**

SELAH.

7. **Hear, O my people and I will speak."**

We are asked by this *Selah* to note well what is the important matter for us to consider when God is about to judge. He is the accuser as well as the judge. And it is not by the "outward appearance," on which man looketh; but it is the "heart," by which God judges (1 Sam. xv. 7; Isa. lv. 8).

Hence, His People are admonished to "hear" what is *True worship* (*vv.* 7-15): and the wicked are admonished to "consider" what is *True service* (*vv.* 16-22), when these things come into judgment.

Now observe how this comes out in the second of these two Structures.

The second part of the Psalm.

(*What God says as to the ground of His judgment*) (*v.* 7-23).

B | c | 7-15. "**Hear.**" *True worship* consists not in outward sacrifices "made by hand" but in the Thanksgiving and Prayer which come from the heart. (Hosea vi. 6; Jer. vii. 22, 23. Isa. i. 10-18; lviii. 3-7; lvi. 1, 2. Micah iv. 6-8.) These have the *promise* (*vv.* 14, 15.)

d | 16-22. "**Consider**" (*v.* 22). *True service* consists not in lip-service; with mouth or tongue which are given to evil, deceit (*v.* 19), and slander (*v.* 20.) These have the *threat* (*v.* 22.)

c | 23-. The *True worshippers* will glorify God.

d | -23. The *True servants* will be glorified by God.

Thus are we instructed by this *Selah;* and guided to the true scope of the Psalm, regarded as a whole, by which we learn its deepest truths.

PSALM lii.

There are two Selahs in this Psalm.

(1). Between verses 3 and 4.

(2). Between verses 5 and 6.

The Psalm has a historical title, which tells us of its origin. It was written with special reference to the cruel tongue and sword of Doeg the Edomite (1 Sam. xxi. 7 and xxii. 18).

The *sub*-scription (which, in the Versions) stands over the next Psalm, liii.), connects it with "the death of the champion" Goliath,* and the "Great Dancing" that followed, when the women sang:—

"Saul hath slain his thousands,
And David his ten thousands."

It was this (1 Sam. xviii. 6, 7), and its repetition (xxi. 11; xxix. 5), that led to Saul's hatred and jealousy, to Doeg's tongue, and to the murder of the priests at Nob (1 Sam. xxii. 18-22).

Hence, it appears, that Psalm lii., written immediately after this double event, has also a double reference to Doeg and to Goliath, as shown by the *super*-scription and the *sub*-scription.

The First Selah.

The evil tongue of Goliath, "the mighty man" (*v.* 1) is referred to as *defying* and *boasting* against the Living God; and is seen in *vv.* 1-3; then, the *Selah* passes on to the *devouring* and *deceitful* tongue of Doeg (*v.* 4).

3. **"Thou lovest evil rather than good, lying rather than speaking righteousness.**

SELAH.

4. **Thou lovest all devouring words,**
O thou deceitful tongue."

The Second Selah

connects God's judgment of both (*v.* 5) with the seeing and the saying of the righteous onlookers (*vv.* 6, 7); and marks the change from the *aprostrophe* (singular) to the praise (plural).

---

* See under *Mahalath*, pages 35-39.

5. **God shall likewise destroy thee for ever,**
He shall seize thee and pluck thee out of thy dwelling,
And uproot thee out of the land of the living.

SELAH.

6. **The righteous shall both see it and fear,**
They shall laugh him to scorn [saying],
7. **'Behold the man who took not God for his strength,**
But trusted in the abundance of his riches,
And prided himself in his wealth.' *

Without the second *Selah* we should not have thought of the tongues of the two persons, Goliath and Doeg, both being so closely connected with the same great event in David's history; the one being the cause, the latter the effect.

PSALM liv.

The *Selah*, in this Psalm, occurs between verses 3 and 4.

In this Psalm we have another usage of *Selah*.

We have seen it connecting *verses* and *Psalms*, here it seems to be used entirely in relation to the Structure connecting the *subjects* of the two preceding members with the two corresponding pairs which follow.

The first pair of members relate to *David's God* (*vv.* 1, 2), and the second to *David's enemies* (*v.* 3).

Then comes the *Selah* bidding us note that the same two themes are to be repeated twice, the following two pairs of members.

---

* So it should be, with the Aramaic and Syrian Versions. See Ginsburg's Text and Note, and compare Psalm cxii. 3.

A[1] | 1, 2. David's God. Prayer to Him.
  B[1] | 3. David's enemies. Their enmity.

SELAH.

A[2] | 4. David's God. Jehovah his Helper.
  B[2] | 5. David's enemies. Their evil rewarded.
A[3] | 6. David's God. Praise to Jehovah.
  B[3] | 7. David's enemies. Their destruction.

Thus in A[1] A[2] and A[3] we have David's God; and in B[1], B[2], and B[3] we have David's enemies. In each pair we find some fresh fact and truth revealed.

PSALM lv.

There are two *Selahs* in this Psalm.

(1) Between verses 7 and 8.
(2) In the middle of verse 19.

The *super*-scription tells us that it is for *Instruction*;* and the *sub*-scription which stands (in the versions) over Psalm lvi. tells us that it relates to the moaning of David, like a dove, in the distant woods.†

This connects it with a definite storm of trouble; viz., the rebellion of Absalom, and David's flight from Jerusalem.

The circumstance to which it relates is fixed for us; and at once gives us the scope of the Psalm and the key to its interpretation.

The Psalm must reflect David's inward experiences caused by his outward trouble; and this is exactly what we see.

---

* See under *Maschil*, above, page 85.

† See under *Jonath elem rechokim*, above, page 53.

The Structure of Psalm lv.

A[1] | 1-11. Despondency (1-7 Selah), with reference to his trouble (8-11).

B[1] | 12-15. The Treachery of Ahithophel.

A[2] | 16-19-. Encouragement (16, 17) with respect to his deliverance (18, 19-). Selah.

B[2] | -19-21. The Treachery of Ahithophel.

A[3] | 22, 23. Encouragement (22), with reference to his deliverance (23).

We thus see that the Psalm perfectly reflects David's experiences when passing through that "stormy wind and tempest" (*v.* 8), which was the greatest he was called to pass through; viz., the rebellion of Absalom.

THE FIRST SELAH

passes us on from his despondency to the cause of it: his trouble and escape from it.

6. **And I said, Oh! that I had wings like a dove;**
Then would I fly away and be at rest.
7. **Lo, then would I wander far off,**
I would lodge in the wilderness.

SELAH.

8. **I would haste me to escape**
From the stormy wind and tempest.

It was not merely rest he moaned for, but deliverance.

THE SECOND SELAH

occurs in the middle of verse 19.

Without this *Selah*, here, the verse is inexplicable, and leads even conservative translators to believe that the text is corrupt; while others go so far as to take the liberty of transposing the verses.

The Structure shows us that David, in verses 16—19, is encouraging himself in God with respect to God's humbling his enemies. After a parenthetical reference to God, who of old has sat enthroned as King and Judge, the second *Selah* brings us back, or rather passes us on, to the definition of the "them," as being those who have not remained loyal to David, and who have not kept their oath with him.

18. **He hath redeemed me* in peace out of the conspiracy that was against me:**
For there were many [that had risen up] **against me.**

19. **God shall hear and humble them,**
(Even He who sitteth [enthroned] **of old).**

SELAH.

[The men] **who keep not their oath,†**
And who fear not God.

The second *Selah* at once connects God's judgment on the rebels with Ahithophel; the member B[2] (*vv.* -19-21), corresponding with the member B[1] (*vv.* 12-15).

PSALM lvii.

This Psalm of David is "Michtam"‡ warning us that we have private, personal, and impressive truth concerning David himself, and David's Son and Lord.

---

* Heb., *my soul.*

† Schultens refers the word חָלַף (*chālaph*) to an Arabic root, which means *covenant*, or *oath*; in this case it would refer to *faithfulness* in keeping a covenant; and our verse would refer to the disloyal men who had not kept their covenant with David, but had gone over to Absalom.

‡ See under *Michtam*, above, page 83.

The *sub*-scription (which in the Versions stands over Psalm lviii.) is *Al-taschith*,* *Destroy not.*

The historical title connects the Psalm with a definite event in David's history: viz., "When he fled from Saul into the cave" (1 Sam. xxii. 1; Psalm cxlii. title).

We thus have the scope of the Psalm clearly stated for us.

There are two *Selahs*.

(1) In the middle of verse 3.

(2) Between verses 6 and 7.

THE FIRST SELAH

tells us that David was not merely praying for deliverance from the hand of Saul; but that Jehovah's "mercy and truth might be sent forth."

3. **He shall send from heaven and save me.**
[Though] **he that would swallow me up hath reproached.**

SELAH.

God shall send forth His mercy and truth.

THE SECOND SELAH

is connected with the Structure; for, after having for the second time compared himself to a hunted animal, the *Selah* at the end of verse 6 tells us that the original theme of "mercy and truth" is not to be lost sight of, but repeated; and having before been declared, is now to be praised. This is seen from

The Structure of Psalm lvii.

A | a | 1-3. Address to Jehovah ("Mercy and Truth").
  | b | 4. Hunted animal.
B | 5. "Be Thou exalted."
A | *b* | 6. Hunted animal.
  | *a* | 7-10. Address to Jehovah ("Mercy and Truth").
B | 11. "Be Thou exalted."

* See under *Al-taschith*, above, page 58.

The force of the second *Selah* will now be seen:

6. **" They prepared a net for my steps;**
My soul was bowed down:
They digged a pit before me;
They fell into the midst of it themselves.

SELAH.

7. **My heart is fixed, O God,**
My heart is fixed.
I will sing, yea I will sing praises."

Here the contrast between what David's enemies had done, and what he would do, is most marked and striking. And it is this contrast which is marked by the second *Selah*.

PSALM lix.

There are two *Selahs* in this Psalm.

(1). Between verses 4 and 5.

(2). Between verses 13 and 14.

The *super*-scription describes it as *Michtam**, which shows that its object is *to teach;* and that it is personal and private, with special reference to David, as David's Son and Lord.

The *sub*-scription which (in the Versions) stands above the next Psalm (Psalm lx.) is "relating to *Shushan-Eduth*," which shows that, beyond the object of its original composition, it was formally handed over to the Chief Musician as being appropriate for special Liturgical use at the Feast of Weeks or Pentecost.

THE FIRST SELAH,

besides marking the end of the first Prayer, connects verse 6 with verse 5, and having mentioned their

* See under *Mitchtam*, above, 83.

enemies and asked for them to be punished, passes on to describe their character, as dogs of the Gentiles.

A | **"THOU, therefore, O Jehovah, God of hosts,**
the God of Israel,
Arise, to visit all the heathen:
Be not merciful to any wicked transgressors (*v.* 5)
SELAH.

B | **They return at evening:**
They growl like a dog,
And go round about the city (*v.* 6).
Behold they boast aloud with their mouth:
Swords are in their lips,
For who [say they] doth hear?" (*v.* 7).

The other *Shushan-Eduth* Psalm is Psalm lxxix. Both Psalms were for use "in the land," as was the Feast itself. This is seen from the Structure, and the two *Selahs* mark out the Structure as well as *connect* the leading thought.

They mark the end of the two Prayers which commence the two parts of the Psalm.

The Structure of Psalm lix.

A | 1-5. Prayer. Enemies with them in the Land. (Selah).
 B | a | 6. Comparison to a dog. } Character of Enemies.
  b | 7. Doggish character. Barking.
   C | c | 8-9-. David's trust in Jehovah.
    d | -9-10. Reason. "God my defence."

A | 11-13. Prayer. Enemies with them in the Land. (Selah.)
 B | *a* | 14. Comparison to a dog. } Character of Enemies.
  b | 15. Doggish character. Greediness.
   C | *c* | 16-. David's trust in Jehovah.
    d | -16-17. Reason. "God my defence."

THE SECOND SELAH

marks the end of the second prayer; and, like the first, passes on to describe the character of their enemies with them in the land.

A | 13. **"Consume them in Thy wrath, consume them that they may perish:**
And let them know that God ruleth in Jacob,
Unto the ends of the earth.

SELAH.

B | 14. **And at evening let them return,**
Let them growl like a dog,
And go round about the city.
15. **Let them prowl up and down for good,**
And, if they be not satisfied, then let them whine."*

PSALM lx.

This Psalm is *Michtam*, *to teach*, and it has a historical title, connecting it with David, "when he strove with Aram-Naharaim and with Aram-Zobah, when Joab returned, and smote of Edom in the valley of salt twelve thousand."

The reference is to the defeat of the Edomites.

In this title a particular incident of the campaign is mentioned. The whole campaign is summarised in one or two verses in the historical books.

In 2 Sam. viii. 13, 14 it is of course *David's exploit* that is recorded.

In 1 Chron. xviii. 3, 12, *Abishai's command* is referred to.

In the Title of this Psalm it is *Joab's exploit* which is mentioned.

* So it should be with Septuagint and Syriac Versions. See Ginsburg's Hebrew Text and Note.

While the whole campaign totalled 18,000 of the enemy slain, Joab's part was 12,000. But he took six months longer in finishing up his task (1 Kings xi. 15, 16); and the 18,000 doubtless summarises the total losses of the enemy.

Like Psalm xliv., it has a composite subject. Trouble and triumph. In Psalm xliv. the triumph comes first; in Psalm lx. the trouble comes first.

In each of these Psalms the two subjects are at once marked off and connected by *Selah*.

After rehearsing the trouble through which the nation had passed (*v.* 1-3), verse 4 prepares us for the change; and then the *Selah* introduces the change itself.

From "the truth" we are transferred to the Beloved, who is The Truth. The banner is displayed; but the *Selah* gives the object of it.

4. "**Thou hast given a banner to them that fear Thee,**
That it may be displayed because of the truth.
SELAH.

5. **That Thy beloved may be delivered,**
Save with Thy right hand and answer me.*"

The word *Michtam*, in the Title, shows that it points specially to David and David's Son and Lord.

The word *Neginah*, which is the proper *sub*-scription of the Psalm (and stands at present in the Versions as the *super*-scription of Ps. lxi.) shows that it was to be accompanied by stringed instruments.†

* It is *written* "us" in the Hebrew Text; but it is marked, in the margin, to be *read* "me." In some Codices, with four early printed editions; Aramaic, Syriac, Sept. and Vulgate Versions, it is both *written* and *read* "me." See Ginsburg's Hebrew Text and note.

† Some Codices, with Aramaic, Sept. and Vulg. Versions read it as plural. See Ginsburg's Hebrew Text and note.

PSALM lxi.

In this Psalm we have one *Selah*. It comes between verses 4 and 5.

Verses 1-4 give the prayer. The *Selah* points us to the ground on which the prayer is based in verse 5.

4. **"I would dwell in Thy tabernacle for ever,**
I would seek refuge in the covert of Thy wings.

SELAH.

5. **For Thou, O God, hast hearkened to my vows,**
Thou hast given [me] the heritage of those that fear Thy name."

PSALM lxii.

There are two *Selahs* in this Psalm.

(1) Between verses 4 and 5.

(2) Between verses 8 and 9.

They are both connected with the Structure, which consists of a *Repeated Alternation* of two subjects.

Trust in God; and
The enmity of David's foes.

A¹ | 1, 2. Trust in God.
  B¹ | 3, 4. Enmity of foes. *Selah*.
A² | 5-8. Trust in God. *Selah*.
  B² | 9, 10. Enmity of foes.
A³ | 11, 12. Trust in God.

THE FIRST SELAH

marks the change from the consideration of the enmity of his foes, to his trust in God.

4. **"They only consult to thrust him down from his dignity;**
They delight in lies:
They bless with their mouth, but curse inwardly.

SELAH.

5. My soul, wait thou in silence upon God only;
For my expectation is from Him.
6. He only is my rock and my salvation;
[He is] my high tower; I shall not be moved."

THE SECOND SELAH

marks the change from his trust in God to a further consideration of the nothingness of his foes.

8. "Trust in Him at all times, ye people;
Pour out your heart before Him:
God is a refuge for us.

SELAH.

9. Surely men of low degree are only a breath,
And men of high degree are a lie!
In the balances they will kick the beam,
They are altogether lighter than a breath."

PSALM lxvi.

In this Psalm there are three *Selahs*.

(1) Between verses 4 and 5.
(2) Between verses 7 and 8.
(3) Between verses 15 and 16.

They are all connected with the Structure, as will be seen from the following:—

A | 1-4. Exhortation to praise. *Selah.*
  B | 5-7. "Come and see." *Selah.*
A | 8-15. Exhortation to praise. *Selah.*
  B | 16-20. "Come and hear."

They mark off three of the four members, and thus fix the scope of the Psalm for us.

THE FIRST SELAH

transfers us from praise to God (*v.* 4), to the invitation

to "come and see" His works, giving this as the reason for the praise.

4. **" All the earth shall worship thee,**
And shall sing unto Thee;
They shall sing to Thy name.
SELAH.
5. **Come and see the works of the God;**
Terrible [is He] in His doing towards the children of men."

THE SECOND SELAH

sends us back to the subject of the first members, and repeats the exhortation to praise God.

7. **" He ruleth in His might for ever;**
His eyes observe the nations:
Let not the rebellious exalt themselves.
SELAH.
8. **O bless our God, ye Peoples,**
And make the voice of His praise to be heard!"

THE THIRD SELAH

returns our thoughts once more from praise to God to the doings of God, and invites us to "come and hear."

15. **" I will offer unto Thee burnt offerings of fatlings,**
With the incense of rams;
I will offer bullocks with goats.
SELAH.
16. **Come and hear, all ye that fear God,**
And I will declare what He hath done for me.*"

---

* Heb., *my soul.*

PSALM lxvii.

In this Psalm *Selah* occurs twice.

(1). Between verses 1 and 2.

(2). Between verses 4 and 5.

The first conducts us from the *prayer* (third person) to the *object* of it, "that" (second person).

The second transfers us from the *answer* to the prayer, to renewed *praise* for that answer.

THE FIRST SELAH.

1\. **"God be merciful unto us and bless us,**
And cause His face to shine upon us.

SELAH.

2\. **That Thy way may be known upon earth,**
Thy salvation among all nations."

THE SECOND SELAH.

After an exhortation to praise, the reason for it is given in verse 4 ("for"), and then the second *Selah* again exhorts us to praise God.

4\. **"For Thou shalt judge the Peoples with equity,**
And govern the nations upon earth."

SELAH.

5\. **Let the peoples praise Thee, O God;**
Let all the peoples praise Thee."

PSALM lxviii.

There are three *Selahs* in this Psalm.

(1). Between verses 7 and 8.

(2). Between verses 19 and 20.

(3). Between verses 32 and 33.

We have seen under "Alamoth" (page 67) that this Psalm was written by David to celebrate his bringing up the Ark of the Covenant from the house of Obed-Edom to the place which God had chosen, and which David had prepared for it in Zion.

It celebrates no victory over enemies after battle (as most commentators seem to think); but it refers to the great event in David's reign, after he had captured Jebus, and made it "the city of David."

This Psalm is one of several which celebrate this important epoch of David's life and reign.

2 Sam. vi. and 1 Chron. xv. should be carefully read, and the following Structure of Psalm lxviii. should be thoroughly examined.

Its great theme is announced in its opening words (verses 1-3), which are the very words prescribed for the setting forth of the Ark whenever it moved or set out on a journey, in Num. x. 35:

"**Rise up, Jehovah,**

And let them that hate Thee flee before Thee."

What more appropriate words could be found as the opening summary of this Psalm, at once setting forth, and combining its subject and its object?

"**Let God arise, let His enemies be scattered,**

And let them that hate Him flee before His face."

This *subject* is independently announced; and is set out as its Theme, apart and distinct from the general Structure of the Psalm itself:—

Theme { 1, 2. The wicked scattered.
3. The righteous made glad.

A | 4. "Sing unto God."

B | 5—14. The goings of God through the Wilderness.

C | 15, 16. Mount Zion desired by God. Contrast with Bashan.

C | 17—19. Mount Zion possessed by God. Contrast with Sinai.

B | 20—31. The goings of God into the Sanctuary.

A | 32—35. "Sing unto God."

It will be seen from this that the one great theme of the Psalm celebrates the procession of 1 Chron. xv. and xvi.

Apart from the Structure and the *Selahs*, there are certain expressions which receive their proper interpretation from the correct understanding of the scope.

(1). The goings of God out of Egypt, through the Wilderness, made it a suitable Psalm for the Passover, to which feast it was appropriated. After it had exhausted its first use with reference to the Wilderness wanderings, it passed on to its use, equally appropriate, in connection with the procession to Zion.

This is seen by its *sub*-scription:—"relating to Shoshannim" (or the Spring Festival), which at present stands as the *super*-scription over Psalm lxix.

A further connection of this Psalm with the Exodus is the use of the Divine name "JAH" in verses 4 and 18. The coincidence is that it occurs in the second book of the Psalms (which is the Exodus book); as it first occurs in the Bible in Ex. xv. 13, in the song which celebrated the Exodus from Egypt and the passage of the Red Sea.

(2). The order of the procession, so minutely described in 1 Chron. xv. 16-21, agrees in all points with the same order as given in this Psalm (*vv.* 24, 25), where the Ark, which more than symbolised the presence of Jehovah, is personified and addressed.

24. They have seen Thy goings O God, the goings of my God, my King, into the Sanctuary.

25. The singers went before,
Behind were the players on instruments.
In the midst were the maidens (the '*Alamoth*) playing with timbrels.

These '*Alamoth* are again referred to in verse 11; which reference is to day so sadly misapplied by many, and taken as the ground for women preaching the gospel!

(3.) The references to Sinai are significant, in verses 8, 17. The latter verse, when correctly translated, according to the scope of the Psalm, accords beautifully with the ascension.

17. The chariots of God are twenty thousand, even thousands upon thousands:
Jehovah,* among them, hath come from Sinai into the Sanctuary.†"

---

* This is one of the 134 places where the Sopherim say they changed "Jehovah" to "Adonai."

† That this represents the primitive text, is quite certain, as Dr. Ginsburg has shown from other examples, and from the testimony of the Massorites. It is merely a question of spelling, and of the division of the words. See *Introduction*, pp. 140 and 161, 162.

The confusion arising from not seeing the true Text is seen in the variety of conjectural translations:

A.V. "As in Sinai in the holy place."
R.V. "As in Sinai in the Sanctuary."
R.V. margin. Or, "*Sinai in the Sanctuary*."
P.B.V. "As in the holy place of Sinai."

(4.) The ascent of the Ark to what had been Jebus, and was now the "mount of God" was literally and physiographically a *going up*, as in Ps. xlvii. 5.

The Ark is personified in the next verse (18): or, Jehovah is addressed as represented by the Ark.

18. "Thou hast ascended up on high,
Thou hast led away a multitude of captives;
Thou hast received gifts consisting of men,
Yea, even the rebellious, that Jah [our] God might be at rest* [in Zion]."

We are now in a position to look at the three occurrences of *Selah* in this Psalm.

THE FIRST SELAH

(between verses 7 and 8) points us (in *v.* 7) to the first of the two great subjects of the Psalm; and in the 8th and following verses proceeds to connect, illustrate, and describe, the goings up of the Ark of God in the wilderness.

7. **" O God, when Thou wentest forth before Thy people,**
When Thou didst march through the wilderness:
SELAH.
8. **The earth trembled,**
The heavens also dropped at the presence of God:
Yon Sinai [trembled] **before God, the God of Israel."**

THE SECOND SELAH

comes between verses 19 and 20.

* Compare Ps. lv. 6.

Verse 19 being an injunction to bless Jehovah, even the God of Salvation, is connected by the *Selah* with verse 20, which proceeds to recite the greatness and goodness of Jehovah, and to declare that His salvation includes all deliverances, even deliverance from death itself:

19. **"Blessed be Jehovah** * day by day;
Who loadeth us [with blessings],
God † Himself is our great Salvation. ‡

SELAH.

20. **He that is our God † is a God † of deliverances;**
And unto Jehovah Adonai belongeth escape from death."

The plural "Salvations" (see note) denotes either "deliverances" as in the next line; or "the *great* deliverance" (as being the plural of majesty).

It will be seen how this second *Selah* calls our attention to the fact that verse 20 is the Divine comment on verse 19; showing how great is the salvation which not only saves from death itself, but includes escape from it in resurrection.

THE THIRD SELAH

comes between verses 32 and 33.

The injunction to "sing unto God" (compare Psalm xlvii. 6-7) in verse 32, is followed by the third *Selah* which fixes our attention upon Him whom we are thus called upon to praise in *verses* 33-35.

---

* One of the 134 passages enumerated by the Sopherim in which they changed "Jehovah" to "Adonai."

† Heb. *El*. the mighty God.

‡ Some Codices, with one early printed Edition, the Septuagint and Vulgate Versions have the plural "Salvations," implying "great Salvation." See Ginsburg's Heb. Text and Note.

32. **"Sing unto God, O ye kingdoms of the earth;**
O sing praises unto Jehovah;*

SELAH.

33. **To Him that rideth upon the heaven of heavens, which were of old:**
Lo, He doth send out His voice, yea, and that a mighty voice!

34. **Ascribe ye strength unto God:**
Whose majesty ruleth over Israel,
And whose strength is in the clouds!

35. **O God! terrible art Thou, from out Thy Sanctuary: †**
Even the God of Israel: He giveth strength and abundant power ‡ unto His People.
Blessed be God."

The singular, "Sanctuary," in verse 35, points us to Zion, which the whole Psalm celebrates, as God's new dwelling-place with His People in the Land. It accords well with Psalm cx. 2. "Jehovah shall send the rod of Thy power out of Zion."

PSALM lxxv.

There is one Selah in this Psalm, and it occurs between verses 3 and 4, dividing the second member, which treats of judgment, into two parts:—what is said to *the righteous*, and what is said to *the wicked*.

---

* One of the 134 passages where the Sopherim changed "Jehovah" to "Adonai."

† It should be singular with Sept. and Vulg. Versions. See Ginsburg's Heb. Text and Note.

‡ The plural "powers" may be well Englished by "abundant" or "much."

"Selah." Psalm lxxv.

A | 1. Praise offered.

B | a | 2, 3-. Spoken to the righteous } Judgment.
  | b | -3-8. Spoken to the wicked }

A | 9. Praise promised.

B | *b* | 10-. Spoken of the wicked } Judgment.
  | *a* | -10-. Spoken of the righteous }

The structure shows that the scope of the Psalm is *judgment*, exercised in righteous rule and government in the earth. It has to do with God, the righteous judge who is celebrated and praised for His righteousness.

Though His throne is stablished in the Heaven, "His name is near;" and His wondrous works declare the fact (*v.* 1).

When He receives the Congregation (*v.* 2, compare Psalm lxxxii. 1) in the Mount of Assembly (Isa. xiv. 13, 1 Kings xxii. 19) it is "above the stars," "in the Recesses (or secret places) of the North," which is stretched out over the empty and desolate place (Job. xxvi. 7), then He "will judge righteously" (Psalm lxxv. 2).

Righteous judgment and "promotion" cometh, not from East, or West, or South; but from the North, from His throne of judgment.

The *Selah*, here, calls our attention to these things, and connects God's judgment on the earth now, with His throne of righteousness in the heavens. It shows that that judgment is of two kinds:—the upholding of the righteous, and the cutting off of the wicked.

2. "**When the set time is come** [saith Jehovah]
I, even I, will judge uprightly

3. [**Though**] **the earth quaketh with all the inhabitants thereof,**

I have established the pillars of it.

SELAH.

4. **I said unto the arrogant, 'Deal not arrogantly:'**
And to the wicked 'Lift not up [your] **horn.'**

5. **Lift not up your horn on high;**
Speak not with a stiff neck.

6. **For not from the EAST, neither from the WEST,**
Nor yet from the SOUTH cometh exaltation.

7. **No! God is the judge;**
He putteth down one; and setteth up another.

8. **For in the hand of Jehovah there is a cup;* and the wine is red.†**
It is full of mixture: and He poureth out of the same:
Surely the dregs thereof, all the wicked of the earth shall drain them out and drink them.

9. **But as for me, I will declare** [God's praises] **for ever,**
I will sing praises to the God of Jacob.

10. **All the horns of the wicked will I cut off;**
But the horns of the righteous shall be exalted."

The force of the *Selah* will be now observed, in connecting the declaration concerning the set time for God's coming judgment with the righteous judgment itself, as it will affect the righteous and the wicked respectively.

---

* The cup is frequently used as a symbol of God's judgment (Psalm lx. 5, Isa. li. 17-23 (comp. xix. 14), Hab. ii. 15, 16, Ezek. xxiii. 32, etc., Jer. xxv. 27; xlviii. 26; xlix. 12).

† Or, *foameth* as in R.V., referring to the froth made by the pouring out mentioned in the next line.

PSALM lxxvi.

In this Psalm of Asaph we have two *Selahs*.

(1). Between verses 3 and 4.

(2). Between verses 9 and 10.

They determine the Structure, and furnish the key to the scope of the Psalm. From this Scope it is seen to be yet another Psalm celebrating the capture of Jebus; and the glory of God in defeating the Jebusites, and setting up His dwelling place in Zion.

It is like Psalm xlvi. with which it should be compared.

Zion had no place in history or song until this great event had taken place. Hence its importance, as shown by the many Psalms relating to it.

The two *Selahs* transfer us, in each case, from the *third* person, to the *second*. This at once calls our attention to an important fact; and bids us follow out the clue thus given.

When we do this we see that the Psalm consists of *seven* members. The 1st, 3rd, 5th and 7th relate to the Jebusite enemies; and are in the *third* person; while the 2nd, 4th and 6th are in the *second* person, and are addressed directly to God Himself.

A[1] | 1-3. The Jebusites' defeat. *(Selah)*.
  B[1] | 4. God. Thou art *glorious*.
A[2] | 5. The Jebusites' defeat.
  B[2] | 6-8. God. Thou art to be *feared*.
A[3] | 8-9. The Jesubites' defeat (*Selah*).
  B[3] | 10. God. Thou art to be *praised*.
A[4] | 11-12. The Jebusites' submission.

Both the *Selahs* pass us on from the Jebusite enemies to God:

THE FIRST SELAH

1. **"In Judah is God known:**
His Name is great in Israel,
2. **In Salem is His Tabernacle,**
And His dwelling-place in Zion,
3. **There* brake He the arrows of the bow,**
Shield, and sword, and weapons of war.†
SELAH.
4. **Glorious art THOU;**
[Thou art] **more excellent than‡ the great mountain§ of the robbers."‖**

THE SECOND SELAH,

in the same way, transfers our thoughts from the judgment of God on the Jebusites, and this help of the helpless in their assault upon that stronghold, and passes them on to the more important point of the Psalm, viz.. that all this was only a ground of praise to God.

8. **"The earth feared, and was still,**
When God arose to judgment,
To save all the humble¶ of the earth.
SELAH.
10. **Surely the wrath of man shall turn to Thy praise;**
[Yea] **the remainder of great wrath** shalt Thou restrain."**

PSALM lxxvii.

In this Psalm we have three *Selahs*.

(1) Between verses 3 and 4.

(2) Between verses 9 and 10.

(3) Between verses 15 and 16.

---

* At Jebus. † Compare Psalm xlvi. 9.
‡ See R. V. margin. § The plural of majesty. ‖ *i.e.*, the Jebusites.
¶ Or, *patient*: *i.e.*, those who patiently and humbly waited on God for His saving strength. ** Plural of majesty.

The first two are evidently connected with the Structure, which is a simple alternation.

A | 1-6. Occupation with self.

  B | 7-9. Its sure result. Misery.

A | 10-12. Occupation with God.

  B | 13-20. Its sure result. Happiness.

The First Selah

exhibits the *act* of self-occupation in verses 1-3. It is all "I" and "my" and "me." Then the *Selah* carries us on to the extension and character of it, which is developed in verses 4-6.

Then, in verses 7-9, we have the consequences of this self-occupation, exhibited in the sure result—*misery*. Then the second Selah passes us on to the only remedy, which is occupation with God (*vv.* 10-12), and its sure result—*Happiness.*

1. **"I will cry unto God with my voice;**
Even unto God with my voice,
And He will give ear to me.
2. **In the day of my distress I sought Jehovah:***
My hand by night has been stretched out [in prayer], **and ceased not;**
My soul refused to be comforted,
3. **I remembered God, and was disquieted;**
I complained, and my spirit was overwhelmed.

SELAH.

4. **Thou hast kept mine eyes watching:**
I am so troubled that I cannot speak."

---

* One of the 134 places where the Sopherim say they changed Jehovah to Adonai.

And so the Psalm goes on to heap together all the expressions which reveal the depth of his misery.

THE SECOND SELAH

ends up all this misery (*v.* 9) by showing the only true way out of it (*v.* 10): viz., by looking up to God. Then it is all "Thy" and "Thou."

He thus ends the description of his misery and leads up to the second *Selah* :—

7. **"Will Jehovah cast off for ever?**
Will He be favourable no more?
8. **Is His loving-kindness clean gone for ever?**
Doth His promise fail for evermore?
9. **Hath God forgotten to be gracious?**
Hath He in anger shut up His tender mercies?

SELAH.

10. **And I said, This is my infirmity;**
That the right hand of the Most High doth change.†
11. [But] **I will make mention of the deeds of Jah;**
For I will call to mind Thy wonders of old.
12. **Yea, I will meditate upon all Thy work,**
And muse on Thy doings.
13. **Thy way, O God, is in the Sanctuary;**
Who is a great god like unto our God?"

And so the Psalm goes on to speak of the greatness and goodness of Jehovah; and, having mentioned the *redemption of His people* in *v.* 15, the *Selah* turns our thoughts back to the history of that redemption, showing how our souls are to feed upon the record of

* One of the 134 places where the Sopherim say they changed Jehovah to Adonai.

† See R.V. margin.

Jehovah's doings as written down in the Scriptures of truth.

If we compare this Psalm (lxxvii.) with Psalm lxxiii. we have a similar lesson: though there are no *Selahs* to point it out.

In Psalm lxxiii. it is distraction instead of misery. It is distraction brought about by our occupation with the things *around* us, instead of the experiences *within* us. But the result is sure and certain.

In verses 2-12 we have the occupation with *others*. In verses 13-16 we have the result, *distraction*. Then in verses 17-28 we have the same remedy for it all, as in Psalm lxxvii. It is found in the Sanctuary (*v.* 17, and compare lxxvii. 13), and occupation with God.

The double-fold lesson of these two Psalms, for all who have ears to hear, is this:—

If you want to be *distracted*
look around.

If you want to be *miserable*
look within.

If you want to be *happy*
look up.

Both Psalms end with happiness through occupation of heart with God, in His Sanctuary, where He is to be found, and where He reveals Himself and communes with our hearts.

PSALM lxxxi.

In this Psalm there is one *Selah*. It is between verses 7 and 8.

Its position shows that it is intended to indicate the Structure, as it comes between the two corresponding halves of the first part of the Psalm.

For, Psalm lxxxi. consists of two parts.

A | 1—10. God speaking *to* His people.
B | 11—16. God speaking *about* His people.

The first Part.

A | C | 1—3. Exhortation to worship the true God.
    D | 4—6. Deliverance from Egypt.
        E | 7. Prayer and answer. *Selah.*
    C | 8, 9. Exhortation not to worship false Gods.
    D | 10-. Deliverance from Egypt.
        E | -10. Prayer and answer.

The Second Part.

B | F | 11. Refusing to hear.
    G | 12. Consequences (Sad).
    F | 13. Hearing.
    G | 14—16. Consequences (Happy).

The *Selah*, as we have said, divides the first part, at end of verse 7, passing us back again to a repetition of the three corresponding subjects.

PSALM lxxxii.

The one *Selah* occurs between verses 2 and 3.

It connects two thoughts by contrasting unrighteous judgment with righteous judgment.

There is much about God, and gods, in this Psalm; and a reference to John x. 34, 35, shows that *Elohim* from אלה *('ālāh) to make or appoint with an oath* is used of those who are set apart with an oath to be *the representatives of another* with a view to carry out certain acts. Hence it is used of *Magistrates*, Ex. xxi. 6; xxii. 8, 9, 28 (quoted in Acts xxiii. 5). It is used of *Moses* (Ex. vii. 1.) And it is even used of *Idols*, because they were used for *representing* a false god.

Hence it is used of the *second* person of the Trinity, inasmuch as He, taking first, *creature-form* for purposes of *Creation*, and afterwards *human form* for the purposes of *Redemption*, specially represented and revealed the Invisible God to His creatures* (John i. 18).

We may therefore render the word *elohim*, by *judges*, as all earthly judges are only delegates or representatives of Him who alone is the Judge, and delegates His authority to such.

1. "**God (*Elohim*) standeth in God's (*El*) assembly;**
He judgeth judges.
2. **How long will ye give wrong judgment,**
And accept the persons of the wicked?
SELAH.
3. **Judge the poor, and fatherless,**
Do justice to the oppressed and the destitute,
4. **Deliver the poor and needy,**
Rescue them out of the hand of the wicked."

Thus, by this *Selah*, God's righteous judgment is contrasted with the imperfect, and often unjust judgment of man. And the Psalm ends with a similar contrast which shows it to be the scope of the Psalm as a whole.

6. "**I myself have said ye are judges (*elohim*)**
And ye are all sons of the Most High;
7. **Nevertheless ye shall die like men,**
And fall like [men] O ye princes.
8. **Arise, O God, judge Thou the earth;**
For all the nations are thine inheritance."

---

* *See* our *Lexicon and Concordance* under the word "WORD," pages 896, 897.

PSALM lxxxiii.

There is one *Selah* in this Psalm, between verses 8 and 9.

It is Structural, and points to the division of the Psalm; separating its two parts; and yet connecting the combination and confederation of God's enemies with their punishment.

This will be seen from the Structure.

A | 1. Vindicate Thyself.

B | 2-8. Enemies. Their combination ("They have said" *v.* 4). Selah.

B | 9-15. Enemies. Their Punishment." ("Who said" *v.* 12).

A | 16-18. Vindicate Thyself.

The sub-scription "relating to Gittith" which wrongly (in the versions) stands over the next Psalm (lxxxiv.) shows that it was for special use at the autumn Feast of Tabernacles. (See above page 10).

PSALM lxxxiv.

There are two *Selahs* in this Psalm.

(1). Between verses 4 and 5.

(2). Between verses 8 and 9.

The Structure is as follows:—

A | a | 1-4. Blessedness of the dwellers. (*Selah.*)
  | b | 5-7. Blessedness of the approachers.

B | 8. Prayer. (*Selah.*)

B | 9. Prayer.

A | *a* | 10. Blessedness of the dwellers.
  | *b* | 11-12. Blessedness of the approachers.

THE FIRST SELAH

connects the *dwellers* in, and the *approachers* to the House of the Lord, and unites them in a common blessing. While

THE SECOND SELAH

divides the Psalm, structurally, into two Parts, connecting the Prayer of verse 8 with the words of the Prayer in verse 9.

8. "**O Jehovah, God of hosts, hear my prayer**:
Give ear O God of Jacob.

SELAH.

9. **Behold our Shield, O God,**
And look upon the face of Thy Messiah."

PSALM lxxxv.

The one *Selah* of this Psalm comes between verses 2 and 3.

It connects the two parts of Jehovah's favour to His People and His Land.

David "being a prophet" (Acts ii. 30) spake of Millennial days; and of the blessing which will then be bestowed on Israel and the Land of Israel.

This is the culminating thought of "the Song of Moses" (Deut. xxxii. 43), which assures us that God "will be merciful unto this Land, and to His People."

2. "**Thou hast forgiven the iniquity of Thy People,**
Thou hast covered all their sin.

SELAH.

3. **Thou hast taken away all Thy wrath:**
Thou hast turned Thyself from the fierceness of Thine anger."

Thus the two sides of the favour, God-ward and man-ward, positive and negative, are set in instructive contrast.

PSALM lxxxvii.

In this Psalm there are two *Selahs*

(1). Between verses 3 and 4.
(2). Between verses 6 and 7.

Under the title *Mahalath Leannoth* (*Shoutings and Dancings*) we have already given the Structure, and a Translation of this Psalm; and shown its connection with the bringing up of the Ark to the Tabernacle which David had prepared for it on Mount Zion.

On referring to that Title (page 39), it will be seen that other dwellings of the Ark having been *spoken of*, and Zion having been *spoken to;* the *Selah* determines the Structure, and shows that these two members form the basis of the subject. The *Selah* serves to return our thoughts to the other nations which are thus set in contrast with Zion.

In like manner the *Selah* at the end of verse 6 returns us to, and leaves our thoughts with, Zion as the culminating subject of the Psalm.

PSALM lxxxviii.

In this Psalm *Selah* occurs twice.

(1) Between verses 7 and 8.
(2) Between verses 10 and 11.

It does not here affect the Structure of the Psalm. It is used in both cases by way of *amplification.* What is stated in the former of the two verses is amplified, emphasised and defined in the latter.

PSALM lxxxix.

In this Psalm we have *Selah* no less than four times.

(1) Between verses 4 and 5.

(2) Between verses 37 and 38.

(3) Between verses 45 and 46.

(4) Between verses 48 and 49.

It is the only Psalm ascribed to "ETHAN THE EZRAHITE."

It was not written, as the commentators suggest, at the close of the Jewish monarchy. There is no occasion for us to resort to what is such an unnecessary speculation; for, within the covers of God's Word we have all the information necessary to guide us to conclusions which are at once deeply instructive, really edifying, and truly satisfying.

The first fact we learn is that ETHAN was a contemporary of Solomon, and was a man noted for his great wisdom. In 1 Kings iv. 31 it is said of Solomon that "he was wiser than all men; than Ethan the Ezrahite, and Heman" and others who are named.

Ethan could not be ignorant of the solemn declaration made by Jehovah to Solomon (1 Kings xi. 9-13).

"Wherefore" (*i.e.* on account of Solomon's idolatry) Jehovah said unto Solomon:—

> "Forasmuch as this is done of thee, and thou hast not kept my covenant and my statutes which I have commanded thee, I will surely rend the kingdom from thee, and will give it to thy servant.
>
> "Notwithstanding, in thy days will I not do it, for David thy father's sake: but I will rend it out of the hand of thy son.
>
> "Howbeit, I will not rend away all the kingdom;

but I will give one tribe to thy son, for David my servant's sake, and for Jerusalem's sake which I have chosen" (1 Kings xi. 11-13).

Nothing is added to this solemn declaration, not a word is said as to the effect of it; either upon Solomon himself, or on his counsellors, or on the people.

Doubtless the effect was great; and far-reaching. The prophecy was one to make men's ears tingle; and to solemnize the hearts of all who heard it.

It must have come as a terrible blow to all who considered the unconditional covenant which God had made with David in 2 Sam. vii.

ETHAN, with his wisdom, must have been deeply moved, and without doubt we have his thoughts and feelings Divinely inspired and written down for our learning in this eighty-ninth Psalm.

In this Psalm he first declares his intention of praising the loving-kindness and faithfulness of Jehovah (verse 1).

He then reminds Jehovah of what He had Himself said to David. "Thou saidst" (not "I have said," see note below) (*vv.* 2-4).

The first *Selah* passes us on to Ethan's own words, in which he fulfils his declared purpose (*v.* 1); and sings Jehovah's praises (*vv.* 5-18).

Once again he reminds Jehovah of what He had promised to David in 2 Sam. vii.

But the second *Selah* points us to a profound contrast; for again Ethan utters his own words, and speaks of the solemn prophecy which has just been pronounced against Solomon, and sets forth what the effect must be with regard to Jehovah's own faithfulness; and how His enemies will take advantage of it in their words and their deeds (*vv*. 38-51).

A third *Selah* after verse 45 turns his words into a prayer (*vv*. 46-48); and a fourth *Selah* after verse 48 emphasises the prayer (*vv*. 49—51.)

The whole Psalm, ending as it had begun, with blessing and praises to Jehovah for evermore.

All this may now be exhibited thus:

A | 1. Eternal praises.

  B | a | 2—4. Ethan reminds Jehovah of the covenant He had made with David. (*Selah*.)

  b | 5—18. Ethan praises Jehovah's faithfulness and mercy and truth.

  B | *a* | 19—37. Ethan reminds Jehovah of the covenant He had made with David. (*Selah*.)

  b | 38—51. Ethan deplores the judgment just pronounced against Solomon (1 Kings xi. 11-13.)

A | 52. Eternal praises.

Now we are in a position to understand the *Selahs*.

THE FIRST SELAH

comes at the end of Ethan's recital of what Jehovah had said to David, between verses 4 and 5.

2. "**For Thou saidst,*** '**For ever shall** [My] **loving-kindness be built up;'**

(Thy faithfulness shalt Thou establish in the very heavens).

3. [Thou saidst] '**I have made a covenant with My chosen,**

---

* Several Codices, with the Septuagint and Vulgate thus read it. Not "I have said" but the 2nd person instead of the 3rd. *See* Ginsburg's Heb. text and note.

'I have sworn unto David My servant:
4. **'Thy seed will I establish for ever,**
'And build up Thy throne to all generations.'

SELAH.

5. **And the heavens shall praise Thy wonders, O Jehovah;**
Thy faithfulness also in the congregation of Thy saints."

And so the praise continues down to the end of verse 18, for all Jehovah's loving-kindness, mercy, and truth.

THE SECOND SELAH,

like the first, comes at the end of the member in which ETHAN again reminds Jehovah of all that He had said to David, and of the covenant which He had made with him: referring especially to 2 Sam. vii.

Every word of that chapter, and of this member of the Psalm (*vv.* 19-37), should be read and studied most carefully.

Then the contrast pointed out by this second *Selah* will be very clearly seen. ETHAN refers to what Jehovah had actually said to Solomon in 1 Kings xi. 11—13.

30. **"'If his children forsake My law,**
'And walk not in My judgments;
31. **'If they break My statutes,**
'And keep not My commandments,
32. **'Then will I visit their transgressions with the rod,**
'And their iniquity with stripes,
33. **'Nevertheless, my loving-kindness will I not utterly take from him,**

'Nor suffer My faithfulness to fail.

34. **'My covenant will I not break,**
'Nor alter the thing that is gone out of My lips

35. **'Once have I sworn by My holiness,**
'I will not lie unto David;

36. **'His seed shall endure for ever,**
'And his throne [shall be] **as the sun before Me.**

37. **'It shall be established for ever as the moon,**
'And [as the sun] **the faithful witness in heaven.'**

SELAH.

38. **But, THOU hast cast off and rejected,**
Thou hast been wroth with Thine Anointed.

39. **Thou hast made void the covenant of Thy servant,**
Thou hast profaned his crown [by casting it] **to the ground."**

And so ETHAN proceeds to speak of the effect of Jehovah's words to Solomon, until, after verse 45, we have

THE THIRD SELAH,

and he turns to prayer (verses 46-51). Between verses 48 and 49 there is

THE FOURTH SELAH

marking an increase of fervour and feeling.

49. **"Jehovah,* where are Thy former loving-kindnesses**
Which Thou swarest unto David in Thy faithfulness?

50. **Remember, O Jehovah,* the reproach of Thy servant;†**

---

* This is one of the 134 places where the Sopherim altered Jehovah to Adonai.

† Some codices with the Syriac Version read "servant" (singular) *See* Ginsburg's Hebrew text and note.

How I bear in my bosom the insult* **of the peoples;**

51. **Wherewith Thine enemies have reproached** [Thee], **O Jehovah,**
Wherewith they have reproached the footsteps of Thine Anointed."

Thus, viewed in the light of the Word of God; and noting the fact that the author of the Psalm was a contemporary of Solomon; and, was doubtless, as one of his wisest counsellors, well aware of the solemn prophecy of 1 Kings xi. 11-13; we arrive at the true scope of the Psalm, and see how it exactly fits into and belongs to a period of Israel's history which fixes its date as at least as early as 984 B.C.

The four *Selahs* also are seen fulfilling their office clearly and perfectly.

PSALM cxl.

There are three *Selahs* in this Psalm.

(1.) Between verses 3 and 4.
(2.) Between verses 5 and 6.
(3.) Between verses 8 and 9.

They are all three connected with the Structure, which compels us to give it.

The scope of the Psalm is "the evil man." It is constructed of three three-fold members: with an epilogue which is independent of the Psalm, and expresses the confidence and trust of David in Jehovah, his God.

* So it should be with Aramaic Version. *See* Ginsburg's Heb. text and note; and compare Ezek. xxxvi. 15.

A[1] | 1. Prayer for deliverance from the evil man.
B[1] | 2. His evil purpose.
C[1] | 3. His evil actions. (*Selah*).
A[2] | 4-. Prayer to be kept from the wicked man.
B[2] | -4. His evil purpose.
C[2] | 5. His evil actions. (*Selah*).
A[3]—6, 7. Prayer for deliverance in the day of battle.
B[3] | 8. His evil desires and devices.
C[3] | 9-11. His evil actions requited.

D | 12. Jehovah's goodness to the righteous.
D | 13. Their gratitude to Jehovah.

It will be seen from the above Structure, that the first and second *Selahs* mark the change back to prayer, thus repeating the triad of members.

The third, on the contrary, instead of marking the Structure, calls attention to the change of thought and subject; pointing out to us, that, whereas the former two *Selahs* turned us back to prayer, after considering the actions of the evil man; we are now carried forward from his evil purposes and desires in *v.* 8, to consider, not his actions, but their failure and the judgment of God upon them (*vv.* 9-11).

PSALM cxliii.

There is one *Selah* in this Psalm (the last in the Book).

It occurs between verses 6 and 7, and is connected with the Structure, which we have first to consider.

It consists of an introversion of four members.

A | 1-4. Petitions and Pleas.

B | 5. Conduct. Remembrance of past mercies.

B | 6. Conduct. Desire for present help. (*Selah*).

A | 7-12. Petitions and Pleas.

It will be seen that, after the consideration of his conduct (verses 5 and 6), the Psalmist turns our thoughts back again (*v.* 7, &c.), to the former subject, Petitions and Pleas.

We have thus come to the end of our examination of every one of the 71 *Selahs* in the Book of Psalms; and have found the same principle governing their use.

We have noted that they neither begin, nor end, a Strophe or Psalm; but that they do *both*, by connecting together either by way of emphasis or contrast, what precedes with what follows; conveying lessons, and proving once more that, "whatsoever was written aforetime was written for our learning" (Rom. xv. 4).

There is, however, remaining, one Model Psalm, which must not be omitted from our consideration.

HABAKKUK iii.

In this Psalm there are three *Selahs*.

(1). In the middle of verse 3.

(2). In the middle of verse 9.

(3). Between verses 13 and 14.

It is this Model Psalm which contains and gives us not only the key to the Psalm-Titles, but the key to the usage of *Selah*; for, as in two out of three occurrences we find it in the middle of passages which were subsequently numbered as verses, *Selah* cannot be claimed either for beginning or ending a subject, but rather for connecting what precedes with what follows.

We find the same law working here as we have seen throughout the Psalms.

Though these three *Selahs* are not connected with the Structure of Hab. iii., it may be well for us to notice the brief outline of its subject-matter, or scope.

Hab. iii.

A | 1-2. "I have heard." Consequent fear.
 B | 3-15. Salvation. The giving of the *Law*.
A | 16. "I have heard." Consequent fear.
 B | 17-19. Salvation. The sending of *Grace*.

THE FIRST SELAH.

The Theme, Salvation, having been announced in verse 3, viz., *The Descent on Sinai*, the *Selah* directs us forward to the consideration of the wonderful details connected with the giving of the Law and of the events which followed it.

THE SECOND SELAH

These details are interrupted by the Second *Selah*, which calls our attention to a remarkable parenthetical statement worthy of our deepest attention, viz. :—

"The oaths to the Tribes were a sure word" (*v.* 9).

And now, lest the thread of these details should be lost by this parenthetical declaration, this second *Selah* at once connects us again with those details which that parenthesis might otherwise have disturbed.

THE THIRD SELAH

transfers our thoughts from the Salvation which had been brought, and celebrated in the destruction of the enemy (verse 13), and bids us consider the magnitude of it when contrasted with the enemy's previous boasting and exultation (*v.* 15).

This completes our investigation of the whole of the 74 passages in which *Selah* occurs.

We are now in a position to consider the question of the etymology of the word.

And if we can fix our attention on what is spiritual rather than on what is material; on the sense rather than on sound; on the subject rather than on music; on the truth rather than on a tune; on the meaning rather than on musical notation; on the matter rather than on a melody, then we shall see something to engage our deepest attention; and something more worthy of the Word of God.

It will be seen to matter very little whether *Selah* is to be derived from סָלָה (*Sālāh*) *to pause*, or from סָלַל (*Sālal*) *to lift up*: For both meanings together do not exhaust their application. We can apply both *to ourselves* and see that it is *we* who are *to pause* and think upon what has been said; and that it is *we* who are *to lift up* our hearts for some deeper additional teaching; and thus learn the lesson which each occurrence of the word *Selah* was intended to teach us.

PART III.

THE SONGS OF DEGREES.

"THE SONGS OF DEGREES."

I.—THEIR VARIOUS INTERPRETATIONS.

OF all the titles of the Psalms those of the so-called "Songs of Degrees" have received the greatest variety of interpretations: and, of all these, only one can be considered as really satisfactory.

Even this was only thrown out casually as a suggestion more than two hundred and fifty years ago, and has never received, so far as we can find, the slightest examination. It was too good; and too Scriptural a solution to attract attention from those who regard the Bible like "any other book;" and who consequently feel at liberty to fall back on imagination and conjecture.

All other interpretations are trivial when compared with the dignity and solemnity of the subject treated of in the Psalms themselves.

Most of them agree in treating them as Post-Exilic; and interpretations which do not tend to bring the date of these Psalms down to later times are treated with scant respect.

(1) David Kimchi and some of the later Jewish expositors refer to the Talmud as supporting the view that these fifteen Psalms were sung on the fifteen steps of the Temple, one on each; but the Talmud only *compares* the fifteen Psalms with the fifteen steps,* and gives a different explanation of the title elsewhere.†

But there is no trace in the Bible, or in history, no authentic tradition of any kind, that there ever were

* *Middoth* (Temple Measures) ii. 5. *Succah* (*Tabernacles*), ib.

† *Succah* 53a.

fifteen steps! They exist only in imagination; and it looks as though the number of steps was an invention in order to make the comparison possible; and to explain the supposed practice of singing these Psalms upon them.

Equally beside the point is the reference, by later writers, to the flight of *seven* steps of the outer court, and the *eight* steps of the inner court: for, though these are mentioned in Scripture, yet they refer, not to Solomon's Temple, or to Herod's, but to the yet future Temple of which we read in the prophecy of Ezekiel xl. 22, 31. So confidently is this reference made that proof of the conclusion is found in the fact that the first of these fifteen Psalms (Ps. cxx.) consists of *seven* verses, and the second (Ps. cxxi.) consists of *eight*.

But, we ask, Is there anything in this ingenuity to interest the mind, to touch the feelings, or to satisfy the heart?

(2). Luther,* followed by some modern interpreters, renders the title, "A song in the higher choir:" the choir being in an elevated position, "on the stairs or some high place," that they might be better heard.

(3). Calvin's idea was that the name was connected with music; and that they were so called because they were sung in a higher key; not that the musical notes rose by degrees in succession.

(4). Bishop Jebb associates these Psalms with the "going up" of the Ark to Mount Zion.

(5). Tremellius says the title means "a most excellent song," *i.e.*, a song of high degree (quoted by John Trapp).

(6). Gesenius, De Wette, Franz Delitzsch, Dr. Edersheim, and others suppose that the term "ascents" refers to a gradation in the synthetic arrangement of the parallel

* *Commentary on the Psalms of Degrees*, 1577.

lines, by which a word or thought in one line is repeated or expanded in the following line.

This latter is very interesting as a philological fact; but whether it has anything to do with the word "ascents" is quite another matter.

However attractive the fact may appear in itself, it is certainly inadequate as an explanation of the word "ascents," inasmuch as (1) that not all of these Psalms possess this feature: and (2) that the same feature is found in other Psalms which are not in this collection.

(7). A very popular, and perhaps the commonest view is that they are all Post-Exilic; and related only to the return of the Exiles from Babylon.

(8). Another view refers them to the going up of Israel to the Feasts at Jerusalem three times in the year. This view is referred by some to the Temple of Solomon, and by others to the Second Temple. This interpretation is as old as Aquila (about 130 A.D.), Symmachus (Cent. II. A.D.), Chrysostom (Cent. IV. A.D.), Theodoret (about 450 A.D.), and Euthymius (about 1118 A.D.) And among Moderns by Ewald, Hengstenberg, Christopher Wordsworth, and others.

It is reflected in the titles of works upon these Psalms: *Songs of the Going-Up*; *The Gradual Psalms*, (Rev. H. T. Armfield, Lond., 1874); *The Pilgrim Psalms* (Dr. N. McMichael, 1860; and Samuel Cox, 1874); *The Songs of the Temple Pilgrims* (Dr. R. Nisbet, 1863); *The Caravan and the Temple, and Songs of the Pilgrims* (E. J. Robinson, 1878); *The Book of Psalms* (Bishop Perowne, 1868); *The Land and the Book* (W. H. Thomson, 1881); *The Treasury of David* (C. H. Spurgeon, 1882).

But this view may be summed up in the words of Professor Wellhausen: "The majority of these Psalms ['Songs of Degrees'] however, have, as it seems, ***nothing at all to do with pilgrimages.*** The meaning of the expression cannot be regarded as finally determined."

(9). A variation of this interpretation is greatly in favour with teachers among the Plymouth Brethren, who see in these Songs of Pilgrimage a reference to the future return of Israel to their Land and Temple, when these Psalms will receive their real application or fulfilment. There may be this future *application*, but it does nothing towards furnishing us with the ***interpretation*** we are seeking.

(10). There is the School of Commentators, who, leaving all conjectures as to the "letter" of Scripture, find only spiritual references in them to the Church or to experience, as they do in all other Scriptures, though they plainly speak only of Israel, Judah, Jerusalem, and Zion.

This view is reflected in such books as "*Ascents of the Soul,*"* which see in these Psalms only language which sets forth the rising of the heart from deepest distress of mind to the highest joy and delight.

Of one and all of these interpretations we may well ask, *Cui bono?* What if any one of them be the correct solution? What then? What is the interpretation associated with their setting? What is the lesson to be learnt from it? What is there worthy of being handed down to us, as "written for our learning"?

Nothing! we cannot be satisfied with such views as these; which are "views" and nothing more.

We must look further for the key to something more instructive, more substantial, and more satisfactory.

**The Ascents of the Soul:* or, *David's mount towards God's House.* The book is in Italian, by Geo. Francesco Loredano, Venice, 1656. Englished by Lord Coleraine, 1681.

La Scala Santa: A scale of Devotion, Lord Coleraine.

The Golden Diary of Heart Converse with Jesus in the Book of Psalms, by Dr. Edersheim, Lond., 1877.

I. Their Various Interpretations.

It is only now that we can form a true judgment as to the value of Dr. J. W. Thirtle's discovery as to the other titles of the Psalms.* Not that the correct interpretation of this title comes in the same category, or is to have its mystery unlocked by exactly the same key.

The key is quite different. It was suggested more than two hundred and fifty years ago (as we have said), but, not until Dr. Thirtle's discovery, were we in a proper condition to use the suggestion. Not until we realised how much there is in all these titles were we disposed and ready to see how much there must be in this.

Indeed it is not many years since Dr. Thirtle himself came across the key in a book by Abraham Wolfson, published in Warsaw, 1882, and referred to at length in the Quarterly Magazine *Hebraica* (predecessor of the *American Journal of Semetic Languages*). He saw it, but put it aside.

Quite recently we came across it ourselves in reading Dr. John Lightfoot's Works; and we should doubtless have passed it by without further thought but for Dr. Thirtle's discovery as to the importance of the titles in general, and his subsequent recognition of the significance of this one in particular.

Although thus twice anticipated by others, Dr. Thirtle's discovery is absolutely independent, causing us to notice Lightfoot's reference, and himself to remember Wolfson's book.

In his work on "The Titles of the Psalms,"* Dr. Thirtle said of this title ("A Song of Degrees"), in a footnote to Ps. cxx. on page 361 :—

"The title is a problem: and the specific purpose of these Songs still awaits satisfactory explanation."

* "*The Titles of the Psalms: Their Nature and Meaning Explained*," by James William Thirtle, LL.D., D.D. London, 1905: Henry Frowde. Price 6s.

Much has been said in the two years since those words were written; and an "explanation" is now forthcoming which is not only perfectly "satisfactory," but which does honour to the Word of God, and is worthy of the great subject of these Psalms.

In a word, the explanation has been advanced and made secure by such a discrimination of the Inscriptions as was contended for by Dr. Thirtle, and made clear to readers of *Things to Come* in a series of papers on the Psalm-Titles in 1905 and 1906.

II.—Their Origin.

We will first show how the discovery was independently made, and then the steps by which the conclusions were reached.*

All the honour and glory belong to the wondrous perfection of God's Word. There is no need to go beyond its covers. All the wisdom and knowledge necessary are treasured up there. There is no need to go to Tradition, or to the Fathers; no need for us to draw on man's imagination; or for him to exercise his ingenuity. There is no need for deep learning or great thoughts. All that is required is a child-like mind and a spiritual understanding. This latter is the gift of God (1 John v. 20); so that all the praise belongs alone to Him. With this spiritual eyesight even a child can understand; without it the wisest man can know nothing; because "the things of the Spirit of God are . . . spiritually discerned."

The first act of the spiritual mind of one who believes God would be like Ezra, to "open the book" and look and see what God has said.

The first question for us to ask, is

What Songs?

On looking at the Titles of these fifteen Psalms, we notice at once the use of the definite article. The Hebrew is—

שִׁיר הַמַּעֲלוֹת (*Shīr hamma'aloth*).

"A Song of THE Degrees."

The importance of this fact cannot be over-estimated; for it is evident that certain special and well-known

* As developed in Dr. Thirtle's book Old Testament Problems. London, Henry Frowde, 6/-

"Degrees" are alluded to. So well-known, indeed, that no further explanation was deemed necessary by the writer.

Those who first used such a Title, and those who were accustomed to read it, knew perfectly well that it was common to take something in a certain Psalm or Song, or some circumstance connected with it, and call the song by that name.*

"A Song of THE Degrees" would therefore be a song about the Degrees, a song relating to certain well-known "Degrees" mentioned in the same Word of God, and therefore likely to be associated with such a song in the mind of the reader.

It is this circumstance to which we owe the otherwise obscure expression, ἐπὶ τοῦ βάτου (*epi tou Batou*), *upon*, *or about the Bush* (Mark xii. 26). "Have ye not read in the book of Moses how, in the Bush, God spake unto him saying," etc. The preposition "ἐπί" (*epi*) does not mean "in," but *on*, as being connected with. The R.V. renders it "at."

It means, "Have ye not read in the book of Moses, how [in the Scripture] relating to the Bush, God spake saying?"

WHAT "BUSH"?

The answer is self-evident; and the reference to Exodus iii. 6 was so obvious that there was no occasion to add anything further by way of explanation.

So also in 2 Sam. i. 18, where it says that David "bade them teach the children of Judah the —— of the bow." What of the "bow?" we may ask; but the usage was so well known by those who read it at the time

* Just as we do to-day. When we speak of "the Song of the Shirt," we mean the well-known song *about* the shirt.

that the Ellipsis would be automatically supplied by all who heard the expression.

Not seeing this idiom, the A.V. supplies the Ellipsis by adding, in italics, the words "*the use of*" the bow. There must be but few readers who have not stumbled, and asked themselves how it could be that, because David lamented over the death of Jonathan and Saul, the children of Judah were to be taught "the use of the bow."*

The R.V., seeing the idiom, rightly supplies the words "[*the song*] of the bow."†

Again we ask:

What "Bow"?

and the answer is clear, viz., "the bow of Jonathan,"‡ mentioned in verse 22.

So, with regard to "a Song of THE Degrees," we ask:

What "Degrees"?

And the only "Degrees" of which the Scripture tells us are the Degrees by which the shadow of the sun-dial of Ahaz went back, as a sign of the fifteen years which were added to the life of Hezekiah.

The record is given in 2 Kings xx. 8-11 as follows; and the emphasis is placed by repetition on the word "Degrees," which is exactly the same Hebrew word in the history as in the titles of these fifteen Psalms.

When Isaiah went in to Hezekiah in his sickness to assure him that he should recover, Hezekiah asked: "What shall be the sign that Jehovah will heal me,

* As though our English expression "a coach and four" could ever be misunderstood as meaning anything but *horses!*

† We should have preferred to supply "the Lamentation of the Bow," for that is what this "song" is called in the previous verse.

‡ Not "the sword of Saul," be it observed.

and that I shall go up into the house of Jehovah the third day?"

And Isaiah said: "This sign shalt thou have of Jehovah, that Jehovah will do the thing that he hath spoken: Shall the shadow go forward **ten degrees**, or go back **ten degrees?**"

And Hezekiah answered:—"It is a light thing for the shadow to go down ten **degrees**: nay, but let the shadow return backward ten **degrees**.

And Isaiah the prophet cried unto Jehovah, and he brought the shadow ten **degrees** backward, by which it had gone down in the **degrees** (marg.) of Ahaz."

What so reasonable as to conclude that these are THE "degrees" or *steps* of the sundial referred to in the Titles of these fifteen Psalms. No others are mentioned in Scripture to which they can be referred.

We give a view of an ancient sundial, such as was doubtless set up by King Ahaz, and known by his name. The reign of Ahaz immediately preceded that of Hezekiah; and the sundial which he set up would be well known, and in the minds of all. There could be no doubt as to what "degrees" were referred to in these Psalm-Titles.

Our view (on the opposite page) shows the steps on which the shadow of the gnomon fell, thus indicating the hour of the day.

But not only have we this evidence. We have the declaration of Hezekiah's purpose recorded in Isaiah xxxviii. 20.

"Jehovah was ready to save me;
Therefore will we sing my SONGS to the stringed instruments
All the days of our life
In the house of Jehovah."

Ancient Equatorial Sundial at the Observatory, Delhi.

Again may we ask :—

WHAT "SONGS?"

Where are these songs? and where are they to be looked for if not here? Can this resolve of Hezekiah mean anything but "therefore will we sing my songs* of, or about the Degrees?"

Instead of reading "A song of the Degrees," we should treat the Genitive as the Genitive of *relation*, and render it "A song relating to THE Degrees."

---

* We are aware that the Hebrew word for "song" in 2 Kings xx. is not the same in Isaiah xxxviii., and in these Psalm Titles. But this is no argument against our conclusion, for the word "song" is clearly implied.

In the Titles, the word is שִׁיר (*shīr*) a song. In Isa. xxxviii. 20 the verb is נָגַן (*nāgan*) *to perform music*, and the noun is cognate נְגִינָה (*negīnah*) meaning (1) *music*, (2) *a song*, and (3) by the Figure of *Metonymy*, *the subject of a song*.

Job xxx. 9. "Now am I *their song*." This refers to *words*, and not merely to an instrument, as is clear from the next line, "Yea, I am their byword."

Psalm lxix. 12. "I was *the song* of the drunkards."

Psalm lxxvii. 6. "I call to remembrance my *song* in the night." It could hardly be *a tune* that he called to remembrance.

Lam. iii. 14. "I have become. . . . their *song* all the day." In verse 63 we have the word שִׁיר (*shīr*) *a song* (the word of the Psalm Title) translated "musick." "I am their musick." (R.V. "I am their song.")

The use of *negīnah* in Isaiah, and *shīr* in the Psalm Titles merely indicates the manner in which Hezekiah's songs were to be sung. They were to be accompanied by an instrument. The expression being cognate it is difficult to reproduce it in translation. We might say :—"Perform Thy performance;" but the rendering of the A.V. and R.V. cannot be excelled—"sing my songs."

It should be noted that *negīnah* is used with *shīr* in the *super*-scription of Psalm lxvi. and Psalm lxvii., which latter is of course the *sub*-scription of Psalm lxvi. The same is seen in connection with Psalm lxxv. and lxxvi.

II.—Their Origin.

The shadow of the sundial went back *ten* degrees; and the years added to Hezekiah's life were *fifteen* years. These numbers are reproduced and preserved in these Psalms; for there are fifteen Psalms altogether, corresponding with the fifteen years; ten of which were by Hezekiah, corresponding with the ten degrees.

It went without saying that they were by Hezekiah. He spoke of them as "MY songs." There was no occasion for him to put his name.

The remaining five, already written by others, and thus ready to his hand, he must have selected as being suitable for his purpose in his arrangement of their order, and he found four of David's and one of Solomon's which answered his purpose, and exactly fitted in with the plan on which he was arranging his songs.

That there is a perfect order is evident. It appears to be as follows:—

There are *fifteen* of them:

Ten by Hezekiah. Five by others (David (4) and Solomon (1)).

There are *five* groups of *three* Psalms each:

Two in each group are by Hezekiah. *One* by others (David's, in the first two and last two groups, and Solomon's by itself in the centre group).

The *subjects* of each group correspond:

The first Psalm of each group is *Affliction.*

The second is *Jehovah our help.*

The third is *Blessing and peace in Zion.*

We need not particularise further, as the reader will easily trace for himself this correspondence.

Surely the miracle Hezekiah was celebrating was

worthy of being commemorated. It was one of the most wonderful that the world had ever seen; for it was not merely the sun standing still, but the actual reversal of the sun's motion.

And Hezekiah was the most remarkable man that ever lived. He was the only man who ever knew for certain that he had fifteen years to live; the only man who lived for that long period in no fear of death.

The miracle itself was stupendous; and evidently produced a deep impression, not only on Judah but on all the surrounding nations, as it was calculated to do. Hence we find the king of Babylon sending letters, and a present, to Hezekiah; for (it says) "he had heard that Hezekiah had been sick and was recovered" (2 Kings xx. 12. Isa. xxxix. 1); and "sent unto him to enquire of the wonder that was done in the land" (2 Chron. xxxii. 31).

Indeed, some who are very clever and quick enough to discover discrepancies, have quibbled at the fact of Hezekiah being in a position to show the messengers of the king of Babylon "his" treasures of gold and silver (2 Chron. xxxii. 27, 28) so soon after he had stripped the house of the Lord, and his own house, in order to appease the king of Assyria (2 Kings xviii. 13-16), though it really deferred the siege only for a short time.

Such objectors have failed to notice one little verse (2 Chron. xxxii. 23), where we read: "And many brought gifts unto the LORD to Jerusalem, and presents (marg., Heb., *precious things*) to Hezekiah king of Judah; so that he was magnified in the sight of all nations from thenceforth." And they fail to remember also that all the treasures found in the camp of the Assyrians would become the property of Hezekiah.

But this one verse is enough to explain how Hezekiah's treasuries were replenished: and, indeed, furnishes us with the only satisfactory reason which can be given for his showing them. It was no arbitrary act of pride in the possession of his treasures, as such; but the pride was shown in *exhibiting them as the evidence of his magnificence* when it was the LORD Who had so signally both healed him and magnified him.*

The miracle itself is recorded in 2 Kings xx., and Isa. xxxviii.

We have already seen enough to justify us in connecting these "Songs of THE Degrees" with that miracle.

It is interesting for us to note, as we have mentioned above, that this connection was more than suggested two hundred and sixty years ago by Dr. John Lightfoot (1602—1675), and, strange to say, it occurs not in a work on the Psalms, but in connection with the chronology of the Old Testament history.†

Lightfoot, in discussing the chronology of Hezekiah's reign, and the fifteen years added to the life of that king, says:

"Hezekiah lived these fifteen years in safety and prosperity, having humbled himself before the Lord for his pride to the ambassador of Babel. The degrees of the sun's reversing, and the fifteen years of Hezekiah's life-prolonging, may call to our minds the fifteen Psalms of Degrees; viz., from Psalm cxx. and forward. These

---

* Note the emphasis placed on the words "his" and "and" in his showing his treasures to the ambassador from Babylon (Isa. xxxix. 2).

† *A Chronicle of the Times and the Order of the Texts of the Old Testament*, 1647, Works (Pitman's edition, 1822), Vol. ii., 268, 269.

were Hezekiah's songs that were sung to the stringed instruments in the house of the Lord (Isa. xxxviii. 20); whether these were picked out by him for that purpose, be it left for censure* [*i.e.*, examination, see note below.] The Jews hold they were called 'Psalms of Degrees' because they were sung upon the fifteen stairs that rose into the Courts of the Temple. Whoso, in reading these Psalms, shall have his thoughts upon the danger of Jerusalem by Sennacherib and her delivery, and the sickness of Hezekiah and his recovery; shall find that they fit those occasions in many places very well. But I assert nothing, but leave it to examination."

The astonishing thing is, not that this suggestive remark should have been made; but that it should have lain so long neglected. It shows how strong are the bonds of tradition when once they obtain a hold on the human mind; and how they positively blind the eyes of the understanding.†

Another writer, Abraham Wolfson, has also connected the miracle with these Psalms in a work (written in Hebrew) published in Warsaw so recently

---

* "*Censure*," 200 years ago, meant only *examination* or opinion. It is only in recent times that it has acquired the lower meaning of *blame* or *condemnation*. It is thus, with many other words, a witness that fallen and falling man drags down and lowers the meaning of words in his use of them. For, we cannot find one which has ever acquired a higher meaning. (See *Figures of Speech*, p. 856-860 and *How to Enjoy the Bible*, Part ii., Canon iii., page 230).

† Tradition is like *a tether* which prevents an animal from reaching a blade of green grass beyond its length. It effectually shuts us up to what we may have received from man, and compels us to interpret in accordance with it, whatever we may afterwards learn from the Word of God.

as 1882,* but, though he merely discusses it, he fails to grasp the matter; being misled (as so many are in the present day) by confining the term "Israel" in these Psalms to the Ten Tribed Kingdom, instead of extending it to "ALL Israel" as Hezekiah himself insists on doing, so significantly, in his keeping of the Passover.

Wolfson does not seem to have heard of Lightfoot's suggestion; so that, like Dr. Thirtle's, his discovery was an independent one.

It does not appear that even Lightfoot himself ever gave the matter the "examination" which he suggested; or, if he did, that he ever published it.

That "examination" has now been made; and having read these Psalms again and again, and compared them with all the facts and circumstances of Hezekiah's history, we may prove the truth of Lightfoot's promise that we "shall find that *they fit those occasions in many places very well*."

In making this "examination," we shall, happily, be leaving the unsatisfactory conjectures and imaginations of men, and shall discover, instead, a wealth of treasure in the Word of God, and find "great spoil" (Psalm cxix. 162).

* It is noticed in *Hebraica*, a magazine devoted to Semitic research, Chicago.

III.—THEIR AUTHORSHIP.

BEFORE we commence the examination suggested by Dr. Lightfoot, and fully justified by the researches to which we have called attention, there is one other matter of intensest interest which arises at this stage.

If Hezekiah was the author of ten of these Psalms, and the editor of the five others; and, if he took the position of being his own "chief musician" or director of the Temple worship, settling what should be sung in the house of the Lord (Isa. xxxviii. 20), may we not conclude that his authorship and editorship did not begin and end there?

Did the Lord lengthen Hezekiah's life for no special purpose? Was Hezekiah the man to devote those fifteen years to his own selfish interests? Surely the zeal with which he commenced his reign by carrying out the reformation of the house of the Lord, would not all die out suddenly, as soon as it was completed. There is evidence that the same zeal was manifested in the worship of the house of the Lord; and in obeying the Word of the Lord. Care was taken that all was done "according to the commandment of David" (2 Chron. xxix. 25); "with the instruments of David" (*v.* 27); and praise was given to the LORD "with the words of David" (*v.* 30).

The Word of Jehovah was evidently his delight; and was at once his authority, and his guide in all the service which he undertook.

It is recorded of Hezekiah, that, "In every work that he began in the service of the house of God, *and in the law, and in the Commandments*, to seek his God, he did it with all his heart, and prospered" (2 Ch. xxxi. 21).

The reformation and the service of the Temple having been completed, and the enemy defeated, how could those fifteen years have been better occupied than in bringing together and editing the sacred books.

This work would need the same Divine guidance and inspiration. And who so qualified for this great work, or so worthy of it, as Hezekiah?

It is recorded of him "that after him was none like him among all the kings of Judah, nor any that were before him" (2 Kings xviii. 5). If human instrumentality was to be used by God, who was more suitable than Hezekiah? and what time more suitable than those special, God-given years?

In any case, it was the first and prime duty of a king to make *for himself* a copy of the Law, by writing it out with his own hand.

This duty was provided for in Deut. xvii. 18: "And it shall be, when he sitteth upon the throne of his kingdom, that he shall write him a copy of this law in a book out of that which is before the priests the Levites."

The Law had been given by Moses into the care and keeping of "the priests the sons of Levi" (Deut. xxxi. 9): and, independently of any copies made by these priestly custodians, the king must make his own copy.

It is certain that Hezekiah would have made his own copy of the Law, in which he took such delight; and, from the study of which he was so impressed with the importance of the Passover being for "all Israel."

And as to qualification for his task; if Sennacherib was able to record his siege of Jerusalem on a cylinder of stone,* surely Hezekiah was able to record his deliverance from that siege, in "the writing," of which he speaks.

It is certain also that he had a guild of men in his employment specially set apart for this work. They are called "the men of Hezekiah," and their work is clearly intimated in Prov. xxv. i.:—"These are also proverbs of Solomon, which the men of Hezekiah, king of Judah, copied out."

From this we learn that these men were copyists, transcribers, and transmitters of the Sacred Text. Their work, as a guild, would scarcely begin and end with the "Proverbs of Solomon." It would surely extend to other books; and Hezekiah himself would, without doubt, take special interest in and oversight of their work in securing, collecting, and settling the Sacred writings.

At any rate, there are three "majuscular" letters which, to this day, are found at the end of many of the books of the Old Testament. No scribe or compositor has dared to ignore these three letters, or word, if it be a word. There they stand to-day, preserved and transcribed, and transmitted in the manuscripts, and even in the printed editions of the Hebrew Bible.

No one can tell us how these three letters came there, or what they mean.

The three letters are *Cheth* (ח-H); *Zayin* (ז-Z), and *Koph* (ק-K).

חזק

* This cylinder may be seen in the British Museum in London. A further account of it, with photographic reproductions, will be found below. (See pages 253 and 255.)

III.—Their Authorship.

Strange to say, these three letters are the first three letters of the Hebrew name of Hezekiah; and they would stand well for the abbreviation of his name (HeZcK.) just as we use our initials to-day.

What is more reasonable than to believe that when "the men of Hezekiah" completed their work of copying out the different books, Hezekiah should himself have affixed his own sign-manual at the end; thus completing and confirming and establishing their work. This, in a word, is Dr. Thirtle's suggestion.

True, there is a verb חָזַק (*chazak*), which means *to confirm or establish*; and it may have originated in Hezekiah's own act of *confirmation*: or, if not, the existence of this verb might well have suggested the initialling to Hezekiah, and thus serve a double purpose.

It was time that such a work should be done, for the days of Judah's kings and kingdom were numbered.

Twelve years before, Shalmaneser, king of Assyria, had taken Samaria, carried away the Ten Tribes, and made an end of the kingdom of Israel.

It looked as though the kingdom of Judah was about to share the same fate as Israel, and to suffer a like calamity at the hand of Sennacherib.

Jezebel had corrupted the kingdom of Israel, and Athaliah had done the same work for the kingdom of Judah. Jezebel's work had already borne its fruit in the casting aside of Israel; and Athaliah's work was fast ripening for the fatal harvest for Judah.

The recent siege through which Jerusalem and Judah had passed would surely serve as a sufficient warning that it was time something should be done to collect, transcribe, and preserve the several sacred books, to bring them into order, and give them their place in the Sacred Canon.

These fifteen years so miraculously given would surely be the very time, of all others, for such a work.

No other man was so qualified as Hezekiah, and no other time so suitable as those God-given years.

We have, in all this, more than a hint as to the authorship of many of the anonymous Psalms.

We have no more authority to *insert* the name of David over a Psalm where it is absent, than we have to *remove* it from those Psalms over which it has been placed.

It is true that "the second Psalm," though it is anonymous, is assigned to David in Acts iv. 26. And it is implied in the word "also" in Acts xiii. 35. But this does not warrant us, *in the absence of any such authority* in assigning any other Psalms to David which have not his name associated with them.

It is common to speak of "the Psalms of David," but this is a non-scriptural expression. It can neither include those which are distinctly stated to be by others, nor entitle us to include any that are not designated as by David, or that are without a name.

In saying this, we are only putting honour upon the exactitude of Holy Writ.

We cannot, of course, be certain how many of these anonymous Psalms were by Hezekiah himself. There were weighty reasons why he should not put his own name. A proper sense of humility would account for its absence, apart from all other considerations.

Unlike modern writers and composers, Hezekiah would naturally abstain from putting himself or his own compositions forward, though he would be punctilious in inserting the names of others.

Moreover, it would not be necessary for his contemporaries, for it would be a well-known fact for a long time after his death.

To return again to the tri-grammaton (HZK.); no proper explanation has ever been given of it, or its use in Scripture. There are, of course, no vowel points in the MSS., but some later transcribers have pointed the word חֲזַק (*chazāk*), making it into the imperative mood, and translating it "*Be strong*." But this is quite arbitrary, and is destitute of authority.

Moreover, the tri-grammaton has been sometimes treated as though it were the heading of the *clausulæ*, appended to each book by the Massorites centuries after. Each of the *clausulæ* contains a summary as to the number of verses in the book, the number of divisions, words, letters, etc., etc.

What connection, the admonition, "Be strong," has with the arithmetical information of these *clausulæ* is not stated; nor is it clear. In fact, it is senseless; and that, we suppose, is considered good enough for a solution of a problem such as this.

The Bible is treated as though any meaningless notion or vain conceit will suffice for an explanation, without inquiry or examination as to its subject-matter, or, as to whether it makes sense or nonsense.

It is true that there are other books, later than Hezekiah, which have these same three letters at the end; but, What is more likely than that Ezra, or the men of the Great Synagogue, or any other editors of the sacred Text, should continue to use this formula, even though the knowledge as to its primary use and significance had been lost?

If only for the sake of uniformity, without knowing its origin or meaning, nothing would be more natural than that the Nakdanim, Sopherim, or Massorites should not depart from a practice which had thus come down to them.*

There are several Psalms which could be pointed

---

* The use of this tri-grammaton is uniform and continuous at the end of each book, until we come to the death of Hezekiah. Not until after that, at the end of the book of Kings, do we meet with any departure from the addition of these three letters. There, for the first time, we find a different formula. Instead of the simple sign we find two words, making a sentence—instead of forming the initials.

At the end of Kings, we have חֲזַק וְנִתְחַזֵּק (*chazāk venith-chazzēk*) *be strong, and we will be strong.*

This looks as though the subsequent editors, whether Josiah, Ezra, or others (for, of all Judah's kings, none can be named who had greater love for God's word than these) understood the *tri-grammaton* as a solemn injunction transmitted to them; and that they took up the work and carried it out in the same spirit in which it had come down to them, as though Hezekiah being dead yet spoke to them, and said, "Be strong," and they *responded*, "We will be strong." This same form (of two words) is used at the end of Isaiah and Jeremiah. The one word is used again after Ezekiel, at the end of the Minor Prophets, the Psalms, Proverbs, and Job.

We do not find it after the Song of Solomon, Ruth, Lamentations, Ecclesiastes, or Esther (the five books called the *Megillōth*, or little rolls).

We meet with it again after Daniel, and after Ezra-Nehemiah (always as one book).

After Chronicles (which is the last book in the Hebrew Bible) we find a longer form, which, being translated, means "Be strong and we will be strong. The Lawgiver is not straitened."

out as undoubtedly the work of Hezekiah;* the internal evidence connecting them very closely with himself, his life and his times. Among these are assuredly Psalms xliv., xlvi., xlvii., xlviii., xci., cxix. and many others.

This brings us to the examination of these Songs of the Degrees to see what evidence we can find to prove that they are the work of Hezekiah; the songs which he said he would sing in the House of Jehovah.

This, when proved, will take these "Songs of the Degrees" back far beyond the Babylonian Captivity, and give them their place in the History; effectually disposing of the theories of the "Higher" critics who have laboured so zealously to bring them down to later times; and done their utmost to demolish them as the Word of God, and to discredit them as the work of man.

* For further information on this important subject we must refer our readers to Dr. Thirtle's work; and to our remarks on Psalm xlvi. above, under "Selah."

IV.—THEIR EXAMINATION.

WE come, at length, to such an "examination" as was suggested by Dr. Lightfoot, and abundantly vindicated in Dr. Thirtle's investigations. In carrying this out, we have found the following fifteen points of contact between the history of Hezekiah and his Songs of the Degrees; the same in number as the fifteen Psalms. But there may be others which we have overlooked; for we never profess to exhaust the Divine Word.

In deciding the order in which we should here present them we have been guided by the Songs, and not by the history. In Kings, Chronicles, and Isaiah we have the chronological order of the historical facts. In the Songs we have the Divine order according to their spiritual significance.

We have already noted the fact that the fifteen Psalms are divided into *five* groups of *three* each. And the order in the subjects of the three Psalms is the same, group for group, and Psalm for Psalm.

The *first* Psalm in each group has Distress, Affliction, and Trouble, with Prayer, for its subject.

The *second* has Trust in Jehovah.

The *third* has Blessing, and Peace of Zion.

THE FIFTEEN POINTS ARE AS FOLLOWS:—

1. Rabshakeh's blasphemous tongue.
2. Sennacherib's reproaches.
3. Sennacherib's shame.
4. Hezekiah's earnest prayer.
5. God, "the Maker of heaven and earth."

6. Hezekiah's desire for peace.
7. Jehovah's promised help.
8. "For Thy servant David's sake."
9. Jehovah's sign to Hezekiah.
10. Hezekiah's trust in Jehovah.
11. Hezekiah "like a bird in a cage."
12. "The Captivity of Zion."
13. Hezekiah's zeal for the house of Jehovah.
14. Hezekiah childless.
15. The Passover for all Israel.

The reader must compare what is said under these fifteen heads, with the Psalms themselves, and the notes in Part IV.

The two parts are supplemental to each other; and should be studied together. The references also are to be carefully compared.

---

(1) *Rabshakeh's Blasphemous Tongue.*

We know, from the history, that when Rabshakeh's words were heard, they were received with dismay. King Hezekiah and all his ministers rent their clothes, and covered themselves with sackcloth.

He sent word to Isaiah, and said: "It may be Jehovah thy God will hear the words of Rabshakeh, whom the king of Assyria his master hath sent to reproach the living God,* and will reprove the words

* Like the expression "the God who made heaven and earth," the title "the living God" always has reference to Idols. He is so called in contrast with those which had no life. Compare 1 Thess. i. 9.

which Jehovah thy God hath heard: wherefore lift up thy prayer for the remnant that is left" (Isa. xxxvii. 4).

Hezekiah, himself, prayed and said,

"Jehovah, bow down thine ear, and hear:
Open Jehovah, thine eyes, and see:
And hear the words of Sennacherib who hath sent him (*i.e.*, Rabshakeh) to reproach the living God" (2 Kings xix. 16).

We do not have to look far into these Psalms to find references to the scornful, contemptuous, and proud words of Rabshakeh.

In the very first we read:

"Deliver my soul, O Jehovah, from **lying lips**,
And from **a deceitful tongue**,
What shall be given (or done) unto thee,
Or what shall be done unto thee, thou **false tongue?**" (Psalm cxx. 2, 3).

"Have mercy upon us, O Jehovah,
Have mercy upon us:
For we are exceedingly filled with **contempt**.
Our soul is exceedingly filled with the **scorning** of those that are at ease,
And with the **contempt** of the proud" (Psalm cxxiii. 3, 4).

Not only did Hezekiah pray with reference to the disturbers of Zion's peace, and of his own peace of mind; but we have distinct references to Sennacherib's reproaches.

---

(2) *Sennacherib's Reproaches.*

Both in 2 Kings xix., and in Isa. xxxvii., the prophet Isaiah sent to Hezekiah, in answer to his prayer, of Divine message in reply to Sennacherib's reproaches of Jehovah.

The words are nearly the same in both records. They both refer to, and quote, Sennacherib's words; and tell us what he had said as to his conquests of other nations.

But Jehovah, in His reply by Isaiah, reveals the fact that Sennacherib had done only what He had permitted him to do; and how He had *over-ruled* all for the accomplishment of His own counsels.

In 2 Kings xix. 25, 26 and Isa. xxxvii. 26, 27, Jehovah apostrophizes Sennacherib, and asks him:

> "Hast thou not heard long ago, how I have done it,
> And, of ancient times, that I have formed it?
> Now have I brought it to pass,
> That thou shouldest be to lay waste fenced cities into ruinous heaps.
> That is why their inhabitants were of small power,
> They were dismayed and confounded:
> They were as the grass of the field,
> And as the green herb,
> As the **grass on the housetops,**
> And as corn **blasted before it be grown up.**"

Can we have the smallest doubt that, in Psalm cxxix., we have a reference to these words of Jehovah by Isaiah?

Jehovah had said that He had made the enemies of Sennacherib to be as grass before him. So here Hezekiah prays that Jehovah would do the same with all the enemies of Zion.

"Let all that hate Zion be put to shame and turned backward.
Let them be as the grass upon the housetops,
Which withereth before it be grown up:
Wherewith the mower filleth not his hand;
Nor he that bindeth sheaves [filleth] his bosom" (Psalm cxxix. 5-7).

No one can fail to see the close connection between these words of Hezekiah and Isaiah; or fail to admire the beautiful way in which Jehovah's taunt to Sennacherib is turned into a prayer for Zion.

---

(3) *Sennacherib's Shame.*

In the history we read how, after that Jehovah had cut off the hosts of Sennacherib in one night, he "**returned with shame of face** to his own land" (2 Chron. xxxii. 21).

Can we doubt for one moment that Hezekiah refers to this when he says:

"Jehovah is righteous:
He hath cut asunder the cords of the wicked.
Let them all be confounded (R.V. '**be ashamed**') **and turned back**
That hate Zion." (Ps. cxxix. 4, 5).

---

(4) *Hezekiah's Earnest Prayer.*

We learn, from Isaiah xxxviii. 3, that Hezekiah's grief was deep and real.

He "wept with great weeping" (*v.* 3, margin).

"He prayed and cried to heaven" (2 Chron. xxxii. 20).

In this prayer Isaiah joins him. Hezekiah had sent to him for this purpose: "lift up thy prayer for the remnant that are left" (2 Kings xix. 2, 4).

When Hezekiah received Rabshakeh's letter, he "spread it before Jehovah." This prayer is recorded in 2 Kings xix. 15-19. Its earnestness will be noted in verse 16 and 19.

"Jehovah, bow down thine ear, and hear:
Open, Jehovah, thine eyes, and see.
I beseech thee, save Thou us out of his hand."

When threatened with death by "the King of terrors," he "turned his face to the wall, and prayed unto Jehovah again, saying:—

"I beseech thee, O Jehovah . . . .
And Hezekiah wept sore" (2 Kings xx. 2, 3).

Another prayer is recorded in Isaiah xxxviii. 10-20: and verse 14 shows how sore was his trouble.

"Like a crane or a swallow, so did I chatter:
I did mourn as a dove:
Mine eyes fail with looking upward:
O Jehovah, I am oppressed;
Undertake for me."

How can we read these words without at once associating them with the Songs of the Degrees?

The very first words of the first of these Psalms give us the connecting link.

"**In my distress I cried unto Jehovah,**
And he heard me" (Psalm cxx. 1).

"**Unto Thee did I lift up mine eyes** . . .
Our eyes wait upon Jehovah our God,
Until that He have mercy upon us.

Have mercy upon us, O Jehovah,
Have mercy upon us" (Psalm cxxiii. 1-3).

"**Out of the depths have I cried unto Thee, O Jehovah.**
Adonai, hear my voice,
Let thine ears be attentive to the voice of my supplications" (Psalm cxxx. 1,2).

It is hardly necessary to make any comment on these Scriptures. The correspondence is obvious: and he who reads the history and the Songs most minutely will be the most amply rewarded for his study.

We must note, secondly, that this prayer of Hezekiah was made to Jehovah as

---

(5) *God, the Maker of Heaven and Earth.*

Hezekiah prayed unto Jehovah and said:—

" O Jehovah, God of Israel, which dwellest between the cherubim,
Thou art the God, even Thou alone, of all the kingdoms of the earth;
Thou hast made heaven and earth;" (2 Kings xix. 15; Isa. xxxvii. 16).

There is a special reason for thus addressing his prayer.

Rabshakeh had railed against God, and "spake against the God of Jerusalem as against the gods of the people of the earth, which were the work of the hands of man" (2 Chron. xxxii. 19).

Yes, the God of Jerusalem was "the God of Hezekiah" (verse 17), and he was "the God who made heaven and earth." With Him all things are possible.

Well, therefore, did Hezekiah make his prayer unto Jehovah, in sharp contrast with the gods of Assyria, in whose praise Sennacherib had spoken.

Now notice how this is referred to in Psalm cxxi. 1,2; and observe the *full stop* at the end of the first line, and the *Question* at the end of the second.

"I lift up mine eyes unto the mountains.
From whence will come my help?
My help cometh from Jehovah,
Who made heaven and earth" (Ps. cxxi. 1,2).

It will be seen that these four lines are an introversion: in which we have the *Creation* in the first and fourth lines, and the *Creator* in the second and third.

The contemplation of Creation, in the mountains which stand about Jerusalem, turned Hezekiah's thoughts to Him who created them.

The God who made the mountains, made heaven and earth; and He could do all things; and could bring help and deliverance to Hezekiah.

Hezekiah did not do anything so foolish as to think the mountains could help him.

To "lift up the eyes" is a Hebrew form of expression, or idiom, for *considering*; * and hence for doing that which was the result of such consideration. In Psalm cxxiii. 1 we have it again.

"Unto Thee have I lifted up mine eyes,
O Thou that dwellest in the heavens."

And the next verse goes on to explain the act †.

* And the act is put by *Metonymy* of the Adjunct, for what is connected with, and included in, the act. See *Figures of Speech*, pages 253, 606.

† Compare Gen. xiii. 14. Ezek. xviii. 6,15.

There is another Figure of Speech employed in this verse (Psalm cxxi. 6 *). It is called *Anadiplosis* (which means *a doubling*) because a word is *doubled*, or repeated, for the purpose of pointing out the word on which the real emphasis is to be placed. Here it is shown to be on *help*.

"Whence is to come **my help**?
My help cometh," etc.

This Figure conclusively shows that it was not the mountains from whence he was expecting help; but from Jehovah who created them.

In Psalm cxxiv. 8, Hezekiah again expresses the same confidence, and on the same grounds.

The introversion of these four lines shows that Hezekiah looked unto the mountains, not for any help that they could give him (as some have thought), but because they were the work of Hezekiah's God. As he lifted up his eyes and considered them, they told of *Him, the Creator, who made them*; yea, of Him who "made heaven and earth."

In Psalm cxxiv. 8, he again expresses the same hope.

"Our help is in the name of Jehovah,
Who made heaven and earth."

The whole of this series of Psalms ends with a further reference by way of praise:

"**Jehovah that made heaven and earth,**
Bless thee out of Zion" (Psalm cxxxiv. 3).

In Psalm cxxiii. 1, also, Hezekiah's prayer is addressed to Him "that dwelleth in the heavens." This

* See *Figures of Speech*, pp. 251-255.

For other examples compare Gen. i. 1,2 (earth); Psalm cxxii. 2,3 (Jerusalem); cxxvi. 2,3 (done great things), etc.

is Jehovah before whom he spread Sennacherib's letter, and said :—"O Jehovah Sabaoth, God of Israel, that dwellest between the cherubims" (2 Kings xix. 15; Isa. xxxvii. 16).

---

(6) *Hezekiah's Desire for Peace.*

In his prayer, Hezekiah refers to his longing for peace, in the midst of wars without, and fears within. His sickness came in the midst of the siege: as is clear from the promise given in connection with the sign of the shadow's going back on the Degrees (or steps): "I will add to thy days fifteen years; and I will deliver thee and this city out of the hand of the king of Assyria" (2 Kings xx. 6).

Hezekiah's prayer therefore has reference to the siege as well as his sickness. Hence he prays, and says :

> "Behold, for peace I had great bitterness" (Isa. xxxviii. 17).

So, in the Songs of the Degrees, he says :

> "My soul hath long dwelt with him that hateth peace.
> I am for peace: but when I speak, they are for war" (Psalm cxx. 6, 7).

Is there not here, in the very first of these Psalms, a reference to the history? Yea, to the first beginning of all his trouble.

We read in 2 Chron. xxxii. 1-3, that "when Hezekiah saw that Sennacherib was come, and that he was purposed to fight against Jerusalem (margin, Heb. *His face was to war*), he took counsel with his princes." Who can doubt that, in this *v*. 7, we have a reference to such passages as this, and 2 Kings xviii 19, etc., Isa. xxxvi. 5, etc.

Hezekiah's one desire was for "peace." He prays:

> "**Pray for the peace of Jerusalem.**
> **Peace be within thy walls**" (Psalm cxxii. 6, 7).

> "**And peace upon Israel**" (Psalm cxxv. 5).

> "Thou shalt see thy children's children,
> And **peace upon Israel**" (Psalm cxxviii. 6).

The last Psalm of each of the five groups of three, has blessing and peace for its theme. And his own last prayer (recorded in the history) was that "peace and truth" might be in his days (2 Kings xx. 19).

---

(7) *Jehovah's Promised Help.*

Isaiah had positively assured Hezekiah that Jehovah would certainly deliver him and Jerusalem. He said:

"Thus Jehovah hath said concerning the king of Assyria: He shall not come into this city, nor shoot an arrow there, nor come before it with shield, nor cast a bank against it. By the way that he came, by the same shall he return, and shall not come into this city, saith Jehovah. For I will defend this city, to save it" (2 Kings xix. 32-34).

"I will add unto thy days fifteen years; and I will deliver thee and this city out of the hand of the king of Assyria; and I will defend this city" (2 Kings xx. 6).

This was Jehovah's answer to Sennacherib's challenge, sent on, in advance, to Hezekiah from Lachish (which he was besieging): "Shall your God deliver you out of my hand" (2 Chron. xxxii. 9, 15, 17, Isa. xxxvi. 20; xxxvii. 11).

Now notice how this Divine pledge was taken up, and treasured, and mentioned again and again in these "Songs of the Degrees":

"**My help cometh from Jehovah** . . .
He will not suffer thy foot to be moved:
He that keepeth thee will not slumber,
Behold, he that keepeth Israel shall neither slumber nor sleep.
Jehovah is thy keeper:
Jehovah is thy shade upon thy right hand. . . .
Jehovah shall preserve thee from all evil:
He shall preserve thy soul.
Jehovah shall preserve thy going out and thy coming in
From this time forth, and even for evermore" (Psalm cxxi. 2-8).

"If it had not been **Jehovah who was on our side**, now may Israel say;
If it had not been **Jehovah who was on our side**, when men rose up against us:
Then they had swallowed us up quick, . . .
Blessed be Jehovah, who hath not given us *as* a prey to their teeth" (Psalm cxxiv. 1-3, 6).

"As the mountains are round about Jerusalem,
So **Jehovah is round about his people**" (Psalm cxxv. 2).

"Then said they among the heathen,
Jehovah hath done great things for them,

Jehovah hath done great things for us;
Whereof we are glad" (Psalm cxxvi. 2, 3).

"Except **Jehovah build the house**,
They labour in vain that build it:
Except Jehovah keep the city,
The watchman waketh but in vain"* (Psalm cxxvii. 1).

It was because of this assured promise of Jehovah, sent to Hezekiah, by Isaiah, that we see his firm trust in the word of Jehovah. There was no other ground for his faith: for, "faith cometh by hearing, and hearing by the word of God" (Rom. x. 17).

---

(8) *For My Servant David's Sake.*

"When Hezekiah received the letter of the hand of the messengers, and read it:" he "went up into the house of Jehovah, and spread it before Jehovah" (Kings xix. 14).

Isaiah was sent with Jehovah's answer to that letter: and in it special stress was laid on the grounds on which Jehovah would deliver Jerusalem, and Hezekiah, and His people. He said:

"I will defend this city, to save it, for mine own sake, and for **my servant David's sake**" (2 Kings xix. 34).

So also in answer to his prayer for recovery from his

---

* We have another example of the Figure *Anadiplosis*, or *Doubling* in this Psalm, for the sake of emphasising the vanity:

"The watchman waketh but **in vain**.
In vain ye rise up early."

See *Figures of Speech*, pages 251-255.

sickness, Isaiah was sent with the message: "Thus Jehovah hath said, **the God of David thy father**, I have heard thy prayer . . . I will defend this city for Mine own sake, and **for My servant David's sake**" (2 Kings xx. 5, 6).

See how these words were remembered by Hezekiah, when he "**remembered David**, and all his troubles," and prayed to Jehovah to remember them also (Psalm cxxxii. 1).

Hezekiah remembers them and says:

> "For **thy servant David's sake**
> Turn not away the face of Thine anointed"
> (Psalm cxxxii. 10).

The whole Psalm is taken up with David. The first part is what David sware to Jehovah (*vv.* 2-10): and the second part is what Jehovah had sworn to David (*vv.* 10-18).*

It is all for David, and for David's sake.

Surely this is in close connection with the history as it is recorded in the book of Kings.

---

(9) *Jehovah's Sign to Hezekiah.*

Isaiah suddenly changes his address in 2 Kings xix. 29, and Isa. xxxvii. 30, and turns from Sennacherib to Hezekiah. All is really addressed to Hezekiah: but the apostrophe is addressed to Sennacherib, who is to be turned back by the way that he came.

A sign is then voluntarily given to Hezekiah in the following words:

* See the structure of the whole Psalm in Part IV., pp. 308-311.

"And this shall be a sign unto thee,
Ye shall eat this year such as groweth of itself;
And the second year that which springeth of the same:
And in the third year **sow ye**, and **reap**,
And plant vineyards, and **eat the fruit thereof**."

Here was a sign, indeed, as to the truth of Jehovah's words. A sign that could be clearly understood and evidenced.

Nothing that would be sown would spring up. Only what grew spontaneously would be available for food. The sowers would be disappointed, and would see the fruitlessness of their labour.

How well can we understand the special reference of the following words:

"They that **sow** in tears shall **reap** with songs of joy.
He that keeps going on carrying his basket of **seed**
Shall surely come again with songs of joy,
Carrying his **sheaves**" (Psalm cxxvi. 5, 6).

"For thou shalt **eat the labour of thine hands**:
Happy shalt thou be,
And it shall be well with thee" (Psalm cxxviii. 2).

The continued perseverance of the sowers under the disappointment of their labour was remembered with thanksgiving in this Psalm, which commemorated their sowing in tears and their reaping with songs of joy.

The whole picture presented is not that of exiles in Babylon, a foreign land, but that of peaceful agriculturists, carrying on their operations, at home, in their own land.

(10) *Hezekiah's Trust in Jehovah.*

One of the very first things recorded of Hezekiah was: "He trusted in Jehovah, the God of Israel" (2 Kings xviii. 5).

It was this that formed the subject of all Rabshakeh's appeals to the People, whom he wished to treat with, and detach from Hezekiah; and thus stir up rebellion against him: "Hear the word of the great king, the king of Assyria: Thus saith the king, Let not Hezekiah deceive you: for he shall not be able to deliver you out of his hand: Neither let Hezekiah make you trust in Jehovah, saying, Jehovah will surely deliver us, and this city shall not be delivered into the hand of the king of Assyria. Hearken not to Hezekiah" (2 Kings xviii. 28-31).

Indeed the whole chapter must be read, as well as the parallel chapters in 2 Chronicles and Isaiah, if we wish to form a true estimate of Hezekiah's trust in Jehovah.

Again and again it is spoken of in all the three records. (See Isa. xxxvi. 18; xxxvii. 10.)

And note the ground of his trust: Isaiah brought him the promise by "the word of Jehovah." Hezekiah believed the word spoken, and rested upon it. Hence, he could wait, and pray, and look upward.

Now see how this trust is reflected in these Psalms. It will be found prominently in the second of each group of three Psalms

> "He will not suffer thy foot to be moved:
> He that keepeth thee will not slumber"
>
> (Psalm cxxi. 3.)

> "They that **trust in Jehovah** shall be as Mount
> Zion,

Which cannot be removed, but will abide tor ever.
As the mountains stand round about Jerusalem
So Jehovah is round about His People
From henceforth even for ever.
For the rod of the wicked will not rest upon the lot of the righteous" (Psalm cxxv. 1-3).

I.e., the rod of the Assyrian will not rest upon Israel. This was the expression of Hezekiah's trust in God's promise sent by Isaiah. (*See* Notes, p. 293).

"Except Jehovah build the house, they labour in vain that build it:
Except Jehovah keep the city, the watchman waketh in vain" (Psalm cxxvii. 1).

"I wait for Jehovah,
My soul doth wait,
And in his word do I hope.
Let Israel hope in Jehovah:
For with Jehovah there is mercy,
And with Him is plenteous redemption.
And He will redeem Israel from all his iniquities" (Psalm cxxx. 5-8).

---

(11) *Hezekiah like a Bird in a Cage.*

Perhaps the most beautiful and striking of all these fifteen points, and the most conclusive which can be afforded of the truth of our position, is that which is supplied, not from the Scripture history of Hezekiah, but from from the Assyrian record of Sennacherib himself.

IV.—Their Examination.

There may be seen to-day, in the British Museum in London,* a Hexagonal Cylinder of this very Sennacherib, King of Assyria (B.C. 705—681).

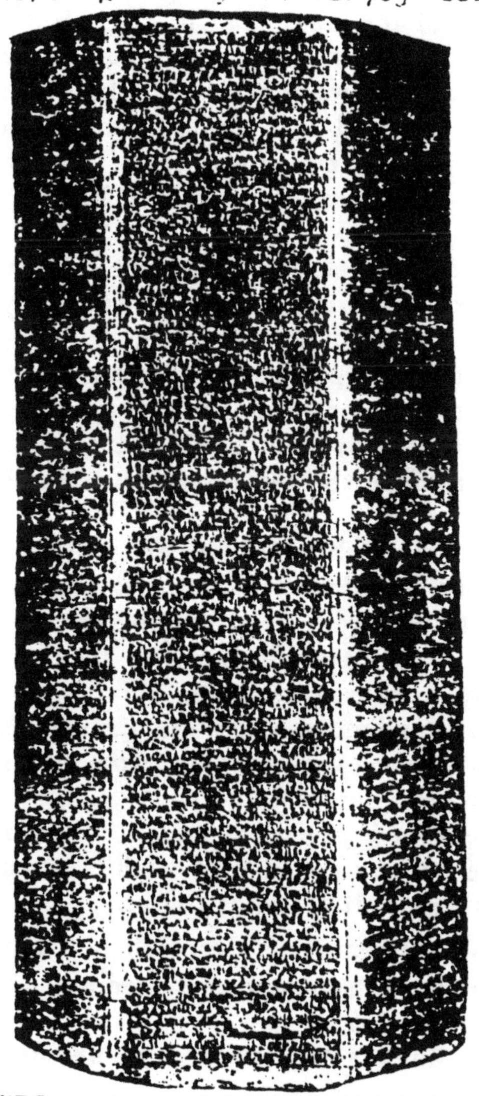

* 55—10—3, 1.

By the kind permission of the Oxford Press, we are privileged to give a reproduction of a photograph of this Cylinder.

It is "one of the finest and most perfect objects of its class and kind ever discovered, and its importance as an historical document can hardly be over-rated. It contains four hundred and eighty-seven lines of closely written but legible cuneiform text, inscribed in the Eponymy of Belimuranni, prefect of Karkemish about 691 B.C."

The text records eight expeditions of Sennacherib. Among them is his description of this very siege of Jerusalem in the reign of Hezekiah.

By the same kind permission of the Oxford Press, we are enabled to give (on the opposite page) a photographic facsimile of that portion of the Cylinder, beginning with the eleventh line of the central column, which is shown in our illustration on page 253.

The words we wish to refer to are in the seventeenth to the twenty first lines: After speaking of the cities which he had besieged, Sennacherib says:

17. . . . I captured 200,150 people, small and great, male and female,
18. horses, and mules, and asses, and camels, and men,
19. and sheep innumerable from their midst I brought out, and
20. I reckoned [them] as spoil. [Hezekiah] **himself like a caged bird within Jerusalem,**
21. **his royal city, I shut in,** &c.

Now read the words of Hezekiah in Psalm cxxiv. 7.

"Our soul is escaped as a bird out of the snare of the fowlers:
The snare is broken, and we are delivered."

LINES 11-24 OF THE CENTRAL COL. OF CYLINDER, SHOWN ON P. 253.

This takes the Psalm right back to the very days of Hezekiah and Sennacherib.

Indeed, it takes us back beyond the days of Hezekiah and Sennacherib: for *it is a Psalm of David.*

Some 350 years before Hezekiah, David had found himself in similar trouble. He was hunted like a partridge in the mountains, pursued as a dog, and sought as a flea, by Saul. He had been shut up in his hiding places.* At such a time it was that David penned this Psalm (cxxiv.) At such a similar time of

* Read 1 Sam. xxiii. 1-13; 19—xxiv. 12; xxiv. 14; xxvi. 1—20.

Hezekiah's need, shut up in his house by sickness, and besieged in Jerusalem by Sennacherib, he was indeed "like a caged bird:" what Psalm could more suitably express the sense of his need, and his praise for Divine deliverance?

He had no need himself to write another "Song." Here was one ready to his hand. Indeed David's reference to his escape "as a bird out of the snare of the fowlers" would be seized on by Hezekiah as exactly suiting his deliverance from the "snare," as well as from the siege of Sennacherib.

It makes the history live again before our eyes.

We can see the vain boasting of his enemies; and hear his own praise, as he exclaims:—

> "Blessed be Jehovah, who hath not given us as a prey to their teeth." (Psalm cxxiv. 6*).

Thus put back into its own historic setting, it demolishes all the artifices of the "higher" critics whose one aim is to bring these Psalms down to Post-Exilic days; and writes "folly" on their vain imaginations. Here is evidence that what they would bring down to B.C. 150 could have been written only by David himself; and, used here by Hezekiah who was concerned in the events referred to, is thus proved to have been written more than 1000 years before Christ.

If these critics prefer Hammurabi to Moses, then let them prefer Sennacherib to themselves. We prefer the testimony of Sennacherib's Cylinder to all their imaginations; while we welcome the additional evidence it affords as to the truth of the Word of God.

---

* The anonymous Psalm, lxvi., may also be by Hezekiah. If so, verse 11 would refer to the same deliverance from "the net," wherewith birds are caught.

(12) "*The Captivity of Zion.*"

This expression, which occurs twice in these Psalms (Psalm cxxvi. 1, 4), finds its connection with Hezekiah's history.

The ten tribes had, twelve years before, gone into captivity, on account of their idolatry.

The coming up of a large remnant of them to Jerusalem to keep the Passover after Hezekiah's Reformation was a happy token of hope that the rupture between Judah and Israel might possibly be healed: that the Tribes, who, when they went to Bethel and Dan had their backs turned on the house of Jehovah at Jerusalem, might yet again assemble within its walls.

As we shall see in our last point of comparison, Hezekiah was most particular in emphasising the fact that the Passover was for "ALL Israel." Again and again is this stated. (See 2 Chron. xxx. 1, 9, &c.)

No wonder, then, that he exhorted the remnant of the ten tribes to "turn again unto Jehovah;" assuring them that, if they did so, their brethren would "find compassion before them that led them captive, so that they should come again into this Land" (2 Chron. xxx. 9).

That there was a literal captivity Sennacherib tells us. And, we have seen on the Cylinder which records his invasion (see pages 253 and 255 above) that he had captured and taken away 200,150 people from the Tribes of Israel. And it was Israel, "all Israel," that occupied the thoughts and filled the breast of Hezekiah.

In 2 Kings xix. 2, 4, Hezekiah entreats Isaiah to lift up his prayer "for the remnant that are left:" referring of course to the thousands which had been carried away into captivity.

There is therefore no need whatever to introduce the later captivity of Judah in Babylon. There is also an Idiomatic use of the expression which we are considering.

"To turn the captivity" was the Idiom for making an end of any trouble or affliction.* It might be better Englished "to turn the fortunes" of a person or nation. Captivity was a calamity: and when it was "turned" it was over. So the term "captivity" was used of any great trouble †; and its "turning" was the ending of the trouble and a returning to a former estate. (Compare Ezek. xvi. 53 with 55; and see Ez. xxix. 14, Jer. xxx. 3; xxxiii. 11, Zeph. iii. 20).

Hence, it was said of Job, that "Jehovah turned the captivity of Job" (Job. xlii. 10). Job was never in literal captivity to man; but he was to his afflictions and sorrows. When the Lord "turned the captivity" of Job, it is explained as meaning that "the Lord gave Job twice as much as he had before." It meant that Job had "a happy issue out of all his afflictions."

This is the meaning of Psalm cxxvi. 1.

> "When Jehovah **turned again the Captivity** of **Zion,**
>
> We were like them that dream."

This refers to the ending of the siege of Jerusalem; delivering the city from the hand of the enemy; and

---

*The Figure of Speech made it conveniently expressive as an Idiom שׁוּב שְׁבוּת (*shūv shevōth*) *return the returning.*

† Just as we use the word "affliction," not necessarily of *sickness*, but of any trouble.

giving peace and blessing in Zion. It was this that enabled him to add :—

" Then was our mouth filled with laughter, and
our tongue with singing :
Then said they among the heathen,
' Jehovah hath done great things for them.'
Jehovah hath done great things for us ;
We are glad " (Psalm cxxvi. 2-3).

In the next verse (*v.* 4), Hezekiah turns from praise for the delivery from their outward troubles of the siege, and his sickness, to prayer for deliverance from the internal trouble of a divided nation. He had sown the seeds of re-union in carrying out a Passover for " all Israel ;" and he strengthens his hope by the thought of the fact :

" They that sow in tears
Shall reap in joy.
He that goeth forth and weepeth,
Bearing precious seed,
Shall doubtless come again with rejoicing,
Bringing his sheaves with him."
(Psalm cxxvi. 4, 5, 6)

His assurance is the basis of his prayer in verse 4 ; to understand which we must fill up the *Ellipsis* correctly ; and this will necessitate a change in the translation of the words as they stand in the text.

" **Turn again our captivity**, O Jehovah,
As [Thou turnest] the torrents * in the *Negeb*."

---

* ***Aphikim*** means the *torrents restrained* in a narrow natural or artificial channel, open or covered, either in a gorge or defile, or in pipes or aqueduct, and therefore inaccessible. In Psalm

The word rendered "rivers" *Aphīkīm* is from אָפַק (*āphak*) to *restrain by force* (Gen. xliii. 31; xlv. 1; Est. v. 10).

The word rendered "south" is, in the Hebrew, *Negeb*. That it does not and cannot mean "South" is clear by comparing Gen. xii. 9, with xiii. 1.*

In Gen. xii. 9 "Abram journeyed going on still toward the *Negeb*." This was in the direction of Egypt, which was South of Canaan. But,

In Gen. xiii. 1, "Abram went up out of Egypt, he and his wife and all that he had, and Lot with him, into the *Negeb*." But this was *North* from Egypt, on his return journey to Canaan: and therefore if translated "South" (as in the A.V.) it directly contradicts ch. xii. 9.

That the *Negeb* was the hill country South of Judea (and North of Egypt) is clear from other passages.

It may therefore be rendered, in connection with these, *torrents*, either in *gorges* or *ravines*, which restrained by their force the rushing torrents. This water ran, not "in the hills" but, between them, in the rocky ravines.

A careful study of our New Version and notes given in Part iv. will show the nature of Hezekiah's prayer.

He prayed that, as Jehovah, the mighty God, turns the torrents of water hither and thither in their rocky confines, in the *Negeb* or hill country of Judea, so He

---

xlii. 1., the panting thirsty hind brayeth for the waters which she hears rushing below, but cannot get at. The word occurs in the following passages: and is rendered *Channels*, 2 Sam. xxii. 16; Psalm xviii. 15; Isiah viii. 7. *Streams*, Job vi. 15; Psalm cxxvi. 4. *Mighty*, Job xii. 21; *Strong pieces*, Job xl. 18; *Water-brooks*, Psalm xlii. 1; *Rivers*, Joel i. 20; Song v. 12; Ezek. vi. 3; xxxi. 12; xxxii. 6; xxxiv. 13,; xxxv. 8; xxxvi., 4, 6; Joel iii. 18 (iv. 18 Heb).

* See *Figures of Speech*, pages 82—84, by the Editor.

would turn the hearts of His People unto Himself, as well as turn away all their troubles from them.

---

(13) *Hezekiah's Zeal for the House of Jehovah.*

Perhaps the most prominent feature in Hezekiah's character was his zeal for the house of Jehovah. It was the chief concern of his life. It occupied his thoughts; it claimed his attention; it filled his heart.

Hezekiah stands out in peculiar contrast with the other kings in whose reigns Isaiah prophesied.

The names of Ahaz, and Hezekiah, are linked together in a very special manner by Isaiah's ministry.*

Of Ahaz it is written (2 Chron. xxviii. 24): "**He shut up the doors of the house of Jehovah.**"

Of Hezekiah it is recorded (2 Chron. xxix. 3): "**He opened the doors of the house of Jehovah and repaired them.**"

This is mentioned as the very first act of Hezekiah: "in the first year of his reign, in the first month."

His Reformation of the Temple and its services, as recorded in the book of the Chronicles, occupies three whole chapters; and we are told, with the greatest minuteness, how complete was that work, and how thoroughly it was carried out.

After the Reformation of the Temple, he continually resorted thither.

---

* Of Jotham it is written (2 Ch. xxvii. 2) "He entered not into the House of Jehovah": but this is said in his praise; and the context shows that he did "all that Uzziah his father did," except that he did not sin as his father did (*see* 2 Chron. xxvi. 16-24) by entering into the temple of the Lord to burn incense, &c. Only the Priests could enter the "Temple."

When he first heard of Rabshakeh's words, Hezekiah "rent his clothes, and covered himself with sackcloth, and **went into the House of Jehovah**" (Isa. xxxvii. 1).

When he "received the letter of the King of Assyria from the hand of the messengers, and read it, Hezekiah **went up into the House of Jehovah**, and spread it before Jehovah." (Isa. xxxvii. 14).*

When smitten by his sickness unto death, and when Isaiah came to him and promised him recovery, his first question was:—"What shall be the sign that Jehovah will heal me, and that **I shall go up into the House of Jehovah**?" (2 Kings xx. 8, Isa. xxxvii. 22).

His "writing" which he wrote "when he had been sick, and was recovered of his sickness," ended with his resolve: "Therefore will we sing my songs to the stringed instruments all the days of our life, **in the House of Jehovah**." (Isa. xxxviii. 20).*

This is the "*going up*" referred to the "Songs of the Degrees." These are the "Ascents" of Hezekiah: which correspond with the *ascent* of the sun which turned the shadow back and down on the steps of the sundial of Ahaz. As the shadow went backward, and was brought back again, the number of the degrees by which

* Alas! in the matter of the letter of the King of Babylon this was not the case. When the King of Assyria came against him with a summons to surrender the city, Hezekiah went up into the House of the LORD, and spread it before the LORD.

When "the King of Terrors" came, with his solemn summons to surrender his life, Hezekiah "turned his face toward the wall, and prayed unto the LORD."

When "the King of Babylon" sent letters and a *present*, Hezekiah did neither the one nor the other: on the contrary, he was "glad of them;" and showed them "his house," and "his treasures," instead of the House of the Lord, and His mercies. (See *The Vision of Isaiah*, by the same author and publisher).

it had *gone down*, the sun must have gone up, *ascended* in the heavens again;* so these steps or degrees were well fitted to illustrate and symbolize these continued *ascents* of Hezekiah, when he ascended and went up into the House of Jehovah.

When we read, in these Psalms, the references to "the House of Jehovah," we cannot fail to notice how remarkably they receive their natural interpretation when taken in connection with Hezekiah's history:

> "I was glad when they said unto me,
> Let us go into **the House of Jehovah**. . . .
> Because of the **House of Jehovah** our God I will seek thy good." (Ps. cxxii. 1, 9).

> "Behold, bless ye Jehovah, all ye servants of Jehovah,
> Which by night stand in the **House of Jehovah**.
> Lift up your hands in the Sanctuary,
> And bless Jehovah." (Ps. cxxxiv. 1, 2).

---

(14) *Hezekiah Childless.*

There is another subject in connection with Hezekiah which finds a prominent place in these Psalms. Surely we must often have noticed the references to children; and wondered what they could possibly have to do with these "Songs of Degrees," whatever explánation of them might be adopted.

The explanation is that, at the time of this calamity, *Hezekiah was childless.*

Psalm cxxxii. shows that he remembered "the sure mercies," promised to David when God said, "I will set

*See the Illustration already given above, page 221.

up thy seed after thee, which shall proceed out of thy bowels, and I will establish his kingdom" (2 Samuel vii. 12).

He knew the sure word of Jehovah that there should never be wanting one to sit upon David's throne: and yet, at this very moment, at this critical point in his history, when his life was in the utmost danger, (for he was "sick unto death") *there was no heir to David's* throne; no heir to Hezekiah's kingdom. This must have caused him great disquietude.

Like Abraham, when he had "no seed," Hezekiah must have longed for a son. He could not be otherwise than anxious until he had received the Lord's promise of a son and heir. (See 1 Kings viii. 25,26; xi. 36. 2 Chron. vi. 16; vii. 18).

He trusted in Jehovah for Victory over his enemies.

He trusted in Jehovah for His recovery from His sickness.

So likewise he trusted in Jehovah for His faithfulness to His promise to David. This is shewn in Psalm cxxxii. 11.

> "Jehovah hath sworn in truth to David;
> He will not turn from it:
> **Of the fruit of thy body will I set upon thy throne."**

It was not until three years after Hezekiah's deliverance from Sennacherib, and his recovery from his sickness, that, among the words of Isaiah spoken to Hezekiah "at that time" (2 Kings xx. 12), was the promise:—concerning "**thy sons that shall issue from thee, which thou shalt beget,**"* (2 Kings xx. 18, Isaiah xxxix. 7).

* Hezekiah's trouble came in the 14th year of his reign; and, as he lived 15 years longer, his whole reign lasted 29 years, (2 Kings

How well can we now understand the references to the birth of children as being "the gift of God" in these Psalms. Those who interpret them of the goings-up of Tribes to Jerusalem (past or future) must be puzzled to know what to do with these references to God's gift of children. Surely, in the days of the captivity, the birth of children must have been a cause of mourning rather than of rejoicing!

But, when we think of the experiences of Hezekiah, the wonder would be if there were no such references in his rejoicings!

When we think of Hezekiah's circumstances and times, how well we can enter into his feelings as they are reflected in Psalm cxxvii. 3-5:

"**Lo, children are an heritage of Jehovah:**
And the fruit of the womb is his reward.
As arrows are in the hand of a mighty man;
So are children of the youth.
Happy is the man that hath his quiver full of them:
They shall not be ashamed,
But they shall speak with the enemies in the gate." *

In the next Psalm (cxxviii.) Hezekiah dwells upon this, as his own great blessing wherewith Jehovah had blessed him.

"Blessed is every one that reverenceth Jehovah;
That walketh in His ways.
For thou shalt eat the labour of thine hands:

---

xviii. 2). His son Manasseh was 12 years old when Hezekiah died: so that he must have been born in Hezekiah's 17th year, (or in the third of the 15 added years).

* Margin, Or, *shall subdue*, as Psalm xviii. 47, or, *destroy*.

Happy shalt thou be, and it shall **be well with thee.**
Thy **wife** shall be **as a** fruitful vine
By the sides of thine house:
Thy children like olive plants
Round about thy table.
Behold, that **thus shall the man be blessed**
That reverenceth Jehovah.
Jehovah **shall bless thee** out of Zion:
And **thou shalt see** the good of Jerusalem
All the days of thy life.
Yea, **thou shalt see thy children's children,**
And peace upon Israel."

These concluding words take us back to the promise of Isaiah (Isa. xxxix. 8) that Hezekiah should have "children;" for his immediate reply was: "Good is the word of Jehovah which thou hast spoken. . . . For there shall be peace and truth in my days."

This was setting his seal to the promise of children: while the "peace" which Hezekiah should "see" was true, and was "truth."

---

(15) *The Passover for "All Israel."*

We have already noticed some allusions to this remarkable event; but we have not exhausted the references to it in these Psalms.

The last two Psalms (Psalms cxxxiii. and cxxxiv.) relate almost exclusively to that Passover.

Its special feature was, that the ten tribes (which had been separated for so long), had cut themselves off from the House of Jehovah, and His worship in the Temple at Jerusalem. Ever since their separation from Judah, it was impossible for them to keep the Feasts of the Lord.

It was therefore a Divine and blessed resolve on the part of Hezekiah, after he had "opened the doors of the house of Jehovah" (which had been shut up in the reign of Ahaz), and had cleansed it, and purged it of idolatry and idolatrous symbols, to keep the feast of the Passover.

It was already past the proper time of keeping it; and there were other reasons preventing it (2 Chron. xxix. 34); but, so great was his zeal, that he availed himself of a Divinely appointed provision, by which those who could not keep it on the fourteenth day of the *first* month, might keep it on the fourteenth day of the *second* month. (Compare Ex. xii. 18 with Num. ix. 10, 11).

Hezekiah had resolved, therefore, rather than wait eleven months longer, "to keep the Passover in the *second* month" (2 Chron. xxx. 1-3).

But the Passover was not merely a Feast instituted for Judah and Benjamin. It was for "all Israel:" and Hezekiah and his princes would not hear of any of the children of Israel being excluded. Nay, "they established a decree to make proclamation throughout ALL ISRAEL, from Beer-sheba to Dan, that they should come to keep the Passover unto Jehovah, God of ISRAEL, at Jerusalem: for they had not done it of a long time in such sort as it was written. So the posts went with the letters from the king and his princes throughout ALL ISRAEL and Judah" (2 Chron. xxx. 5, 6).

The result of this was that a multitude of the people, even many of Ephraim and Manasseh, Issachar and

Zebulun, and also of Asher, "humbled themselves, and came to Jerusalem" (2 Chron. xxx. 11, 18):

And we read that "also in Judah"

> "The hand of God was to give them ONE HEART to do the commandment of the king and of the princes, by the word of Jehovah" (verse 12).

No wonder that we read in verses 25, 26:

"All the congregation of Judah, with the priests and the Levites, and all the congregation that came out of Israel, and the strangers that came out of the land of Israel, and that dwelt in Judah, rejoiced. So there was great joy in Jerusalem."*

Is not all this unity exquisitely expressed in Psalm cxxxiii.?

It is a Psalm of David: and expressed David's own delight at the unity of the twelve tribes, "all Israel," after a period of hostility and separation, when "all the people were at strife throughout all the tribes of Israel" (2 Sam. xix. 9) were once more re-united, and David's message "bowed the heart of all the men of Judah, even as the heart of ONE MAN" (*v.* 14).

But it was a Psalm which Hezekiah found exactly suited to his own circumstances, when the Tribes so

---

* We have not space here to make the obvious and powerful application of all this to Christians in the present day. Religious differences keep them separate from one another; and hence, jealousies and envyings and bitterness and strife and hostility are manifested; and deplored by many. But they do not see the only remedy: that, as God gave Israel "one heart" so He has given us, now, one Head; and made us members of one spiritual body. Not until we "all" humble ourselves, will bickerings and strife give place to the "great joy" which will be found in the acknowledgement of the truth of the "one Body"; typified, conveyed, and emphasised by the repeated expression "all Israel."

long separated in enmity and strife had come under the hand and blessing of God, to give them "ONE HEART" (2 Chron. xxx. 12).*

We print the Psalm according to its structure.

Psalm cxxxiii.

A | 1. Behold, how good and how pleasant it is for brethren to dwell together, and that in unity.

B | a | 2-. [It is] like the precious (or sacred) oil upon the head,

b | -2. Which descend upon the beard, even Aaron's beard, which descended to the edge† of his garments:

B | *a* | 3-. [It is] like Hermon's dew,

b | -3-. Which descendeth upon the mountains of Zion:

A | -3. For there Jehovah commanded the blessing:‡ —Life, for evermore.

In A and *A* we have the blessings of "unity," and "life for evermore." In B and *B*, the two illustrations: of the Holy Oil, in B; and in *B*, of Hermon's dew.

The point of the first comparison lies not in the preciousness or fragrance of the oil, but in its *abundance*; not resting or remaining on the head, but descending

* Dr. Thirtle calls attention, in a valuable note, to Josephus (*Ant.* Book ix. ch. xiii. § 2). Josephus tells how Hezekiah "sent to the Israelites, and exhorted them to leave off their present way of living, and return to their ancient practices, and to worship God, for he gave them leave to come to Jerusalem, and to celebrate, ALL IN ONE BODY, the Feast of unleavened bread: and he said this by way of invitation only; and to be done, not out of obedience to him, but of their own free will, and for their own advantage, because it would make them happy."

† The collar, or neck. See Exod. xxviii. 32.

‡ Deut. xii. 5, 11, 14, 18, 21. Compare Psalms cxxviii. 6; cxxxiv. 4.

even to the garments: thus sanctifying the whole, in all its parts; all the members sharing in the blessing.

The point of the second comparison lies not in the refreshing nature, or all-pervading influence, of dew; but in the fact that it falls alike on both mountains; and descends upon the loftier Hermon in the north, and upon the lowlier mountains of Zion in the south. The same dew extends from Hermon to Zion, and covers both mountains alike.

Israel's unity was a *corporate* unity;* having Jerusalem for its one place of worship; and all blessings being commanded there.

The unity of the Church of God to-day is a *spiritual* unity (Eph. iv. 3); having Heaven for its one place of worship; and all spiritual blessings treasured up "in the heavenlies," there, in Christ (Eph. i. 3).

All Israel was united in one corporate Nation. The Church of God is united in one spiritual Body. And, as the anointing oil ran down even to the garments of Aaron, even so the anointing of the true Aaron, Christ, our Head, flows down to and reaches not the skirts of His garments only, but the "feet." These humblest members share in His grace. All the members of His body are thus anointed and sealed; not with the material element as "oil," but with *pneuma hagion*, with spiritual power, and Divine gifts.

---

* The Hebrew is יַחַד (*yāchad*) *unity:* (not אֶחָד *'echād*) which means *a composite unity, an only one*, implying *uniqueness*. So that Israel's corporate *unity* is viewed as manifested in the one Nation, just as the spiritual unity of the Church of God is seen in the one spiritual Body of Christ (Eph. iv. 1-4). *Yāchad* is not used therefore of Jehovah. In Deut. vi. 4 it is *echād*, a composite unity: Father, Son and Holy Spirit.

The teaching of "the dew of Hermon" is the same. Hermon is four times higher than Mount Zion: the air on its summit is always much colder; and hence it has to part with its moisture in the form of "summer-sea-night-mist." This is uniformly rendered "dew," both in the A.V. and R.V.

The Rev. James Neil has shown * that this rendering "dew," cannot stand; and was made in ignorance of the natural phenomena of Palestine.

The *night-mist* is much more copious than the "dew" which we are acquainted with in Western Lands; and resembles recent rain rather than our scanty "dew."

What the illustration means is, that the unity of brethren (and in our case *spiritual* unity), is more blessed among brethren than when these copious summer-sea-night mists that are known on the summit of Hermon 10,000 feet high, fell on the drier Zion.

It is not that the same dew which fell on Hermon came and fell on Zion; but the same cloud and mist descended upon *both* mountains, *uniting them* in its one embrace, extending the same refreshment and blessing to both, and over all between.

The *Ellipsis* is filled up in the A.V. by the supply of the words "*and as the dew*." But there is no occasion to supply anything, as we have shown above.

This unity of the brethren manifested by the coming down of multitudes of "all Israel" from the most Northern parts round Hermon, was as copious on Zion as Hermon's dews were upon mount Hermon.

Zion's own "dews" were the children of Judah. But the multitudes from Asher, Ephraim, Manasseh,

---

* See *Palestine Explored*, by the Rev. James Neil (Nisbet & Co.), pages 129—151. Tenth Edition.

Zebulun, and Issachar, made it like Hermon's dews. For the tribes, coming from the north, were from the land of Hermon.

Could any illustration be more beautiful, or more truly poetical?

CONCLUSION.

THOSE who profess to treat the Bible "like any other book" do nothing of the kind. They do nothing so honest, and nothing so honourable. In fact, they treat it *as they treat no other book.* While professing to treat the Bible as ordinary *literature*, they treat its authors as forgers, and their work as the work of illiterates; though, with strange inconsistency, they continue to write Commentaries upon it!

That most wonderful "Law of Correspondence," they call, and treat as, mere "*poetry;*" while these Psalms, which are full of the most exquisite and *real poetry*, they neither understand nor appreciate.

But we appeal to those who have read what we have said on these Songs of THE Degrees and ask: Is any further evidence needed to prove that these fifteen Psalms of the Degrees are so called, because they were commemorative of Hezekiah's great deliverance, o. which the going back of the Shadow on the Degrees (or steps) of the Sun-dial of Ahaz was the sign? Did not this great prophetic sign become at once the historic symbol of that deliverance, and the Title of these fifteen Psalms?

Notice how the very word "Degrees" is repeated *five times* in 2 Kings xx. 9-11, and Isa. xxxviii. 8.

"Behold, I shall cause (lit. am causing), the shadow on the **Degrees** (or steps) which is gone down on the **Degrees** (or steps) of Ahaz, by the Sun, to return backward, ten **Degrees.** So the Sun returned ten **Degrees,** by which **Degrees** it had gone down."

The marvel seems to be, not that the key is now at length obtained to these fifteen Psalms, but that it was ever lost! And that, having been suggested by Lightfoot two hundred and sixty years ago, it should have been neglected through all those years, until Dr. Thirtle's discovery of the significance of the Titles, as a whole, led him to investigations regarding this title in particular, and to an examination of the Songs themselves.

And yet, we can discern the cause. Lightfoot is very little read in our days, and is in small request. His thirteen volumes can be bought for a few shillings: while modern works on the Bible, worth nothing, fetch as many pounds.

Dr. Lightfoot believed God. He believed God's Word: and never seems so happy as when he is showing that what seems a discrepancy is really a wonderful harmony.

While his solid monumental works are neglected for the flimsy imaginations of the "higher" critics, the lifeless Gospel of humanity, or the frothy mixtures which occupy their readers with themselves and their experiences, instead of on God and His Word, we can understand the prevailing ignorance of the Scriptures of truth, and the consequent errors which flow therefrom.

What we have written here on the subject of the Titles of the Psalms in general, and of these fifteen Songs of the Degrees in particular, shows us why the Critics labour to take these Psalms from their true historic setting, and bring them down as far as possible to the days that are Post-Exilic, or about 160 B.C.

Their one great object is to get rid of the supernatural from Scripture. That is why they disdain, and will ignore, any evidence which connects these Psalms with the Miracle, and puts them right back to the very days of Sennacherib, Isaiah and Hezekiah.

We have shown that that is the only key to the plain understanding of them.

This must be clear beyond dispute.

When Hezekiah wrote (Isa. xxxviii. 20):—

> "Jehovah was ready to save me:
> Therefore will we sing MY SONGS to the stringed instruments
> All the days of our life in the House of Jehovah":—

where are we to look for these "Songs," if not in the "Songs of THE Degrees?"

PART IV.

THE SONGS OF THE DEGREES.

Psalms cxx. to cxxxiv.

A NEW TRANSLATION, WITH THE STRUCTURES, NEW REFERENCES, AND NOTES.

"The LORD was ready to save me:
Therefore we will sing MY SONGS to the stringed instruments all the days of our life in the House of the LORD." (Hezekiah: in Isa. xxxviii. 20).

PART IV.

THE SONGS OF THE DEGREES: THEIR STRUCTURE, AND TRANSLATION.

INTRODUCTORY.

THE Songs of the Degrees are fifteen in number, corresponding to the fifteen years added to the life of Hezekiah King of Judah, of which the Miracle of the shadow of the sun's going backward ten degrees, on the Sundial of Ahaz, was the sign given by Jehovah.

Of these fifteen Psalms, ten are by Hezekiah, and five by others: viz.: four by David, and one by Solomon.

The Psalm by Solomon occupies the centre; and, of the seven on either side, two are by David.

In each seven the name of Jehovah occurs *twenty four* times; and Jah *twice*, (once in the third Psalm of each seven).

In the central Psalm Jehovah occurs *three* times.

They are arranged in five groups: each group consisting of three Psalms. The subjects of each group of three Psalms are:

1. Distress and Prayer, in the first.
2. Trust in Jehovah, in the second.
3. Deliverance, Blessing, and Peace in Zion, in the third.

They all refer to the days when The Temple Worship was going on; when Jerusalem was surrounded by the armies of Sennacherib; and when Hezekiah was crying to, and trusting in, Jehovah, and longing and praying for the peace of Jerusalem.

The first Psalm of all combines all these three subjects.

We have in our New Translation uniformly transliterated the Divine and other proper names.

The connection of these Psalms with Hezekiah has shown us their proper *scope*; and has led therefore to a revision of some of the Structures as formerly published in *A Key to the Psalms.**

GROUP I. First Psalm.

PSALM cxx.

DISTRESS.

A | 1. Hezekiah and Jehovah.

B | 2. His prayer to Jehovah.

B | 3, 4. His Apostrophe to Rabshakeh.

A | 5-7. Hezekiah and Man.

---

* Eyre and Spottiswoode, 33 Paternoster Row. Price Five Shillings.

GROUP I. FIRST PSALM (CXX).

Psalm cxx.

A Song of the Degrees.

A | 1. Unto Jehovah, in the distress[1] that came upon me, I cried,[2] and He answered me.

B | 2. 'O Jehovah, deliver me[3] from a lying lip[4] and from a deceitful tongue.'

B | 3. What [judgment] shall be given unto thee, or what [punishment] shall be heaped upon[5] thee, thou deceitful tongue? 4. Sharp arrows[6] of the Mighty one,[7] with coals of fire.[8]

A | 5. Woe is me that I sojourn among the Moschi,[9] and dwell beside the Kedarenes.
6. Too long have I dwelt[10] with them[11] that hate peace. 7. **I**, [even I, am] for peace: but, when I speak, they [are] for war.[12]

[1] distress]. 2 Kings xix. 3. Isa. xxxvii. 3. "This day is a day of trouble, and of rebuke, and of blasphemy." "Trouble" is the word rendered "distress" in verse 1 of this Psalm.

[2] cried]. 2 Kings. xix. 3, 4, 14—19. 2 Ch. xxxii. 20. Isa. xxxvii. 15—20; xxxviii. 2, 3.

[3] me]. Heb. *my soul, i.e.*, myself. "Deliver" refers to 2 Kings xviii. 30, 32. "Jehovah will surely DELIVER us."

[4] lying lip, &c.]. The reference is to Rabshakeh. 2 Kings xviii. 19—35; xix. 8—15. 2 Ch. xxxii. 10—19. Isa. xxxvi. 4—21; xxxvii. 8—14.

[5] heaped upon]. Heb. *added unto.* Compare 1 Sam. iii. 17; xx. 13, &c.

[6] sharp arrows]. Ps. xlv. 5; cxxvii. 4. Jer. i. 9.

[7] Mighty one]. *i.e.*, God: agreeably to the Talmud.

[8] fire]. Heb. *broom*, put by Metonymy for *fire*, the roots of which are used for fire.

[9] Moschi and Kedarenes]. Put by Metonymy for the *cruel* and *merciless* character of these people: just as we use the terms Tartars, Vandals, Goths, Philistines, Barbarians, &c. These "delight in war" (Psalm lxviii. 30).

[10] have I dwelt]. Heb. *hath my soul had her dwelling*.

[11] them]. So some Codices, with Sept., Syriac, and Vulgate. *See* Ginsburg's Heb. Text and note.

[12] They are for war]. See 2 Kings xviii. 19. Isa. xxxvi. 5. 2 Chron. xxxii. 1, 2, margin.

Group I. Second Psalm.

PSALM cxxi.

TRUST IN JEHOVAH.

A | 1, 2. Jehovah's help proclaimed.
A | 3—8. Jehovah's help promised.

A (*vv.* 1, 2). *Jehovah's help proclaimed.*

A | a | 1-. Contemplation of Creation.
  b | -1. Whence can help come? (Question).
  b | 2-. Whence help cometh. (Answer).
 a | -2. Contemplation of the Creator.

A (*vv.* 3—8). *Jehovah's help promised.*

A | c | 3, 4. What Jehovah will *not* suffer. (Negative).
  d | 5. What He will do. Jehovah the Keeper.
 c | 6. What He will *not* do. (Negative).
  d | 7, 8. What He will do. Jehovah the Keeper

Psalm cxxi.

A Song for the Degrees.

A | a | 1-. I lift up mine eyes unto the mountains.[1]
b | -1. From whence cometh my help?[2]
b | 2-. My help [cometh] from Jehovah,
a | -2. Who made heaven and earth.[3]

A | c | 3, 4. Let Him not suffer thy foot[4] to be moved: Let not[5] Thy Keeper slumber. Behold, He that keepeth Israel will neither slumber nor sleep.

d | 5. Jehovah [is] thy Keeper; Jehovah [is] thy Shade upon thy right hand.[6]

c | 6. By day, the sun will not smite thee: nor the moon by night.[7]

d | 7, 8. Jehovah will keep thee from all evil; He will preserve (or keep) thy life.[8] Jehovah will keep thy going out, and thy coming in, from this time forth, even for evermore.[9]

[1] the mountains]. The correspondence is with the member *a.*, the Creation: the contemplation of the work of Jehovah producing trust in the power of the Creator.

The question is asked: and in *b* the answer is given.

[3] In this member we have the definite connection of the Psalm with the prayer of Hezekiah. Hezekiah had made his prayer to the living God—"Thou hast made heaven and earth." (1 Kings xix. 15, and Isa. xxxvii. 16.) This was the basis of his prayer; in vivid contrast to the Idols and Gods of the heathen, which were "the work of men's hands" (2 Kings xix. 18; 2 Ch. xxxii. 19; Isa. xxxvii. 19). Rabshakeh had reproached "the living God:" which is always the Divine Title when Idols are the subject of the context.

See further references to this in Psalms cxxiv. 8; and cxxxiv. 3.

[4] thy foot]. Some Codices read "*thy feet*," See Ginsburg's Heb. Text, and note.

[5] Let Him not]. The negative in *v.* 3 is אַל (*al*). But in *v.* 4 it is לֹא (*lō*).

[6] This was the repeated promise of Jehovah to Hezekiah by the mouth of Isaiah. *See* 2 Kings xix. 20—34, Isa. xxxvii. 6, 7, 22—35.

[7] It is this member that almost compels us to believe that the Anonymous Psalm, xci. is also by Hezekiah.

[8] Heb. *thy soul, i.e., thee.*

[9] This was the promise; and the performance of it is seen in 2 Chron. xxxii. 22: where Jehovah saved His People out of the hand of all their enemies, and "guided them on every side."

GROUP I. THIRD PSALM (cxxii.)

GROUP I. Third Psalm.

PSALM cxxii.

DELIVERANCE, BLESSING, AND PEACE

A | 1. The House of Jehovah.

  B | 2. Jerusalem spoken to.

    C | 3. Jerusalem spoken of.

      D | 4. Description.

      D | 5. Description.

    C | 6-. Jerusalem spoken of.

  B | -6-8. Jerusalem spoken to.

A | 9. The House of Jehovah.

Psalm cxxii.

A Song of the Degrees. David's.[1]

A | 1. I rejoiced with them that said unto me: "Let us go into the House of Jehovah."[2]

B | 2. Our feet have stood [and shall still stand][3] within thy gates, O Jerusalem!

C | 3. Jerusalem! that art the city built as a city compact in itself.

D | 4. Whither have ascended, Tribes, the Tribes of Jah, according to the ordinance[4] for Israel, to give thanks to the Name of Jehovah.

D | 5. For there was set the Thrones[5] of judgment, even the Throne of the house of David.

C | 6-. Pray for the peace of Jerusalem.

B | -6-8. They shall prosper that love thee. Peace be within thy walls, [and] prosperity within thy palaces. For my brethren's and companions' sake, let me, now, speak; [saying]: Peace [be] within thee.

A | 9. For the sake of the house of Jehovah our God let me seek good for thee.

Title [1] **David's**]. Some Codices, with Aramaic, Sept. and Vulgate omit "David's."

[2] **House of Jehovah**]. This was the great subject that filled the heart and thoughts of Hezekiah, as it had of David. David spoke of the Tabernacle as "the house of Jehovah," as others had constantly done before him. (See Ex. xxiii. 19. Josh. vi. 24. Judg. xviii. 31. 1 Sam. 1, 7, 24; iii. 15. 2 Sam. xii. 20. Pss. v. 7; xi. 6). Hezekiah commenced his reign by "opening the doors of the house of the Lord" (2 Chron. xxix. 3). Then he restored it for Jehovah's service. Seventeen times it is mentioned in the three chapters which give the account of his Reformation (2 Chron. xxix., xxx., xxxi.).

When he received Sennacherib's letter, "Hezekiah went up into the house of Jehovah, and spread it before Jehovah" (Isa. xxxvii. 14).

When his mortal sickness came on him, Isaiah's promise was:—"on the third day thou shalt go up to the House of Jehovah" (2 Kings xx. 5).

When he asked for a sign, it was not a sign, merely, of his recovery, but a sign "that I shall go up into the House of Jehovah" (2 Kings xx. 8, Isa. xxxviii. 22).

After he was healed, his promise was: "therefore will we sing my songs . . . in the house of the LORD."

[3] **have stood**]. Is a strict perfect, *i.e.* have stood and shall still stand. This refers to the Passover which had been kept for "All Israel." (See above, pp. 266-270).

[4] **Ordinance**]. Ex. xxiii. 17; xxxiv. 23. Deut. xvi. 16. Psalm lxxxi. 4 (5), 5 (6).

[5] **Thrones**]. Heb. *pl.* of majesty. *The great* throne or seat of judgment. Compare 1 Kings ii. 19: where the word rendered "seat" is the same as that rendered "throne" in the same verse.

Group II. First Psalm.

PSALM cxxiii.

DISTRESS.

A | 1. Prayer to Jehovah.

B | 2-. As the eyes of servants look: } Comparison.
B | -2. So our eyes look.

A | 3, 4. Prayer to Jehovah.

Psalm cxxiii.[1]

A Song of the Degrees.

A | 1. Unto Thee have I lifted up mine eyes, O Thou that dwellest in the heavens![2]

B | 2-. Behold, as the eyes of menservants [look] unto the hand of their masters; [and] as the eyes of a maidservant [look] unto the hand of her mistress;

B | -2. Even so our eyes [look] unto Jehovah our God, until (lit. till such time as) He have mercy upon us.

A | 3, 4. Have mercy upon us, O Jehovah, have mercy upon us: for we are exceedingly filled with contempt. We[3] are exceedingly filled with the scoffing[4] of those that are at ease[5], and with the contempt of the proud.[6]

Group II. First Psalm (cxxiii.).

[1] In this Psalm we have reference again to the scoffing of Rabshakeh; as in the first Psalm of the first group; which has the same subject: "Distress."

[2] dwellest in the heavens]. This was the very language of Hezekiah, when he spread the letter of Sennacherib before Jehovah, and prayed: "O Jehovah Sabaoth, God of Israel, that dwellest between the cherubim" (2 Kings xix. 15, Isa. xxxvii. 16).

[3] We]. Heb. *our soul.*

[4] contempt, scoffing]. This member refers to the words of Sennacherib and Rabshakeh in 2 Kings xviii. 19-35; xix. 8-13. 2 Chron. xxxii. 10-19. Isa. xxxvi. 4-21; xxxvii. 8-13.

[5] The word is the same as that rendered *arrogancy* in 2 Kings xix. 20, 28, and Isa. xxxvii. 21, 29 (margin, *careless ease*).

[6] proud]. This is what is *written:* but the *k'ri*, *i.e.* what is *read* is *proud oppressors:* taking the one word as two words.

GROUP II. Second Psalm.

PSALM cxxiv.

TRUST IN JEHOVAH.

A | 1, 2. Jehovah, our help.
  B | a | 3. Voracity of enemies.
      b | 4, 5. Comparison: Waters.
        C | 6-. Blessed be Jehovah.
  B | *a* | -6. Voracity of enemies.
      b | 7. Comparison: Fowlers.
A | 8. Jehovah, our help.

Psalm cxxiv.

A Song of the Degrees. David's.[1]

A | 1, 2. If it had not been Jehovah who was on our side, let Israel, now, say:[2] If it had not been Jehovah who was on our side when men rose up against us:

B | a | 3. They had swallowed us alive, when their wrath was kindled against us.

b | 4. Then the waters had overwhelmed us: yea, the torrent[3] would have passed over us[4]; yea, the proud waters[5] had passed over us.

C | 6-. Blessed be Jehovah,

B | *a* | -6. Who hath not given us over a prey to their teeth.

b | 7. We[6] are escaped as a bird out of the snare of the fowlers.[7] The snare is broken, and we are escaped.

A | 8. Our help is in the name of Jehovah, who made heaven and earth.[8]

Group II. Second Psalm (cxxiv.).

Title. [1]Some Codices, with Syriac and Vulgate omit "David's." See Ginsburg's Heb. Text, and note.

[2]Let Israel now say]. Compare Psalm cxxix. 1.

[3]torrent]. Compare Psalm xviii. 16; lxix. 2; cxliv. 7; Hab. i. 11.

[4]over us] (twice). Heb. *our soul.*

[5]proud waters]. Compare Psalm cxlv. 3; lxxxix. 9.

[6]we]. Heb. *our soul.*

[7]snare of the fowlers]. See above pages 253 and 255.

[8]who made heaven and earth]. Compare Psalm cxxi. 2, and cxxxiv. 3. (The Second Psalm of first Group, and see pages 242-244).

Group II. Third Psalm.

PSALM cxxv.

DELIVERANCE, BLESSING AND PEACE.

A | 1-3. Israel's security.
  B | 4-. Jehovah's goodness.
    C | -4. The upright.
    C | 5-. The perverse.
  B | -5-. Jehovah's judgment.
A | -5. Israel's peace

Psalm cxxv.

A Song of the Degrees.

A | 1-3. They that put their trust in Jehovah are like Mount Zion[1]; which cannot be moved, [but] standeth fast for ever. As the mountains are round about Jerusalem, so Jehovah is round about His People, from this time forth, and for evermore. For the sceptre[2] of the lawless one[3] will not continue over[4] the inheritance of the righteous[5], lest the righteous put forth their hands to [do] wickedness.[6]

  B | 4-. Do good, O Jehovah,

    C | -4. To such as are good, and to such as are upright in their hearts.

    C | 5-. But as for such as turn aside unto their crooked ways.

  B | -5-. May Jehovah drive them forth with the workers of iniquity.

A | -5. [But] peace be upon Israel.

[1] are like Mount Zion]. Some Codices, with one early printed edition, and Syriac, read *are in Mount Zion*. See Ginsburg's Heb. Text, and note.

[2] sceptre]. Heb. *rod*: the *rod* of the Assyrian, put by *Metonymy* for the Assyrian oppression. (Isaiah xxx. 31.

[3] continue over]. *i.e., rest*, so as to *lie heavily upon*, or oppress: with the idea of continuance, as in Isa. xxv. 10. It refers to the promise of deliverance from the Assyrian invasion of Sennacherib.

[4] lawless one]. So, some Codices, with Sept., Syr. and Vulgate.

[5] righteous]. *i.e.*, Hezekiah, and Israel: referring to the Land, as Israel's inheritance.

[6] wickedness]. By mingling with the heathen, and learning their works, and practising their abominations. We generally associate "wickedness" with social evil; but in Scripture it is nearly always religious "iniquity," and spiritual "wickedness."

GROUP III. First Psalm.

PSALM cxxvi.

DISTRESS.

A | 1-. Distress: its ending
  B | -1. Comparison. Dreams.
    C | 2, 3. Joy.
A | 4-. Distress: its ending.
  B | -4. Comparison. Torrents.
    C | 5, 6. Joy.

EXPANSION of C (*vv.* 2, 3).

C | a | 2- Gladness.
  b | -2- Great things
  b | 3-. Great things
  a | -3. Gladness.

EXPANSION of *C* (*vv.* 5, 6).

C | c | 5-. Sowing in tears.
  d | -5. Reaping in joy.
  c | 6-. Sowing in tears.
  d | -6. Reaping in joy.

Psalm cxxvi.

A Song of the Degrees.

A—1-. When Jehovah turned the fortunes[1] of Zion,
  B | -1. We were as those who dream.[2]
    C | 2, 3. Then was our mouth filled with laughter.[3] And our tongue with songs of joy.[4] Then said they among the nations,[5] 'Jehovah hath done great things for them.' [Yea,] Jehovah hath done great things for us; We are become full of joy.
A | 4-. Turn our fortunes, O Jehovah,
  B | -4. As[6] [thou turnest] the torrents[7] in the gorges.[8]
    C | 5, 6. They that sow in tears, will reap with songs of joy. He that keeps going on,[9] weeping, carrying his basket of seed, will surely come again with songs of joy, bearing his sheaves.

[1]turned the fortunes]. This has no reference to any Captivity of Israel in Babylon or elsewhere. It is a Hebrew idiom, for *an ending of distress:* a restoring to the former estate after trouble. See Job xlii. 10. "Jehovah turned the captivity of Job." How? When He turned Job's fortunes; and when He "gave Job twice as much as he had before."

Compare Ezek. xvi. 53. In verse 55 it is three times explained as "return to your former estate."

In Jer. xxxiii. 11: "I will cause to return the captivity of the land, as at the first, saith Jehovah."

The great point is the *Distress.* The form of it is only a circumstance. Job was never a "captive." The land was never removed away; It was still there; but its trouble was removed or turned away. See pages 257—260

[2]dream]. It was like waking from a dream: for "It came to pass that night, that the angel of Jehovah went out, and smote in the camp of the Assyrians an hundred, four-score and five thousand: and when they arose early in the morning, behold, they were all dead corpses. (2 Kings xix. 35. 2 Ch. xxxii. 21. Isa. xxxvii. 36). It all seemed like a dream, when they awoke, and found their enemies gone, and their trouble ended.

[3]laughter]. Compare Job viii. 21.

[4]songs of joy]. These are the "My Songs" of Isa. xxxviii. 20.

[5]nations]. 2 Ch. xxxii. 22, 23, show that the news of these "great things" which Jehovah had done for Israel produced a great sensation; and caused Hezekiah to be "magnified in the sight of all nations from thenceforth."

[6]As]. There is an Ellipsis here, and the verb has to be supplied from the line immediately preceding.

"As [thou turnest]." Wellhausen can think of nothing but a *lacuna* in the Text!

[1] torrents]. Heb. *aphīkīm*: the rushing and turbulent streams that are forced to turn hither and thither, constrained by their rocky boundaries which they cannot move. See page 259.

[2] gorges]. Heb. *the Negeb*, *i.e.*, the rocky or "hill country" south of the hill country of Judea, (Gen. xii. 9), and north of Egypt, (Gen. xiii. 1).

In Deut. i. 7, it is one of four topographical names. The *plain* (ARABAH, the Jordan Valley); in the *hills* (the HILL COUNTRY of Judah); the *vale* (SHEPHELAH, Philistia), the *south* (the NEGEB, south of the hill country of Judah). See page 260.

[3] keeps going on]. Heb. *going on, let him go on*, implying continuance and perseverance, in spite of his tears.

More literally: A going forth let him go, weeping,
Bearing his basket of seed:
A coming in he will come, rejoicing,
Bearing his sheaves:

The figure *Polyptoton* (the repetition of the same verb in different inflections, is used for the sake of emphasis, which we have marked by the word *keeps*, in the first instance, and by the word *surely* in the second.

Group III. Second Psalm.

PSALM cxxvii.

TRUST IN JEHOVAH.

A | 1-. The vain builders of the house.
  B | -1. The vain defenders of the city.
    C | 2-. The vain diligence of the labourers.
} Insufficiency of Man.

    C | -2. The gifts of Jehovah without labour.
A | 3. The builders of the city, children, the heritage of Jehovah.
  B | 4, 5. The defenders of the city, children, the reward of Jehovah.
} Sufficieny of Jehovah.

Psalm cxxvii.

A Song of the Degrees. Solomon's.[1]

A | 1-. Except Jehovah build a house, in vain have its builders laboured thereon.

B | -1. Except Jehovah watch over a city.
In vain hath a watchman watched.[2]

C | 2-. Vain is it for you to rise up early, to sit up late, to eat the bread [gained] by wearisome [labour].

C | -2. [Jehovah] giveth to His beloved[3] while they sleep.[4]

A | 3. Behold! an inheritance[5] from Jehovah are sons;[6] [and His] reward [is] the fruit of the womb.

B | 4,5. As arrows in the hand of a mighty man, so are [our] sons, the young men.[7] Happy is the man who hath his quiver full with them. They[8] will not be put to shame, should they meet[9] their foes in the gate.

Title. [1] Solomon's]. A Psalm written by Solomon regarding the gift of the Lord to him while he slept (1 Kings iii. 5, etc.); which "the men of Hezekiah" doubtless "copied out" as most suitable for its place here, referring as it does so suitably to his childless position during the siege of the city, and *His* "gift" from the Lord afterward. Verse 2 refers to the name "Jedidiah," *beloved of Jehovah* (2 Sam. xii. 25). Here, *Yedīd* means Jehovah's beloved one.

The Psalm is divided into two parts:—

The insufficiency of man (*vv.* 1,2-).

The sufficiency of Jehovah (*vv.* -2-5).

Thus it treats of the true ground of trust in Jehovah, which is the subject of the Psalm. The trust here referred to is not Hezekiah's trust as to deliverance of the city; but his trust as to the building up of his own house in the gift of a son as promised by Jehovah through Isaiah.

The Deliverance celebrated in the next (the third Psalm of this Group), refers to the same subject.

[2] **Watchman watch**]. Heb., *keep awake; be alert.*

[3] **beloved**]. Heb. *Yedīd*, the name of Solomon (2 Sam. xii. 25), given to him by the LORD. Solomon was given because David was *beloved of Jehovah;* and the child was given as a proof that David was beloved, notwithstanding his sin.

[4] **while they sleep**]. It is the accusative, not of the object, but of *the time*, as is frequently the case. It answers the question—When? *Early in the morning* (Psalm v. 4). *At noonday* (Psalm xci. 6). *On one and the same day* (Gen. xxvii. 45). At the *beginning of barley-harvest* (2 Sam. xxi. 9).

It was while Solomon slept that Jehovah gave him all those great and wonderful gifts, even more than he had asked (1 Kings iii. 5-15).

It was while Adam slept that He gave him a wife (Gen. ii. 21, 22); and while Abraham slept that He gave him the Land by an unconditional covenant (Gen. xv. 12-16).

And yet all that Wellhausen can say is:—"the Hebrew words are unintelligible." We believe him: for, "the things of the Spirit of God . . . are spiritually discerned" (1 Cor. ii. 14). Unless one understands what the free grace of God is, these "Hebrew words are unintelligible."

[5] **inheritance**]. Referring to his "house": the subject of A. (*v.* 1).

'sons]. Referring to the real builders and defenders of the house. (See Ruth iv. 11; Psalm lxxxix. 4. 1 Sam. ii. 35. 2 Sam. vii. 27. Jer. xviii. 9 ; xxxiii. 7). Comp. Isa. lxii. 5, "so shall thy sons *possess* or *build* thee."

'the young men]. We take "of youth" or "of young men" as the Genitive of Apposition.

'they]. *i.e.*, the sons, the young men.

'meet]. Heb., *speak*, or *plead* their cause. (Josh. xx. 4. 2 Sam. xix. 29. Jer. xii. 1).

But the meaning of the word must be decided by the context, which shows that it is more than mere *talk*. If with "enemies," it must either be to *negotiate* or *confer*, if not to fight. A.V. Margin has "or, *subdue*." It is probably used idiomatically, as "looking one another in the face" is used of fighting (2 Kings xiv. 8, 11). In 2 Kings xi. 1, it means *to destroy*, or *to pronounce sentence of death*. Compare Psalm ii. 5.

Our rendering, *meet*, is neutral, and satisfies the context.

GROUP III. Third Psalm.

PSALM cxxviii.

DELIVERANCE, BLESSING, AND PEACE.

A | 1. Blessedness of those who reverence Jehovah (3rd pers.).

  B | a | 2. Thou.

    b | 3-. Thy house and thy wife.

      c | -3. Thy children. Peace.

A | 4. Blessedness of those who reverence Jehovah (3rd pers.).

  B | *a* | 5-. Thee.

    b | -5. Thy City and thy life.

      c | 6. Thy children's children. Peace.

Group III. Third Psalm (cxxviii).

Psalm cxxviii.[1]

A Song of the Degrees.

A | 1. Blessed is every one that revereth Jehovah; that walketh in His ways!

B | a | 2. For thou wilt eat the labour of thine hands:[2] Blessed wilt thou be, and it will be well with thee.

b | 3-. Thy wife [will be] like a fruitful vine, within[3] thine house.

c | -3. Thy children like olive-plants, round about thy table.

A | 4. Behold! thus will the man be blessed that revereth Jehovah.

B | *a* | 5-. May Jehovah bless thee out of Zion.

b | -5. And thou [shalt] behold the prosperity of Jerusalem,[4] all the days of thy life.

c | 6. And [thou wilt behold] thy children's children: Peace [will be] upon Israel.

[1]This is the third Psalm of the third group; and, as in the second, Hezekiah again declares his sense of the blessing he received in the promise and gift of a son, and an heir to David's throne.

[2]the labour of thine hands]: *i.e.*: thine own hands, in contrast with the opposite in Lev. xxvi. 16. Deut. xxviii. 30-33, 39, 40. See also Amos v. 11. Mic. vi. 15.

[3]within], *i.e.*, in the innermost parts of thy house.

[4]Jerusalem]. In this member Jerusalem is in correspondence by contrast with the house in "b."

GROUP IV. First Psalm.

PSALM cxxix.

DISTRESS.

A | 1, 2-. Distress caused by enemies.

B | -2. Failure of enemies.

A | 3. Distress caused by enemies.

B | 4-8. Failure of enemies.

Psalm cxxix.

A Song of the Degrees.

A | 1. Many a time have they distressed[1] me from my youth up (may Israel now say): (2-). Many a time have they distressed me from my youth up:

B | -2. Yet have they not prevailed against me.

A | 3. The plowers plowed upon my back: they made long their furrows.

B | 4-8. [But] Jehovah [is] just[2]! He hath cut asunder the cords of the wicked (5) Let all that hate Zion be put to shame[3], and turned backward. (6) Let them be as the grass upon the housetops,[4] which withereth before it be grown up; (7) wherewith the mower filleth not his hand, nor he that bindeth sheaves his bosom. (8) Neither do they that go by say, "The blessing of Jehovah be upon you; we bless you: in the name of Jehovah."

GROUP IV. FIRST PSALM (cxxix).

The first Psalm of the fourth group returns to the subject of distress; and Hezekiah includes Israel in the theme.

[1] **distressed].** Heb. *have been adversaries to me*, or fought against me.

[2] **just].** It is the thought of a just God judging His enemies.

[3] **shame].** The reference here, is to 2 Chron. xxxii. 21. "So he *returned with shame of face* to his own land."

[4] **as grass on the housetops].** This is in reference to the words of Jehovah concerning Sennacherib, Isa. xxxvii. 27. See above, pages 238—240.

Group IV. Second Psalm.

PSALM cxxx.

TRUST IN JEHOVAH.

A | 1—3. Waiting on Jehovah.
 B | 4. The reason. כִּי (*ki*) For.
A | 5—7-. Waiting for Jehovah.
 B | -7, 8. The reason. כִּי, (*ki*) For.

Psalm cxxx.[1]

A Song of the Degrees.

A | 1. Out of the depths[1] have I cried unto thee, O Jehovah. (2.) Adonai,[2] hear my voice: let thine ears be attentive to the voice of my supplications. (3.) If Thou, O Jah, shouldest mark iniquities, O Adonai, who will stand?

B | 4. For,[3] with Thee, there is forgiveness[4], that Thou mayest be revered.

A | 5. I have waited for Jehovah: I myself have waited: and in His word[5] have I hoped. (6). I myself[6] [have waited] for Adonai, more than watchmen watching for the morning.[7] (7-). Wait, O Israel, for Jehovah:

B | -7. For with Jehovah there is loving-kindness; and with Him is plenteous redemption.[8] (8). And Himself will redeem Israel from all his iniquities.

GROUP IV. SECOND PSALM (CXXX).

[1] This Psalm is pervaded by a manifestation of trust in Jehovah deep and strong, in the time of greatest distress.

[1] **depths**]. Deep waters are used as symbolical of distress. *See* Ps. lxvi. 12 ; lxix. 1 ; xlii. 7.

[2] **Adonai**]. One of the 134 places where the Massorah reads Jehovah inste d of *Adonay*. (The same in verse 6).

[3] **For**]. The same commencement as the member giving the reason for waiting on God.

[4] **forgiveness**]. Heb. *the forgiveness* : not only the forgiveness pledged to the nation, on the condition of national repentance, but the forgiveness given thanks for by Hezekiah in Isa. xxxviii. 17.

[5] **His word**]. As sent by Jehovah to Hezekiah through Isaiah.

[6] **I myself**]. Heb. *my soul*. So in verse 6.

[7] Compare Isa. xxxviii. 12, 13. "From day even to night."

[8] **plenteous redemption**]. Not only from the King of Assyria (Isa. xxxvii)., but from the king of Terrors (Isa. xxxviii).

Group IV. Third Psalm.

PSALM cxxxi.

BLESSING AND PEACE.

A | 1.- Jehovah my comfort and peace.

B | -1. I have not turned for comfort to others.

B | 2. But I have comforted myself on Thee.

A | 3. Jehovah—Israel's comfort and peace.

Psalm cxxxi.[1]

A Song of the Degrees, David's.

A | 1-. O Jehovah,

B | -1. My heart is not haughty, nor mine eyes lifted up; neither have I exercised myself in great matters, and in things too wonderful for me.

B | 2. But I have soothed and comforted[2] myself, as a weaned child [rests] upon his mother; yea, as the weaned child, [so] upon[3] [Jehovah] I myself[4] [rest].

A | 3. Wait, O Israel,[5] upon Jehovah, from henceforth and for ever.

GROUP IV. THIRD PSALM (cxxxi.)

As David looked back with feelings of humiliation and shame, so Hezekiah "humbled himself for the pride of his heart" (2 Kings xx. 12-19. 2 Chron. xxxii. 25-31. Isa. xxxix. 1-8). In Chron. xxxii. 25, 26, we have the very same Hebrew words for the "lifting up of heart."

[1]The Third Psalm of this fourth Group speaks of peace: not in Zion, as in some of the others, but in himself. Hezekiah takes a Psalm of David, which exactly expresses his feelings, and serves his purpose.

He enjoys peace with Jehovah. He found it, not by occupation with other objects within or without; but in resting on Jehovah, just as a child that is being weaned finds comfort and rest on his mother's breast.

[2]comforted]. Some codices, with Sept. and Vulgate, read "uplifted:" we have expressed it by the word *comforted.* Compare Isa. xxxviii. 13, R.V.

[3]upon]. Heb. not *of* (A.V.), or *with* (R.V).

[4]myself]. Heb. *my soul.*

[5]Israel]. It may seem forced to introduce Israel here. But, if it does, it shows design: for "Israel" is the word which links the three Psalms of this fourth group together:—Ps. cxxix. 1; cxxx. 8; and cxxxi. 3.

GROUP V. First Psalm.

PSALM cxxxii.

BLESSING SOUGHT FOR THE HOUSE OF JEHOVAH.

THEMA.

DAVID'S CHOOSING A PLACE FOR THE TABERNACLE.

A | 2. David sware to Jehovah.

  B | 3-5. What David sware.

    C | 6,7. Search for, and Discovery of, a Dwelling-Place for the Ark of the Covenant.

      D | 8. Prayer to enter into rest.

        E | 9-. Prayer for Priests.

          F | -9. Prayer for Saints.

            G | 10. Prayer for the Anointed.

A | 11-. Jehovah sware to David.

  B | -11, 12. What Jehovah sware.

    C | 13. Designation of the Dwelling-Place.

      D | 14, 15. Answer to Prayer to enter into rest.

        E | 16-. Answer to Prayer for Priests.

          F | -16. Answer to Prayer for Saints.

            G | 17, 18. Answer to Prayer for the Anointed.

Group V. First Psalm (cxxxii).

Psalm cxxxii.

A Song of the Degrees.

Thema.

O Jehovah, remember, for David,[1] all his afflictions.[2]

A. | 2 How he sware to Jehovah, and vowed a vow[3] to the mighty [God] of Jacob.[4]

B | 3-5. "Surely I will not enter into the tent, my house,[5] I will not lie down on the couch, my bed; I will not give sleep to mine eyes, or slumber to mine eyelids: Until I find out a place for Jehovah: A [great] tabernacle for the mighty [God] of Jacob."

C | 6, 7. Lo, we heard of it [*i.e.*, the Ark] at Ephrathah.[6] We found it in Jaar's fields [*i.e.*, Kirjath-Jearim],[7]: (7) [And said]: "Let us come to His Tabernacle.[8] Let us bow ourselves before His footstool."

D | 8. Arise, O Jehovah, into Thy resting-place, Thou, and the Ark of Thy strength.[9]

E | 9-. Let Thy priests be clothed with righteousness;

F | -9. And let Thy saints shout for joy."[10]

G | 10. For Thy servant David's sake, turn not away the face of Thine Anointed.

A | 11-. Jehovah hath sworn[11] unto David. [He is] Truth: He will not depart from it.

B | -11, 12. Of the fruit of thy body shall I set upon Thy Throne. If thy sons keep My covenant, and My testimonies,[12] that I shall teach them, Their sons also shall sit upon Thy throne for evermore.

C | 13. For Jehovah hath chosen Zion; He hath desired it as a Dwelling for Himself.

D | 14, 15. This is My place of rest for evermore. Here shall I dwell, for I have desired it. Her provision I shall abundantly bless. Her poor shall I satisfy with bread.

E | 16-. Her priests also shall I clothe with Salvation.

F | -16. And her saints will shout aloud for joy.

G | 17, 18. There shall I make a horn for David to grow; I have prepared a lamp for Mine Anointed. His foes shall I clothe with shame: But upon Himself let His crown flourish.

[1]Unlike the other Songs, this has a theme, or special separate Title, viz.: David's distress, troubles, and anxieties concerning the House of Jehovah: that House in which Hezekiah took such great delight. See pages 261—263.

It traces David's efforts and prayers in connection with it; and dwells on Jehovah's answers to those prayers; for in those answers Hezekiah, who was childless, found the ground of his hope; and saw the pledge of its realisation, in his having a son to sit upon his throne.

"Distress" is the subject of this Psalm as in the first Psalm, in each group: but it is not the predominant or pervading thought of the Psalm: hence, actual distress is separated from it, and placed at the head of it, as though to mark the change of subjects in this group. Where we have:—

(1). Blessing sought FOR the House of Jehovah (cxxxii).

(2). Blessing IN the House of Jehovah (cxxxiii.).

(3). Blessing FROM the House of Jehovah (cxxxiv).

[1] **Remember for David**]. So as to fulfil the promises made to David, "the sure mercies of David." This was the Theme of Solomon's great prayer at the Dedication of the Temple (1 King viii. 15-21; Isa. lv. 3).

[2] **afflictions**]. Anxieties about his own House, and the Ark and House of Jehovah.

[3] **vow**]. 2 Sam. vii. From the commencement of his reign in Zion we see these anxieties which troubled him (1 Ch. xiii. 3; 2 Sam. vii.; 1 Ch. xxi. 18—xxii. 1).

[4] **The mighty [God] of Jacob**]. The God to whom Jacob vowed his vow. Only here and Gen. xlix. 24; Isa. i. 24 (Israel); xlix. 25; lx. 16.

[5] tent, my house]. Heb. *tent of my house*: which we have taken as the Genitive of Apposition. In this member we have David's vow.

[6] Ephrathah]. Another name for Ephraim; in which tribe Shiloh was, where the Tabernacle was first placed. Samuel, the son of Elkanah, was an Ephrathite, (1 Sam. i. 1), and came up to Shiloh in Ephraim. Jeroboam was an Ephrathite of the tribe of Ephraim (1 Kings xi. 26). Moreover, he set up one of the Calves in Bethel; which, though assigned to Benjamin (Josh. xviii. 22), seems to have been conquered and possessed by Ephraim (Judges 1. 22-26). We may note, however, that David's father is also called an Ephrathite. So there would seem to have been an Ephrath belonging to Judah. *See* Gen. xxxv. 19.

David had "heard" all his life about the Tabernacle being in Shiloh, yet he "found" it in

[7] Jaar, or Kirjath-Jearim (1 Ch. xiii. 5).

[8] Tabernacle]. Heb., plural of Majesty.

[9] Ark of Thy strength]. Only here, and 2 Chron. vi. 41.

[10] shout for joy]. This is the word connected with the bringing up of the Ark. See the Psalm-Title *Mahalath-Leannoth* (Psalm lxxxvii). *Dancings with Shoutings.* (See page 39).

[11] sworn]. 2 Sam. vii. 8-17.

[12] My testimony]. The Massorah punctuates it "this my testimony." But, in some Codices, with Aramaic, Sept., and Vulgate "these my testimonies" (pl). See Ginsburg's Hebrew Text, and note.

Group V. Second Psalm.

PSALM cxxxiii.

Trust.

BLESSING IN THE HOUSE OF JEHOVAH.

A | 1. The blessing enjoyed. Unity pleasant.
  B | a | 2-. Comparison to anointing oil.
       b | -2. The descent of the oil.
  B | *a* | 3-. Comparison to Dew.
       b | -3-. The descent of the Dew.
A | -3. The Blessing. Life for evermore.

Psalm cxxxiii.[1]

A Song of Degrees. David's.

A | 1. Behold, how good and how pleasant it is for brethren to dwell together, even in unity.

  B | a | 2-. [It is] like the precious (or sacred) oil upon the head,

       b | -2. Descending upon the beard, Aaron's beard; which descended to the edge of his garments.

  B | *a* | 3-. [It is] like Hermon's dew

       b | -3-. Which descendeth upon the mountains of Zion.

A | -3. For there Jehovah commanded the blessing:—life, for evermore.

[1]This exquisite Psalm of David's, which celebrated the assembling of "all Israel" in his day, when the kingdom was not yet divided, was most suitable for Hezekiah's purpose; when he, for one brief commemoration of the Passover, assembled again the tribes from "all Israel."

For notes upon the special points of the Psalm see pages 266-270.

PSALM cxxxiv.

BLESSING.

BLESSING FROM THE HOUSE OF JEHOVAH.

A | 1-. Blessing given TO Jehovah. Enjoined.
 B | -1-. The servants.
 B | -1, 2. Their service.
A | 3. Blessing given BY Jehovah. Enjoyed.

Psalm cxxxiv.[1]

A Song of the Degrees.

A | 1-. Behold! Bless ye Jehovah,
 B | -1-. All ye servants of Jehovah:
 B | -1, 2. Ye that stand[2] in the house of Jehovah in the night. Lift up your hands in the Sanctuary, and bless ye Jehovah.[3]
A | 3. Jehovah bless thee[4] out of Zion: Maker as He is of Heaven and Earth.

[1]To understand this last Psalm we must go back to the history as recorded in 2 Chron. xxix, xxx. and xxxi. for in those three chapters we have,

(1) The Reformation of the House of Jehovah.
(2) The Ordering of its Worship.
(3) The Passover for "all Israel."

In those chapters we have,

1. The cleansing of the House (2 Chron. xxix. 3-19).
2. The Restoration of its worship (*vv.* 20-36).

According to the Commandment of David (2 Chron. xxix. 25), with the Instruments of David (2 Chron. xxix. 26, 27), with the Words of David and of Asaph (*v.* 30), and the Priestly Courses of David. (2 Chron. xxix. 30; xxxi. 2, 15).

When we have carefully read those three chapters, we shall understand the scope of this brief but beautiful Psalm.

[2] ye that stand]. 2 Chron. xxix. 11; xxx. 16; xxxi. 2.

[3] bless ye Jehovah]. 2 Chron. xxx. 21, 25; xxxi. 8.

[4] Jehovah bless thee]. 2 Chron. xxx. 27; xxxi. 10.

Thus we have the last of these fifteen "Songs of the Degrees," and are left in the House of the Jehovah, so dear to Hezekiah's heart. Yea, we are left in the midst of the worship of Him, in praise of whose wonderful deliverances Hezekiah had said:

> "JEHOVAH was ready to save me:
> Therefore we will sing MY SONGS to the stringed instruments all the days of our life in the house of Jehovah" (Isaiah xxxviii. 20).

Printed in the USA
CPSIA information can be obtained
at www.ICGtesting.com
LVHW040024080424
776712LV00025B/167